W9-CSJ-020

The Grand Central Baking Book

The Grand Central Baking Book

Breakfast Pastries, Cookies, Pies, and Satisfying Savories
from the Pacific Northwest's Celebrated Bakery

PIPER DAVIS AND ELLEN JACKSON

PHOTOGRAPHY BY JOHN VALLS

TEN SPEED PRESS

BERKELEY

To my mother, Gwenyth Bassetti,
for her unconditional love and delicious food

Copyright © 2009 by Piper Davis and Ellen Jackson
Photography copyright © 2009 by John Valls

All rights reserved.

Published in the United States by Ten Speed Press, an imprint of the Crown Publishing Group,
a division of Random House, Inc., New York.
www.crownpublishing.com
www.tenspeed.com

Ten Speed Press and the Ten Speed Press colophon are registered trademarks of Random House, Inc.

Library of Congress Cataloging-in-Publication Data
Davis, Piper.
  The Grand Central baking book : breakfast pastries, cookies, pies, and satisfying savories from the Pacific
Northwest's celebrated bakery / Piper Davis and Ellen Jackson ; photography by John Valls. — 1st ed.
      p. cm.
  Includes index.
  Summary: "More than 100 recipes from the Pacific Northwest's first artisan bakery and now the region's
most popular bakery chain, accompanied by easy-to-follow pointers on baking for breakfast and brunch,
cookies, fruit desserts, cakes, pies, and more"—Provided by publisher.
  1. Baking. 2. Grand Central Baking Company. I. Jackson, Ellen, 1964- II. Title.
  TX763.D35 2009
  641.8'15—dc22
                        2009014377
ISBN 978-1-58008-953-1

Printed in China

Cover and text design by Nancy Austin
Food styling by Ellen Jackson
Prop styling by Ellen Jackson. Special thanks to Julie Richardson and Sweet Wares for props.

10 9 8 7 6 5 4 3 2

First Edition

Acknowledgments

From Piper

Thanks must first go to my mother, Gwenyth Bassetti. She raised me to love good food, and I'm greatly indebted to her for opening the doors of the original bakery in 1972 with her business partners, Marion Boyer and Marian Mastretti. Their entrepreneurial spirit and sheer guts led to that beginning in Seattle's Pioneer Square neighborhood, and gave birth to the first in the family of Grand Central bakeries in Portland and Seattle.

Through the years, countless talented bakers have contributed knowledge, hard work, and expertise to our endeavor and we are profoundly grateful to them. I'd like to give special thanks to a few bakers who have left an indelible mark on Grand Central: Doug Courter, Leslie Mackie, Donna Boechler, Pandora DeGreen, Julie Richardson, and Laura Ohm. Laura contributed innumerable delicious recipes to our product line, and she also allowed me the time and energy to work on this book.

I am grateful for my business partners: my brother, Ben Davis; Claire Randall; Bob Kerr; Gillian Allen-White; and Gabriel Morehead. They've all supported this project, and excused me from countless meetings while I was working on this book.

The Grand Central Baking Book never would have gotten off the ground had Ellen Jackson not suggested we write it together. I am also grateful to Ellen for bringing John Valls to the project. His photography and good nature have been a pleasure.

From Ellen

To Allison Fishman, who encouraged me to imagine a life outside of the kitchen; to Janie Hibler, who helped me to realize the possibilities over lunch; to Brigid Callinan, who inspired me with her accomplishments; and to Vitaly Paley, who allowed me to test my wings on his project. This book is better for that experience.

Of course there are never thanks enough for family and friends. I am especially grateful for my husband, Steven, who believes in me unconditionally, supports my endeavors unselfishly and keeps me laughing. Thank you for enduring entire meals built around sweets with a smile. And for my parents, Tom and Dianne McFarland, who raised me to love good food and find the right word, and have cheered me on through it all.

Most of all, my thanks and gratitude go to Piper Davis, who made the whole experience a pleasure. I'm so glad I asked!

Contents

Introduction ... 1

1. Stocking the Larder ... 2

2. Breakfast and Brunch ... 14

3. Keeping the Cookie Jar Full ... 52

4. Mealtime ... 92

5. Everyday Fruit Desserts ... 118

6. Cake ... 142

7. Time for Pie ... 170

Index ... 196

Introduction

My mother, Grand Central Baking Company founder Gwenyth Bassetti, is a home baker. A mother of four, she integrated baking seamlessly into her busy schedule, mixing countless batches of wheat-flecked bread dough that she baked into sandwich loaves, butter-rich dinner rolls, and, on Sunday mornings, gooey caramel cinnamon rolls. In addition to filling our lives with bread, she served up blueberry pancakes hot off the griddle, oatmeal raisin cookies by the dozen, and flaky buttermilk biscuits alongside roast chicken. She's the sort of baker who doesn't plan to make dessert but always manages to turn out a delicious peach cobbler, fragrant berry crisp, or perfect apple pie—and makes it look effortless. I grew up watching her and learning from her expertise and intuition as she manipulated ingredients, temperature, and time to suit her needs. Her only secrets were a well-stocked larder, solid natural instincts, and an understanding of basic baking principles.

I share my mother's compulsion to feed others and enjoy the pleasure that comes from doing so, and I feel lucky to have inherited her sensibility as a baker. Her commonsense approach, natural efficiency, and pursuit of tasty food have become the trademarks of my baking. I'm not a fussy baker, and Grand Central isn't a fussy bakery. Our rustic style can be mastered by the average cook in an ordinary kitchen without high-tech equipment, sophisticated techniques, or hard-to-find ingredients. The uncomplicated sort of baking I learned from my mother and grew up eating is the foundation of the unpretentious style that has made Grand Central Bakery a Northwest favorite.

The bakery and family recipes in this book are designed to showcase easy-to-find local and seasonal ingredients with ease and elegance while offering a thoughtful balance of practical wisdom and professional expertise. We hope that this book, loaded with original information, including unique professional pointers and clever techniques, becomes an invaluable resource for bakers in search of ways to fuse food made from fresh, flavorful ingredients into already full lives.

1

Stocking the Larder

Setting up and maintaining a well-stocked larder is the first step to blending baking seamlessly into everyday life. I know many wonderful cooks who don't bake. They say that it's too detail oriented or requires too much special equipment, or that they simply don't have time for it. I don't buy that. Anyone can incorporate baking into the daily routine. Having certain basic ingredients on hand will help you avoid last-minute trips to the store, so this is a good place to start.

I encourage new home bakers to develop their own thing. You might make muffins every Sunday for a month. Or maybe you'd like to stock your freezer with portioned cookie dough so you can bake cookies on impulse. Become the baker whose pie crust is legendary, or spend the summer mastering crisps and crumbles. You can set yourself up to bake your favorite treats whenever the mood strikes by having key ingredients in your larder and a couple of basic pieces of equipment in your *batterie de cuisine*. Then start baking regularly. It won't be long before you develop good instincts and a feel for baking that allows you to whip up pie dough, a breakfast pastry, or a quick dessert without a second thought.

Starting from Scratch 4

Baker's Larder Basics 4

In the Cupboard 4

In the Refrigerator........................... 6

In the Freezer.................................. 6

Basic Ingredients 7

Building Blocks 8

Ready-to-Bake Items 8

General Equipment 9

STARTING FROM SCRATCH

Part of my job as Grand Central's bakery cuisine manager is to educate the retail staff about our approach to baking. I always begin the discussion by asking if anyone knows what it means to "start from scratch." It's one of those figures of speech that everyone knows but many people have trouble putting into words. After a bit of prodding, they tentatively offer suggestions:

"Homemade?"

"Using only good ingredients?"

"Not using any premade stuff?"

"Organic?"

Once they've wrestled with the concept, I share the term's historic origins. "Starting from scratch" is a literal reference to a line scratched in the dirt at the beginning of a race. I always imagine an ancient PE teacher blowing a whistle and yelling, "All of you, line up and start from the scratch!"

Starting from scratch means starting from the beginning. For me, to begin at the beginning when baking means leading off with the most pure yet practical ingredients available. For instance, I don't advocate using whole vanilla beans or raw cocoa on a regular basis; some ingredients benefit from a certain amount of refinement. Generally speaking, however, using fresh fruit and berries in season, real butter, and local farm-fresh eggs will yield baked goods that taste better.

I grew up eating out of a garden on our farm and making frequent trips to local fruit stands in the Yakima Valley. I didn't know that you could find a peach in the grocery store in January. Our family's commitment to seasonality carried over to the bakery and has always been reflected in our menu. We buy from both big and small vendors, and much of the year we're lucky enough to purchase produce directly from farmers who bring their goods to the bakery's door. Choosing ingredients produced close to home supports the local economy, preserves farm land, and offers an exciting difference in flavor that will make your baking come alive.

So I encourage you begin at the beginning and bake from scratch. If you can open your cupboard and find a few baking staples, or turn to your refrigerator or freezer for partially prepared items, the idea of baking spontaneously and responding to the seasonal bounty is not only less daunting, but also full of possibility.

BAKER'S LARDER BASICS
In the Cupboard

All-purpose flour

Unbleached all-purpose flour is probably the only flour a home baker needs for success. If you're serious about baking bread and yeasted baked goods, you'll also want to purchase bread flour, which has a higher gluten content.

Bread flour

Keep bread flour in your pantry for pizza dough, cinnamon rolls, and bread. If you think you'll be making yeasted pastries on a regular basis and don't want to keep more than one kind of flour on hand, go with bread flour. (Using a gentle hand will ensure that nonyeasted pastries made with bread flour are tender, despite the fact that it contains more gluten.) My mother, who has baked her share of bread, cookies, pies, and pastries, fills her flour drawer with bread flour and uses it for all of her baking.

Whole wheat flour

Whole wheat flour is made by grinding the entire wheat kernel, including the bran, germ, and endosperm. Store whole wheat flour in the refrigerator or freezer for up to six months.

At the bakery, we use whole wheat flour in hearty whole grain breads and in cinnamon rolls. Due to the increasing interest in the nutritional value of whole grains, I'm often asked about substituting whole wheat flour for white. To be honest, I haven't tried baking Grand Central Bakery pastries with whole wheat flour. I'm content to get my fiber and nutrients from other sources.

Once when I was teaching a class in pie baking, one of the women in the class asked about making pie dough with whole wheat flour. Knowing she was eager to give her kids the most wholesome version of everything she made, I wanted to help, yet I couldn't resist suggesting that she serve them a heaping pile of broccoli with dinner and stick to making pastry with white flour. There is plenty of goodness in homemade pastry, and dessert is not where we should be looking for supplemental nutritional value, anyway.

Granulated white sugar

The two most common sources of refined sugar are sugarcane and sugar beets. Sugar beets are widely used in the production of white and light brown sugars because they are cheaper, more prolific, and easier to grow than sugarcane. Cane sugar tastes better in its raw form, which is key to the flavor of less refined sweeteners like dark brown sugar and molasses.

We use superfine granulated cane sugar at the bakery. It has the same composition and sweetness as regular granulated sugar, but it is ground into smaller grains, allowing it to dissolve more quickly. Regular granulated white sugar from the baking aisle in the grocery store can be used for all of the recipes in this book.

Brown sugar

There is an unfounded notion that brown sugar is less processed than white and therefore must be healthier. In fact, most of the brown sugar available is fully refined white sugar with molasses added back into it for flavor and texture. Brown sugar's high moisture content accounts for its distinctive texture; keep it in an airtight container to prevent hardening.

Active dry yeast

Yeast is an essential ingredient in pizza dough, cinnamon rolls, and most breads. Active dry yeast is a form that has been dehydrated to extend its shelf life. Because yeast is a living organism that eventually dies, replace your yeast supply every six months. If you use it only occasionally, buy the $1/4$-ounce packages found in the grocery store and be certain that the sell-by date has not passed, and always keep your yeast refrigerated. To ensure that your yeast is still viable, you can proof, or activate, it just prior to use by soaking it in tepid water (about 70°F). Sometimes this is called "blooming" because the yeast opens up as it dissolves.

Salt

We tested the recipes in this book with fine-grain sea salt. I don't recommend kosher salt for baking, as the large grains don't dissolve easily. If you do use kosher salt, dissolve it in any liquid called for in the recipe rather than mixing it with the other dry ingredients. Also, because kosher salt is less compact than other forms of salt, if measuring by volume use a bit more than the recipe calls for, mounding it in the measure to make a generous teaspoon, for example.

Spices and flavorings

Buy spices in small amounts from the bulk aisle, and don't get more than you'll use in about six months. When fresh, spices are vibrant in color and have a potent aroma. Keep dried herbs and spices away from light, heat, and humidity.

Measuring: Scoop and Sweep

Measure dry ingredients in cups intended for dry goods. The cups should have straight sides and rims, so that contents can be leveled off with a straight edge. We like to measure flour like this: Dip a small scoop or a spoon (or your measuring cup) into the container and use it to fill your measuring cup with flour. When it appears full, gently shake the cup or lightly rap it on the counter, to settle the contents. Do not pack the flour. Then, use the edge of the scoop, the spoon handle, or a knife to level the cup, leaving you with a cup of flour that weighs $4^1/2$ to 5 ounces. All flour measurements are based on unsifted all-purpose flour.

Pure vanilla extract

Yes, pure vanilla extract is expensive. But it's also readily available, consistently good, and worth the extra pennies. A small bottle will last a good long time. If imitation is your only choice, skip it.

Chemical leavening agents

Many of the recipes in this book call for baking soda, baking powder, or both. Baking soda is sodium bicarbonate, which begins producing carbon dioxide as soon as it's combined with moisture and an acidic ingredient, such as yogurt or buttermilk. Items leavened solely with baking soda should be baked immediately after mixing to take advantage of the full potential lift. Baking powder is partially sodium bicarbonate but also contains starch and cream of tartar, which acts as its acidifying agent. Most baking powder is labeled "double-acting," meaning that it's been formulated to release some carbon dioxide when a liquid is added at room temperature, but the majority of its leavening is delayed until the dough is subjected to heat.

Like spices, chemical leavening agents deteriorate with age and should be replaced every six months or so. If you think your leavening is slightly older, add a bit more than the recipe suggests.

In the Refrigerator

Butter

Butter is one of the great basic ingredients of baking and plays a key role in the flavor and texture of nearly all baked goods. All butter is not created equal, however, and grocery store brands vary in flavor, butterfat content, and saltiness. The recipes in this book were tested with unsalted butter. If you only have salted butter on hand, reduce the amount of salt called for in the recipe by one-half.

Given the choice, I like to buy European-style butter (Plugrá, Challenge, and Straus Family Creamery are a few nationally available brands), especially for items like puff pastry and pie dough. These butters are enriched with a culture much like cheese and conse-

quently have a more complex and dynamic flavor. In the Northwest, we're particularly lucky to have locally produced Cremerie Classique from Larsen's Creamery in Oregon City available in most of our grocery stores.

Even though I enthusiastically endorse unsalted European-style butter, in a pinch I have made delicious pastry from whatever salted table butter I could round up. I'm only emphatic that you use real butter. If it's fresh, most butter tastes good and will keep in the refrigerator for about seven days. Freeze butter or store it in a resealable bag to preserve its fresh flavor longer.

Eggs

We've always had chickens running free on our family farm. I took the bright yellow yolks and robust flavor of farm-fresh eggs for granted until I left home. Now I realize this was due to a diet high in protein (from bugs) and carotene (from grass). Count yourself lucky if you have access to a good source of farm-fresh eggs and are able to use them in all of your baking. If you don't, you can use commercial eggs for cookies, cakes, quick breads, and other baked goods that don't showcase the quality of the eggs they contain. But for intensively eggy items like lemon curd, custard, popovers, and clafouti, using good eggs pays off. The recipes in this book were tested using large eggs.

In the Freezer

I grew up in a baking household, but I didn't fully understand the importance of a freezer until I became a professional baker. In a busy, high-volume bakery, freezers are used to hold raw ingredients, partially prepared items, and finished products. Because we are a commercial bakery with multiple outlets, our aim at Grand Central is to produce an assortment of seasonal, made-from-scratch baked goods daily, as efficiently as possible.

Controlling labor costs is one of the biggest challenges that a production bakery faces. A larger chunk of time than you'd imagine is spent gathering ingredients, setting up to bake, and cleaning up. In that light, it makes sense to prepare, say, a week's worth of a product once you're in the groove, and freeze it. That way, when you run out, there's more waiting in the freezer, ready to bake. For the home baker, having partially and fully prepared items in the freezer is the key to including baked goods as a quick, easy side note while preparing a meal.

BASIC INGREDIENTS

Most of these ingredients can be found in my freezer at any given time, although I don't necessarily have a specific plan for how or when I'll use them.

Berries

In the Northwest, we're blessed with an abundance of local fruits and berries but the season is never long enough. I use the freezer to extend my baking calendar by packing it with produce as it comes into season. Nothing cheers up a dark winter night quite like a warm peach cobbler or a juicy berry crumble baked from fruit that was frozen at its peak.

I like to buy organic berries. It's crucial that they be dry when they're frozen. Since I know I'm going to cook them before they're eaten, I don't wash them. Put the entire container, basket and all, in the freezer for several hours before transferring the frozen berries to a heavyweight resealable bag. When properly stored, frozen berries taste remarkably good right up until the next season rolls around.

Peaches

Canned peaches are one of my favorite winter treats, straight from the jar or spooned over vanilla ice cream. When it comes to satisfying a wintertime craving for peach pie or coffee cake, however, I use frozen sliced fruit.

Wait until one of the freestone varieties like Red Haven or Elberta is available to make splitting and slicing a breeze. Toss the sliced peaches with lemon juice and sugar—about $1/4$ cup of lemon juice and 1 cup of sugar for every 4 pounds of fruit—before scooping them into heavy freezer bags. This formula preserves their color and flavor and will work for any stone fruit.

Rhubarb

I adore rhubarb and find its season much too short to fit in all of the baking I want to do with it. I especially like to combine rhubarb with other fruits, like apples and raspberries. Happily, rhubarb freezes like a dream. Wash and dry the stalks, slice them crosswise, then pack the pieces in a freezer bag.

Butter

When butter's on sale, I stock up and keep the extra in my freezer. The coated cardboard box that it comes in protects it adequately, but if you are putting a stick that has been cut in the freezer, make sure to wrap it well.

Nuts

Because nuts have a high natural oil content, they can turn rancid quickly. Freezing nuts (either raw or toasted) slows down the rate at which they spoil. Store them in an airtight container with a lid that makes them easy to get to.

Egg yolks and egg whites

Making curd or custard will leave you with leftover egg whites, while a batch of meringue or macaroons means extra yolks. If you can't make use of those leftovers right away, store them in the freezer in airtight containers, where they'll keep for up to six months.

When freezing yolks, add a little bit of sugar to prevent them from becoming lumpy and grainy when thawed. Whisk in 1 teaspoon of sugar per each 3 yolks until blended, then transfer the mixture to a small freezer container.

BUILDING BLOCKS

A baker's basic building blocks don't vary wildly from one recipe to the next. Keeping some of the following items in your freezer is the real secret to becoming an everyday baker. With ready-to-use pie dough, streusel, or shortbread dough in the freezer, a home baker is poised to transform delicious fruit from the market (or the freezer) into a delicious dessert at a moment's notice.

Pie dough

Having a stash of frozen dough takes the most time-consuming step out of the pie-baking process. Open any serious pie baker's freezer and you're likely to find disks of dough, wrapped in plastic and ready to go. Those in the know will tell you that pie dough loves to be frozen. In fact, I think it makes the dough flakier by causing excess moisture to evaporate, leaving butter alone to hydrate the dough. Once the dough is made, you can easily put together a rustic tart, fruit pie, or batch of hand pies. Just be sure to defrost the dough overnight in the refrigerator or for an hour on the counter, until it's pliable enough to roll without cracking.

Shortbread dough

When you have a chunk of classic shortbread dough in the freezer, you're halfway to a fruit tart or crumble tart or cute, decorated cookies.

Puff pastry

Making puff pastry is a big project requiring a serious time commitment. If you're going to the trouble, I highly recommend that you make a big batch of our Rough Puff Pastry (page 178) and store what you don't use right away in the freezer.

Streusel and crumble topping

I like to mix up large batches of the caramely streusel included in the coffee cake recipe (page 30) and store it in my freezer. The same streusel that is delicious on a coffee cake transforms fresh or frozen fruit into a crisp, one of my favorite desserts. When I'm cooking for two, I like to make individual crisps in small, ceramic ramekins.

READY-TO-BAKE ITEMS

A cache of pie dough or bag of streusel in the freezer is one thing—and a wonderful thing at that—but full liberation for the home baker comes from knowing that the freezer is filled with a few ready-to-bake items. We use this trick at the bakery for a number of the items we produce regularly. None of the following baked goods suffer from spending a period of time in the freezer before baking.

Cake batter

We used to freeze whole, baked cakes, pulling them from the freezer daily to glaze and serve at the bakery. This was an okay solution for maximizing efficiency, but the frozen cakes didn't hold the same appeal as one fresh from the oven.

Then, one of the many ace bakers who have passed through Grand Central Bakery's doors shared this secret: Don't freeze the cake, freeze the batter. What a revelation! We began mixing large batches of batter that we portioned into individual cakes and froze. This allowed us to defrost the batter for an individual cake overnight and bake it fresh the next day. When you're mixing up a batch of cake batter, double the recipe or bake half and freeze half. You can also freeze already-baked cake layers, just like we used to at Grand Central.

Cookie dough

Use a scoop or spoon to shape cookie dough into balls, place them in a single layer on a baking sheet, and then chill or freeze them. Once they're firmly set up, transfer the balls of dough to resealable bags and store them in the freezer for baking in small batches. Logs of dough for the shortbread tea cookies freeze well too. You'll find the technique fully outlined on page 65.

Whole pies

If you're gearing up to bake a fruit pie, make two. Bake one immediately and freeze the other. I put the whole pie on a baking sheet in my chest freezer and wrap it in plastic wrap once it's frozen solid. When I have a hankering for pie, I take it straight from the freezer to a preheated oven. A frozen pie takes a little bit longer to bake, but the bottom crust never gets soggy since it's closer to the pan and begins to bake before the fruit begins to defrost.

Savory hand pies and rustic tarts

Handheld pastries and individual rustic tarts are perfect candidates for the freezer. In fact, it's easier to make these recipes in batches. Finished hand pies don't take much freezer space, and the convenience of baking a few at a time combines the ease of fast food with the nutrition and deliciousness of home cooking.

Quick breads

Fully baked banana, pumpkin, and cranberry orange pecan quick breads all keep remarkably well when wrapped in plastic wrap and frozen for up to three months.

Baked cookies

Nothing beats a cookie warm from the oven, but if you have baked cookies you want to keep fresh for more than a few days, freeze them in a resealable bag. I'd be surprised if anyone turned one down.

GENERAL EQUIPMENT

What you plan to bake will determine what equipment will be essential to your *batterie de cuisine*. The list that follows is not all-inclusive, but it does cover the equipment required for the recipes in this book. More specific or specialized tools are discussed in the recipes requiring them.

Baking pans

In addition to a couple of baking sheets, it's handy to have a modest collection of baking pans in a few basic sizes. If you don't have the exact size called for in a recipe, be certain to choose a pan that holds an equivalent volume. As a general rule of thumb, a round cake pan is three-quarters the volume of a square cake pan of the same size. The list below gives the volume of various sizes of pans.

Standard 12-cup muffin pan, $2^3/_4$ by $1^3/_8$ inches (scant $^1/_2$ cup each, or a bit less than 6 cups total)
8 by 8 by 2-inch square baking pan (8 cups)
9 by 5 by 3-inch loaf pan (8 cups)
9 by 13 by 2-inch rectangular baking pan (13 cups)
10 by $3^1/_2$-inch original Bundt pan (10 to 15 cups)
10 by 4-inch tube pan (16 cups)
9 by 3-inch springform pan (10 cups)
9 by $1^1/_2$-inch pie pan (4 cups)

A wide variety of round cake pans:
6 by 2 inches ($3^3/_4$ cups)
8 by 2 inches (7 cups)
9 by 2 inches ($8^2/_3$ cups)
10 by 2 inches ($10^3/_4$ cups)
12 by 2 inches ($15^1/_2$ cups)

Baking sheets

Once I'd baked with commercial baking sheets, I knew I could never go back to the flimsy, light-gauge metal pans sold for cookie baking. A 12 by 18-inch pan with 1-inch sides (also called a half sheet pan) is slightly larger than a conventional cookie or jelly roll pan, but not so much that it won't fit in your oven. I recommend it to the home baker for its size (large enough to maximize baking surface and oven space, small enough to slip in the freezer) and weight, which is sturdy enough for pizza. Chicago Metallic makes half sheet pans in nonstick and traditional aluminum.

THE **GRAND CENTRAL** BAKING BOOK

I prefer the traditional finish. I'm not sure it's possible to have too many of these; between two and four is ideal, so that you can have a couple in the oven while the others are cooling or being loaded with new items to bake.

Bamboo skewers

Bamboo skewers—the same ones used for kebabs—make the best cake testers.

Bench knife

Also called a bench scraper or dough scraper, this short metal sheet attached to a heavy, rounded wooden handle is my favorite kitchen tool. Use a bench knife any time you are tempted to use a knife blade to scrape or pry. It is indispensable for keeping sticky dough from adhering to your work surface. I also use it divide dough, chop nuts, and scrape my worktable during cleanup.

Bowl scraper

A round, plastic bowl scraper is an inexpensive, handy tool. It's useful for getting the last bit of dough or batter out of a bowl or scraping down the sides of a mixing bowl when creaming butter and sugar or incorporating eggs.

Electric stand mixer

I didn't get a fancy watch, a piece of luggage, or a fat check when I graduated from college. I got a heavy-duty, white, five-quart Classic KitchenAid stand mixer, and I still have it. For me, an electric stand mixer, with its beating, whipping, and kneading abilities, is a must-have for the home baker, even if it's a bit extravagant. A handheld mixer is an acceptable substitute when whipping egg whites or cream or mixing very soft butter, but most handheld mixers aren't up to the task of mixing stiff batters or large volumes properly. If a handheld mixer is the only mixer you have, be sure to use a mixing bowl with high sides to contain the ingredients when you mix. Use it to cream the butter and sugar, then rely on a strong arm and proceed by hand.

Fine-mesh sieve

Sieves and sifters come in all sizes, but it's most important to have one with a fine mesh in your collection, for sifting dry ingredients. Go ahead and invest in one with a stainless steel mesh, as other metals rust easily.

Freezer

Ellen and I both have chest freezers. They're efficient and economical, and we keep them packed to the gills. My dream freezer would probably be an upright model. A freezer with shelves allows you to store baking sheets, which is especially handy when chilling berries or cookies before transferring them to freezer bags. The downside of upright freezers is that they are more expensive and less efficient. A side-by-side configuration is, in my opinion, the least useful of the three, as its shelves don't accommodate regular-size baking pans and they tend to be inefficient in the same way that upright freezers are.

Graduated mixing bowls with high sides

Having bowls of at least three different sizes is essential to the home baker. I find bowls with a deep profile most useful, since the high sides help contain the ingredients when mixing. It's especially convenient to have extra-large and extra-small options. You can find inexpensive nested bowls made from many different materials; they usually come in sets of three, five, or seven bowls. A hodgepodge of bowls works too.

Kitchen scale

For a serious baker, there is no more accurate way to measure ingredients than to weigh them. I never used a scale before I began baking professionally. After using one daily in the bakery, I purchased a scale for my home kitchen and prefer to use it for all of my measuring. Once you're accustomed to working with one, not only is a scale more efficient and easy to use, you'll have fewer dishes to wash. If you don't have a kitchen scale, consider treating yourself. It's an inexpensive luxury, and soon you won't know how you lived without it.

We have provided weight equivalencies for volume measures for many of the ingredients in the recipes in this book because certain ingredients are most accurately measured by weight.

Knives

It takes just three knives to accomplish most of a baker's tasks: a paring knife, for peeling and cutting small fruits; a 6- or 8-inch chef's knife, for chopping nuts and chocolate and slicing and dicing fruit; and a long, gently serrated knife for cutting cakes into layers.

Measuring cups

When measuring by volume, it's important to use the correct container and the same method every time. For liquids, use a glass liquid measuring cup with clear markings. Rest the measuring cup on a flat surface and allow the liquid to settle before gauging the level. Choose the smallest measure suited to the job for the greatest accuracy; if you're measuring $1/4$ cup of liquid or less in a 4-cup measure, it's less likely to be accurate.

Dry measuring cups usually come in nested sets that include $1/4$-cup, $1/3$-cup, $1/2$-cup, and 1-cup measures. Choose cups with flat tops and straight rims, which allow you to sweep a level edge across the top for the most accurate measure.

What About a Food Processor?

Many well-respected bakers use a food processor for all kinds of things, including making pie dough, shortbread, and even cake batter. I reserve the use of my food processor for grinding nut meal and making pesto and mayonnaise. I understand why it is an attractive and effective shortcut for cutting butter into a dry mix; use the pulse feature judiciously to avoid overmixing. My rule of thumb is to use it for projects that take longer to complete by hand than than it takes to wash out the food processor bowl.

Measuring spoons

Amounts of ingredients requiring measurement in spoons are small by nature, so precision is the key. A complete set of graduated measuring spoons includes $1/8$ teaspoon, $1/4$ teaspoon, $1/2$ teaspoon, 1 teaspoon, and 1 tablespoon. The rims should be straight, as with dry measuring cups, so you can level the ingredients.

Microplane grater or citrus zester

Microplane graters and citrus zesters are handheld tools designed to delicately remove the outer, colored skin of citrus fruits. The microplane resembles a woodworker's rasp and is perfect for everything from zesting citrus to shaving chocolate. It removes the zest in short, thin pieces, while a zester removes it in long threads, which usually need to be finely chopped.

Nonstick pan liners

Silicone pan liners do the same job as parchment paper but can be washed and reused, over and over. They are expensive, but last a long time. I have a few Silpat brand pan liners, but I seem to use parchment paper more often.

Oven

The recipes in this book were tested in conventional 30-inch-wide gas, electric, and dual-fuel ovens. Technically, an electric convection oven yields the most consistent results, but I've baked extensively in ovens of all kinds and find that once you get to know your own, you'll be able to achieve success no matter what sort of oven you have. When it comes to the recipes in this book, you can use any standard oven, but it's a good idea to make use of an oven thermometer. Check it the first few times you bake something, paying close attention to the time and temperature suggested in the recipe and how closely those conform to your experience. A thermometer will help you figure out if your oven runs hot or cold (I've found most do one or the other), and identify the spots where the temperature tends to vary.

The problem with any oven is that the minute you open the door, the temperature can drop by at least 25°F and as much as 50°F. You can avoid this sudden dip by preheating your oven 25°F to 50°F above the desired temperature, but be sure to turn it down to the proper temperature as soon as the item is in the oven and the door is closed.

Avoid opening the oven during the first half of the total baking time; after that it's fine to open the door quickly to turn the pan around. This promotes even browning and is especially important if you bake in a still oven (as opposed to a convection oven). Convection ovens have a fan that circulates the hot air into every little nook and cranny of the oven, creating an even baking temperature. In theory, you can load up every shelf of a convection oven without worrying that anything will end up over- or underbaked. In reality, it's best to rotate the pans halfway through the baking time and not to overload your oven—even if it's a professional model. The rule of thumb when using a convection oven is to reduce the suggested oven temperature by 25°F and, sometimes, reduce the baking time by 10 to 15 percent.

The trick is to know your oven and make it work for you, whether you have a high-end dual-fuel oven or a standard model. If you have a gas oven or one with less insulation, preheating may take longer. Bake on the middle rack of a hot, clean (and therefore efficient) oven and rotate the pans at least once, and you'll be successful in your baking endeavors.

Parchment paper

One of the countless secrets I've picked up while working in a commercial bakery is that parchment paper is a baker's best friend. It's functional and convenient and has seemingly endless uses, from lining the bottoms of pans so that cakes release beautifully to keeping baking sheets clean and preventing baked goods from burning and sticking. You can even shape it into a cone for use as a disposable pastry bag. Parchment can be purchased in sheets or in a roll, both of which can be cut to fit any pan.

Pastry brush

I have several natural-bristle brushes in different sizes. They're inexpensive and easy to find, so replace them when they begin to get ratty.

Rolling pin

Having a rolling pin you feel comfortable using is critical. My favorite is a big, heavy, solid maple pin that I've had for years. I know many bakers who like the straight French pins that are 16 to 18 inches long and 2 or $2\,1/2$ inches in diameter. Ellen likes another type of French pin, which is very long, with tapered ends and a diameter of no more than $1\,1/2$ to 2 inches. Again, the body should be about 16 inches long. The conventional wisdom is that French pins are gentler on the dough. Stainless steel, marble, and nonstick pins are good for really sticky dough.

Rubber spatulas

You'll want at least one medium and one large heat-resistant spatula. Get spatulas with durable handles, and don't be tempted by those cheap spatulas you see everywhere; the rubber melts on contact with heat, and they tend to chip off and flake into your baked goods.

Wire whisks

Generally speaking, handheld beaters and stand mixers do the same job as a whisk, but much more quickly and easily. Still, I find that the right whisk also does a good job when paired with a strong, steady arm. A stiff, narrow sauce whisk blends mixtures without incorporating too much air, while a balloon whisk, which is made with finer, more flexible wires, is used to aerate whipped cream and mixtures like eggs and sugar. Having one of each type of whisk is nice.

2
Breakfast and Brunch

Early morning is my favorite time of day. The morning bake was my first shift at Grand Central, and while the obscenely early hour isn't for everyone, I loved it. I found immediate satisfaction in waking up with the bakery, being the first and only person there for several hours, during which I enjoyed three double espressos with Bob Edwards on NPR. Eventually the other workers trickled in, followed by a rewarding stream of customers clamoring for fresh pastries.

I still like to wake up early and coax my friends and family from their beds with the buttery sweet aroma of fresh pastry. The often-requested baked goods in this chapter were some of the first items I mastered as an early morning baker, and I think they're a good place to begin building a solid foundation in baking. Home bakers and loyal customers who want to bring a taste of Grand Central home will find some of the bakery's classics in this chapter, as well as recipes that have been popular in my family for decades.

SHORT DOUGH WORKSHOP **16**

Scones and Short Doughs **20**

Grand Central Bakery Scones 21

Grand Central Bakery Jammers 22

Irish Soda Bread 25

Muffins and Coffee Cake **26**

Blueberry Muffins 27

Anne's Bran Muffins 28

Bread Pudding Muffins 29

Sour Cream Coffee Cake 30

Quick Bread **31**

Banana Nut Bread 32

Pumpkin Bread 33

Cranberry Orange Pecan Bread 34

**Pancakes and
Their Eggy Cousins** **36**

Breakfast Crepes à la Ben 37

Popovers 38

Dutch Babies 39

Leavened with Yeast **40**

The Bakery Cinnamon Rolls 42

Pecan Sticky Buns 46

Gaufres Bruxelloises (Belgian
Waffles) 47

Black Cherry and Raspberry
Kuchen 48

Granola **51**

Megan's Apricot Almond
Granola 51

Minimally mixed, gently shaped, and baked on baking sheets, short dough pastries taste best straight from the oven. Their characteristic flaky texture is directly affected by the amount of shortening used, how it's incorporated into the dough, and how much (or how little) the gluten is developed. In my mind, perfectly mixed short dough bakes into a flaky, hearty pastry with a rich, buttery flavor. The techniques and principles outlined in this workshop can be applied to any biscuit-type pastry, including shortcakes, cream biscuits, and, of course, that trio of Grand Central Bakery favorites: scones, jammers, and Irish soda bread.

Essential Equipment

One of the best things about making short dough at home is that it requires virtually no special equipment. Using a stand mixer is easier for large batches, but I think mixing by hand is a great method. Use a bowl with high sides when mixing by hand.

You'll also need baking sheets. Cookie sheets with raised sides are fine, but I prefer heavy-gauge baking sheets with 1-inch sides, also known as half sheet pans.

Ingredients

All short dough recipes call for flour, shortening (I prefer butter), salt, and leavening. The leavening is usually baking soda or baking powder. Occasionally a recipe will call for both.

FLOUR

There are biscuit recipes that call for bleached flour or pastry flour, but I don't think either ingredient is necessary or even desirable. Both are treated with chemicals to ensure consistent results in a commercial bakery setting. I use unbleached all-purpose flour for most of my pastry baking. Bread flour can be used for short dough with good results too, as long as you're careful

not to overwork the dough. Because bread flour contains a higher percentage of gluten, overworking it will lead to pastries that aren't as tender.

BUTTER

Butter plays a key role in the rich flavor and tender texture of these breakfast pastries. Use unsalted butter unless salted is all you have; if you do use salted butter, cut back on the salt called for in the recipe. (The main reason to use unsalted butter in your baking is so you can control the flavor and ensure consistent results, since the amount of salt added to table butter varies from one brand to the next.)

LEAVENING AGENTS

Short dough pastries are frequently leavened chemically, with baking soda and/or baking powder rather than yeast. These agents cause baked goods to rise by producing carbon dioxide. When the dough captures the gas bubbles, it expands.

LIQUID

All but a few of our short dough recipes call for buttermilk. I think buttermilk is underappreciated. Its acidity activates the baking soda, yielding more volume with less leavening, and it also imparts a complex, tangy flavor. By contrast, the high fat content of heavy cream is desirable in shortcake biscuits and cream scones because it provides additional shortening and also moistens and hydrates the dough.

Technique

When all is said and done, the following technique, though quite detailed, can be summed up in two important principles: keep the ingredients and dough cold, and work quickly, with a light touch.

Prepare the dry ingredients.

When we hire early morning pastry bakers, their first challenge is to finish baking the breakfast pastries before 7:00 A.M., when Grand Central's doors open. Because we pride ourselves on selling the freshest pastries, bakers are encouraged to begin their day around 4:30 A.M. While this hour might seem unimaginably early to some, it actually doesn't leave much time to produce the impressive lineup of delicious breakfast pastries that greet our customers daily.

The key to timing this small miracle is good prep work. In addition to boosting efficiency, prepping short dough prior to mixing and baking helps ensure a flaky, tender texture. We measure out the dry ingredients and butter the day before and refrigerate them until the following morning, which means that the early morning bakers only have to cut in the butter and add the liquid before forming the pastries.

I encourage you to prepare yourself the same way. When baking anything biscuitlike for breakfast, measure the dry ingredients the evening before and refrigerate them overnight. You can even measure the ingredients into the mixing bowl and put the whole thing in the fridge. If you live in an unusually warm climate or have a hot kitchen, cut in the butter the night before so that it remains cool while you're mixing the dough. Warmth leads to soft butter, which results in the fat being absorbed by the flour, rather than encased by the flour, which is the secret to tender flakiness.

Cut in the butter.

Flakiness begins with butter. Because the object is to avoid mixing the fat with the flour, cutting butter into flour is the best technique. Think of the butter and dry ingredients existing separately while inhabiting the same space—next to one another without being a homogenous substance. Recipes for biscuits and pie dough often call for "pea-sized" or "pebbly" butter, but think of the shape and size of butter that has been properly cut in as resembling a dime. The idea is to achieve layers of butter stacked up on one another with flour in between, and as you can imagine, stacking dimes is much easier than stacking peas.

By hand: Dice the cold butter into $1/2$-inch cubes. Add the butter to the dry ingredients and toss everything together to coat the butter pieces with flour. Rub the butter and flour together between your thumbs and fingertips, pressing the butter flat and continuing to toss it with the flour.

(continued)

With a stand mixer: The paddle attachment of a stand mixer does a great job of cutting in as it rubs the butter into the flour and flattens it between the paddle and the bowl. Add the cubed butter to the flour and run the mixer on low speed. It will take a few minutes to incorporate the butter into the flour. If the mixture is no longer cool to the touch, or the butter appears greasy, stop mixing and put the entire bowl in the refrigerator or freezer for 20 to 30 minutes.

Mix the dough.

Recipes often warn not to overwork the dough. I coach new bakers to add the liquid, then mix short dough just until it comes together with a gentle kneading or a few rotations of the paddle. Stop mixing the instant it begins to form larger clumps. If the dry ingredients have been evenly and thoroughly hydrated, the dough has a better chance of coming together with minimal mixing. Still, this step requires careful, even incorporation of the liquid. Don't pour it all into one area, or some spots will be very wet while others are too dry. You can do this step either by hand or with a stand mixer.

Keep It Cold

Refrigeration is essential to slipping a baking project into your day. Feel free to chill dough at any stage; sometimes you'll even improve on the final product by using the refrigerator to "pause" the project. (However, once the liquid has been added, limit the pause to no more than a few hours.) Fully formed short dough can also be frozen. Wrap it tightly, and when you take the dough out of the freezer, let it defrost in the refrigerator; it will be ready to use the following day.

What Is Overworking?

An overworked short dough has been handled in such a way that the gluten in the flour begins to develop. Because hydration and action encourage the gluten to develop, pastries will become tough if the dough is mixed too vigorously after the butter or the liquid is added. This is why I continually emphasize the importance of properly hydrating the dough, and keeping it cool as you work with it. Undermixed dough, on the other hand, will crumble and fall apart, making it difficult to handle.

By hand: When mixing by hand, I use a fork as I introduce the liquid and my hands to coax the dough together. After cutting the butter into the dry ingredients, make a well in the center and pour three-quarters of the liquid into the well, reserving the rest for reluctant dry spots. Use the fork to pull the dry ingredients into the center of the well with a light lifting action, almost as if you're tossing the dry parts through the liquid. As the dough begins to clump, hit the few last dry spots with the remaining liquid, then use your hand or a plastic bowl scraper to make a few swipes around the edge of the bowl, loosening the dough and folding it back on itself until evenly hydrated.

With a stand mixer: Still using the paddle attachment, run the mixer on low speed and pour three-quarters of the liquid around the edge of the bowl in a single circular movement. Stop the mixer after four or five rotations and use a plastic bowl scraper or a rubber spatula to draw the dry bits off the sides and bottom of the bowl and scrape off the paddle. Mix for just a few more rotations while adding the remaining liquid to any visibly dry areas. Stop mixing when the dough begins to pull away from the sides of the bowl.

Form the dough.

Forming the dough properly is the final and most critical step in creating delicate, flaky short dough. Once the dough is hydrated and mixed, lightly dust a work surface with flour and turn the dough out onto it. At this point, many recipes instruct the baker to shape the dough into a ball before forming it into another shape. This seems like an unnecessary step to me, and even undesirable as it creates an opportunity to overwork the dough. Instead, I like to think of gathering and patting the dough.

Try to press the dough out in a manner that encourages flakiness. Use the heel and sides of your palms to gather and compact the dough, adding any stray bits to the top, rather than the sides. Concentrate on creating horizontal layers and handle the dough as little as possible. Use a firm hand to encourage the dough to do what you want while touching and handling it as little as possible.

JAMMERS, PAGE 22

SCONES AND SHORT DOUGHS

Jammers, scones, and Irish soda bread fall into a category we at Grand Central Bakery refer to as "short doughs." These biscuit-like pastries belong to the quick bread family and are leavened without yeast.

Baking with Dried Fruit and Nuts

Use good judgment when adding dried fruit and nuts to baked goods. Depending on the size of the finished item, you may or may not need to chop these ingredients into smaller pieces. The idea is to get a little bit of everything in each bite you take, rather than a mouthful of any one item.

Larger dried fruits, like dates, figs, apricots, and prunes, should always be chopped coarsely before they're added to cookies, bars, muffins, scones, or quick bread. Due to its high sugar content, dried fruit tends to make a gummy, sticky mess of your knife. Avoid this by lightly spraying or brushing a thin film of vegetable oil on the blade before chopping.

A light toasting brings out the best in most nuts, highlighting their naturally rich, sweet flavors. To toast shelled nuts, preheat the oven to 350°F, spread the nuts in a single layer on a baking pan, and bake until the nuts are lightly fragrant and just hot to the touch. They will color only slightly. Depending on the nut, this will take from 7 to 10 minutes. Watch them closely, as they can go from just right to burned in a matter of seconds.

Most nuts will overwhelm individual baked goods like muffins and cookies if you use them in their whole form. Unless you're adding them to an item that benefits from the whole nut's appearance, such as pecan pie, sticky buns, or nut brittle, coarsely chop them (after toasting) before adding them to the rest of the ingredients. Sliced or slivered almonds, pine nuts, and peanuts are usually best left as-is.

Egg Wash

Egg wash can be used as a glue to seal two pieces of dough together, or as a finish. When brushed on an unbaked pastry or loaf, it creates a sticky surface that will help sprinkled seeds or sugar adhere, and an attractive color and sheen once baked.

1 egg
1 tablespoon water
Pinch of salt

Whisk all of the ingredients together and brush onto baked goods before they go in the oven. If you have any leftovers, you can add them to your scrambled eggs at breakfast the next morning.

IRISH SODA BREAD, PAGE 25

Grand Central Bakery Scones

We keep an assortment of dried fruits and toasted nuts in each café's baking station so that pastry bakers can choose their own favorites to feature in that day's scone. Although the combinations are countless, over the years peach-pecan, cranberry-almond, apricot-walnut, and pear-hazelnut have been the most popular. When I make scones at home, I use whatever I have on hand and the results are always different and pleasing. (See Baking with Dried Fruit and Nuts, opposite.)

The size of the scones served in our cafés is generous; together with a cup of coffee, they make for a complete breakfast. This recipe yields 6 Grand Central–size scones, or you can shape the dough into 2 disks and cut 6 from each for smaller scones.

MAKES 6 LARGE OR 12 SMALL SCONES

$2^1/_2$ cups (12.5 ounces) all-purpose flour

$1/_4$ cup (1.75 ounces) granulated sugar

1 tablespoon baking powder

1 teaspoon salt

$1/_2$ teaspoon ground cinnamon

$1/_2$ cup (4 ounces, or 1 stick) cold unsalted butter

1 cup dried fruit

$1/_2$ cup nuts, lightly toasted and coarsely chopped (see sidebar, opposite)

2 eggs

$1/_2$ cup (4 fluid ounces) buttermilk

Egg wash (see sidebar, opposite)

$1/_4$ cup (1.75 ounces) turbinado sugar

Prepare to bake.

Preheat the oven to 350°F. Line a baking sheet with parchment paper.

Combine the dry ingredients.

Measure the flour, sugar, baking powder, salt, and cinnamon into a bowl with high sides or the bowl of a stand mixer and whisk to combine.

Cut in the butter, then add the fruit and nuts.

Dice the butter into $1/_2$-inch cubes. Use your hands or the paddle attachment of the stand mixer on low speed to blend the butter into the dry ingredients until the pieces of butter are the size of almonds. Add the dried fruit and nuts.

Add the eggs and buttermilk.

Whisk the eggs and buttermilk together, then add two-thirds of the mixture to the dry ingredients. Gently mix the dough just until it comes together, then add the remaining buttermilk mixture; the dough will look rough. Scrape the dough from the sides and bottom of the bowl and mix again to incorporate any floury scraps. The majority of the dough will have come together, on the paddle if using a stand mixer. Stop mixing while there are still visible chunks of butter and floury patches. The dough should come out of the bowl in one piece, leaving only some small scraps and flour on the sides.

Form and cut the dough.

Turn the dough out onto a lightly floured surface. Gather it and pat just a few times to get it to come together. The top won't be smooth, but the rough surface creates a crunch that is part of a scone's charm. Gently form dough into a 7- to 8-inch disk (or, for smaller scones, into two 4- to 5-inch disks), brush with the egg wash, and sprinkle with turbinado sugar. Cut the disk into 6 wedges, like a pie.

Bake.

Place the scones on the prepared pan, in a grid with 3 by 2 for large scones and 4 by 3 for small scones. Bake for 30 to 35 minutes (20 to 25 minutes for small scones), rotating the pan halfway through the baking time. The scones should be golden brown.

Grand Central Bakery Jammers

Like any good pastry, jammers are irresistible warm from the oven, and remember, the higher the quality of jam, the better the jammer. I recommend preparing the ingredients the night before. When you bite into a warm biscuit first thing the next morning, you'll consider the time well spent.

MAKES 10 TO 12 JAMMERS

4 cups (1 pound, 4 ounces) all-purpose flour

3 tablespoons granulated sugar

2 teaspoons baking powder

$1^1/_2$ teaspoons salt

1 teaspoon baking soda

1 cup (8 ounces, or 2 sticks) cold unsalted butter

$1^1/_4$ to $1^1/_2$ cups (10 to 12 fluid ounces) buttermilk

About $^3/_4$ cup good quality preserves or jam

Prepare to bake.

Preheat the oven to 350°F. Lightly grease a baking sheet or line it with parchment paper.

Combine the dry ingredients.

Measure the flour, sugar, baking powder, salt, and baking soda into a bowl with high sides or the bowl of a stand mixer and whisk to combine.

Cut in the butter.

Dice the butter into $^1/_2$-inch cubes. Use your hands or the paddle attachment of the stand mixer on low speed to blend the butter into the dry ingredients until the texture of the flour changes from silky to mealy. There should still be dime- to quarter-size pieces of butter remaining. If you're preparing the dough the night before, cover the bowl with plastic wrap and chill overnight; otherwise proceed with the recipe.

Add the buttermilk.

Make a well in the flour mixture and pour in 1 cup of the buttermilk in one addition. Gently mix the dough just until it comes together; it will look rough. Scrape the dough from the sides and bottom of the bowl, then add another $^1/_4$ cup buttermilk and mix again to incorporate any floury scraps. The majority of the dough will come together, on the paddle if you are using a stand mixer. Stop mixing while there are still visible chunks of butter and floury patches. The dough should come out of the bowl in 2 to 3 large, messy clumps, leaving only some small scraps and flour around the sides of the bowl. If the dough is visibly dry and crumbly, add up to $^1/_4$ cup more buttermilk, 1 tablespoon at a time, mixing no more than one rotation after each addition.

Form and cut the dough.

Turn the dough out onto a lightly floured surface. Use the heels and sides of your palms to gather the dough and gently pat it into an oblong shape $1^1/_2$ to 2 inches thick. It won't look smooth or particularly cohesive; that's okay. Use a biscuit cutter to cut the jammers into circles at least $2^1/_2$ inches in diameter. Layer the leftover scraps on top of one another and gently pat them out to a thickness of $1^1/_2$ to 2 inches and again cut into circles.

(continued)

Fill the jammers.

Use your thumb to make an indentation the size of a fifty-cent piece in the middle of each biscuit. While gently supporting the outside edge of the biscuit with your fingers, use your thumb to create a bulb-shaped hole that's a bit wider at the bottom and that goes almost to the bottom of the biscuit (think pinch pot). Try to apply as little pressure as possible to the outside of the biscuit, to avoid smashing the layers, which are the key to flaky jammers. Fill each indentation with 1 tablespoon of jam and put the jammers on the prepared baking sheet with 1 1/2 inches between them.

Bake.

Bake for 35 to 40 minutes, rotating the pan halfway through the baking time. The jammers should be a deep golden brown.

Make-It-Yourself Biscuit Cutter

If you don't have a biscuit cutter, you can use an empty 14-ounce can with a 3-inch diameter. Make sure the top has been cleanly cut away, leaving no jagged edges, and wash the can thoroughly before using it.

Irish Soda Bread

Being a fan of Grand Central's Irish soda bread herself, Ellen will tell you that this crowd is a fiercely loyal bunch, choosing this slightly sweet, crumbly pastry flavored with currants, orange zest, and caraway almost every time they visit the bakery. Less rich than a scone and not as sweet, it's the perfect breakfast when you can't decide between bread and a pastry.

MAKES 8 PIECES

4 cups (1 pound, 4 ounces) all-purpose flour
$1/3$ cup (2.25 ounces) granulated sugar
1 tablespoon baking powder
$1/2$ teaspoon baking soda
1 teaspoon salt
$2^1/4$ teaspoons caraway seeds
$1^1/2$ tablespoons finely chopped orange zest
$3/4$ cup (3.5 ounces) currants
$3/4$ cup (6 ounces, or $1^1/2$ sticks) cold unsalted butter
1 cup plus 2 tablespoons (9 fluid ounces) buttermilk
Egg wash (see page 20)

Prepare to bake.

Preheat the oven to 350°F. Line a baking sheet with parchment paper.

Combine the dry ingredients.

Measure the flour, sugar, baking powder, baking soda, and salt into a bowl with high sides or the bowl of a stand mixer and whisk to combine. Stir in the caraway seeds, orange zest, and currants.

Cut in the butter.

Dice the butter into $1/2$-inch cubes. Use your hands or the paddle attachment of the stand mixer on low speed to blend the butter into the dry ingredients until the texture becomes mealy. If you want to finish baking the soda bread the next day, cover the bowl with plastic wrap and chill overnight; otherwise proceed with the recipe.

Add the buttermilk.

Add $3/4$ cup of the buttermilk all at once, mixing just until the dough comes together, 30 to 35 seconds. Scrape the bottom and sides of the bowl to incorporate any dry ingredients, then stir in enough buttermilk to bring the dough together. You may have buttermilk leftover.

Form and shape the dough.

Turn the dough out onto a lightly floured surface and divide it into 2 chunks. Gently shape the chunks into domed disks and score each one into quarters. Place the each quarter on the prepared pan and brush liberally with the egg wash.

Bake.

Bake for 30 to 35 minutes, rotating the pan halfway through the baking time. The soda bread should be shiny and golden brown. To serve, cut or pull the disks apart where they were scored.

MUFFINS AND COFFEE CAKE

My favorite breakfasts begin with a plate of warm muffins or a fresh slice of yummy coffee cake, followed by eggs and bacon. I like to think of muffins and coffee cake as dessert in reverse—tasty little sweets to be enjoyed before the savory course in the morning.

THE **GRAND CENTRAL** BAKING BOOK

Blueberry Muffins

When it comes to great muffins, no berry is better suited than the blueberry. Practically speaking, fresh blueberries have a physical integrity that holds up to mixing well and won't leave purple streaks when folded into the batter. I love the way the tangy-sweet flavor of blueberries complements this rich, cakelike muffin. To ensure our muffins are as delicate as possible, we mix these with our hands. The tender texture is worth the mess.

MAKES 12 MUFFINS

3 cups (15 ounces) all-purpose flour

3/4 cup (5.25 ounces) granulated sugar

2 teaspoons baking powder

1 teaspoon baking soda

1 teaspoon salt

2 cups blueberries, fresh or frozen (unthawed)

4 eggs

3/4 cup (6 ounces, or 1 1/2 sticks) unsalted butter, melted and slightly cooled

1 teaspoon vanilla extract

1 cup (8 fluid ounces) buttermilk

Prepare to bake.

Preheat the oven to 350°F. Line a standard-size 12-cup muffin tin with paper liners, or lightly grease with butter.

Combine the dry ingredients and berries.

Measure the flour, sugar, baking powder, baking soda, and salt into a bowl with high sides and whisk to combine. Add the blueberries and toss with the dry ingredients until coated. Make a well in the center.

Combine the wet ingredients and add to the dry ingredients.

Lightly whisk the eggs with the butter and vanilla, then pour the mixture into the well. Evenly distribute the buttermilk around the outside edges of the dry ingredients.

Mix the batter.

Using your hands, pull the dry ingredients into the wet ingredients. Use big, slow, circular strokes and scrape the bottom and sides of the bowl with each motion. Stop as soon as the wet ingredients are incorporated; the delicate texture of this batter is achieved through minimal mixing. (Some small patches of flour may still be visible; this is okay, as they'll be absorbed during the baking process.)

Bake.

Scoop or spoon the batter (which will be relatively stiff) into the muffin tin, filling each cup about three-quarters full. Bake for 45 minutes, rotating the tin halfway through the baking time. The muffins should be golden brown and nicely domed, and a skewer inserted in the center of a muffin should come out clean.

Anne's Bran Muffins

Anne Obermeyer, who has been a pastry baker at the Hawthorne Avenue café for years, created this wholesome yet moist and delicious bran muffin recipe. The batter can be mixed up in advance; then you can just scoop and bake the muffins the next few mornings. This batch of batter makes a dozen muffins and keeps well for up to 4 days.

MAKES 12 MUFFINS

1/2 cup (3.5 ounces) packed light brown sugar

1/2 cup (4 ounces, or 1 stick) unsalted butter, melted and slightly cooled

1/3 cup (4 ounces) unsulfured or blackstrap molasses

2 eggs

1 1/4 cups (10 fluid ounces) buttermilk

3/4 cup (2 ounces) wheat bran

1 1/3 cups (6.75 ounces) all-purpose flour

2 tablespoons whole wheat flour

2 teaspoons baking powder

1 teaspoon baking soda

1 teaspoon salt

1 apple or 2 carrots, grated (about 1 cup)

1 cup (5.25 ounces) golden raisins

Prepare to bake.

Preheat the oven to 325°F. Line a standard-size 12-cup muffin tin with paper liners, or lightly grease it, then dust with flour.

Combine the sugar, wet ingredients, and bran.

Whisk the brown sugar, butter, molasses, eggs, and buttermilk together. Add the bran, stir to combine, then set aside to soften while you assemble the dry ingredients.

Combine the dry ingredients.

Measure the all-purpose and whole wheat flours, baking powder, baking soda, and salt into a bowl with high sides and whisk to combine.

Combine the wet and dry ingredients.

Fold the dry ingredients into the wet bran mixture just until combined. Add the apple and raisins and stir to distribute evenly. At this point, the batter can be refrigerated, or you can proceed with the recipe and bake the muffins.

Bake.

Scoop or spoon the batter into the muffin tin, filling each cup three-quarters full. Bake for 25 minutes, rotating the tin halfway through the baking time. The muffin tops should spring back when lightly poked in the center, the edges will darken slightly, and the tops will remain somewhat flat.

Bread Pudding Muffins

Bread pudding is normally found in the dessert chapter of a cookbook. When I was a baker, I arranged my baking schedule so that these bread puddings were still warm when the lunch crowd arrived. But there always seemed to be more customers asking for bread pudding early in the day. Not one to stand in the way of people who enjoy dessert for breakfast, I started baking the bread pudding earlier and earlier, until it wound up in the breakfast pastry lineup. Since Grand Central bread pudding is baked in muffin cups and tastes quite a bit like French toast, this seems fitting.

If you can't think about bread pudding before noon, don't hesitate to bake this for dessert. Finish it with a boozy hard sauce or fresh berries mixed with a bit of sugar to draw out their juices.

MAKES 12 PUDDING MUFFINS

1 pound crusty artisan white bread

$^1/_2$ teaspoon ground cinnamon

6 eggs

$^3/_4$ cup (5.25 ounces) granulated sugar

$1^1/_2$ cups (12 fluid ounces) heavy cream

$1^1/_2$ cups (12 fluid ounces) milk

2 teaspoons vanilla extract

Confectioners' sugar, for dusting

Prepare the bread.

Slice the bread and cut it into 1-inch cubes. Put it in a large bowl and toss it with the cinnamon.

Make the custard and pour it over the bread.

Whisk the eggs, sugar, cream, milk, and vanilla together until well combined, then pour the custard over the bread. Cover and refrigerate for at least 4 hours and up to 24 hours.

Bake.

Preheat the oven to 325°F. Line a standard-size 12-cup muffin tin with paper liners, or generously grease with butter.

Scoop a heaping $^1/_2$ cup of the pudding mixture into each of the 12 muffin cups; each one should be nicely mounded. Top off each pudding with any remaining custard.

Bake for 45 minutes, rotating the tin halfway through the baking time. The puddings should be lightly golden brown on top. Dust them with confectioners' sugar while they're still warm.

Sour Cream Coffee Cake

This moist and delicate coffee cake is topped with fresh fruit and a generous layer of crunchy, sweet streusel. I used spring rhubarb while experimenting with this formula and the result was almost like cake topped with rhubarb crisp. Now that's my idea of a great breakfast! In the summer, try any of the varieties of berries or stone fruits available, or a combination. You can also use frozen berries; just don't thaw them. Apples and pears stand in nicely when fall rolls around. If you take a few minutes the night before to measure out the dry ingredients, you can put this cake together even more quickly the next morning. Serve it hot out of the oven for a special breakfast treat.

SERVES 12

STREUSEL

$^1/_2$ cup (4 ounces, or 1 stick) cold unsalted butter

$^1/_2$ cup (3.5 ounces) granulated sugar

1 cup (7 ounces) packed light brown sugar

$^1/_2$ cup (2.5 ounces) all-purpose flour

Pinch of salt

$^3/_4$ cup (2.75 ounces) rolled oats

COFFEE CAKE

3 cups (15 ounces) all-purpose flour

$^3/_4$ cup (5.25 ounces) granulated sugar

1 tablespoon baking powder

1 teaspoon salt

4 eggs

$^3/_4$ cup (6 ounces, or $1^1/_2$ sticks) unsalted butter, melted and slightly cooled

1 teaspoon vanilla extract

$1^1/_2$ cups (12.75 ounces) sour cream

2 cups diced fresh fruit or berries

Prepare to bake.

Preheat the oven to 350°F. Lightly grease and flour a 9 by 13-inch baking pan.

Make the streusel.

Dice the butter into $^1/_4$- to $^1/_2$-inch cubes, then combine it with the granulated and brown sugars, flour, and salt. Use two knives, a pastry blender, or your fingers to mix the ingredients until crumbly, then mix in the oats. If you're making the streusel ahead of time, cover and refrigerate it until you're ready to proceed with the recipe.

Combine the dry ingredients for the cake.

Sift the flour, sugar, baking powder, and salt into a bowl with high sides. Make a well in the center.

Combine the wet ingredients and mix with the dry ingredients.

In another bowl, lightly whisk the eggs, butter, and vanilla together. Pour the mixture into the well, then add the sour cream by evenly distributing large spoonfuls around the edges of the dry ingredients. Gently mix the batter, using a large spatula to fold the dry ingredients into the wet ingredients. Use big, slow, circular strokes that scrape the bottom and sides of the bowl with each motion. Don't worry if the batter appears slightly lumpy, or if there are streaks of sour cream. The delicate texture of this batter is achieved through minimal mixing. (Some small patches of flour may still be visible; this is okay, as they'll be absorbed during the baking process.)

Finish the coffee cake and bake.

Scrape the batter into the prepared pan. Distribute the fruit in an even layer over the batter, then sprinkle evenly with the streusel. Bake for 45 minutes, rotating the pan halfway through the baking time. The streusel should be crunchy and brown, and a skewer inserted in the center should come out clean.

Serve the coffee cake straight from the oven with plenty of fresh, piping hot coffee.

QUICK BREAD

There are hundreds of recipes for banana bread, pumpkin bread, and cranberry pecan bread, and honestly, I'm not sure the world needs three more. But the number of recipe requests I've received over the years for these three popular items leads me to believe that people want to be able to bake the Grand Central Bakery versions at home.

Quick bread is fast, easy, and forgiving. We bake loaves once a week, on Tuesdays, in batches of hundreds, just enough to get us through until the next Tuesday. Quick bread is the only product we freeze fully baked before we sell it. If wrapped well in plastic wrap, quick bread will still be moist and delicious even after several months in the freezer. Keep this in mind before the holidays roll around; this way everyone on your list can be the happy recipient of a mini loaf—with a minimum of effort and kitchen time on your part.

These recipes yield two loaves each. Since you're going to the trouble of baking anyway, make an extra loaf for your freezer. Eat one now and squirrel the other one away until next week or next month.

Banana Nut Bread

I can't think of a better way to use up overripe bananas. This nutty quick bread is especially delicious toasted, with a schmeer of cream cheese.

SERVES 6 TO 8 PER LOAF; MAKES 2 LOAVES

4 cups (1 pound, 4 ounces) all-purpose flour

1¹/₂ teaspoons baking soda

1 teaspoon baking powder

1 teaspoon salt

2 cups (14 ounces) granulated sugar

²/₃ cup (5 fluid ounces) vegetable oil or canola oil

2¹/₂ cups (1 pound, 4 ounces) banana puree (about 4 small bananas)

4 eggs

2 teaspoons vanilla extract

1 cup (8 fluid ounces) buttermilk

1¹/₂ cups (6 ounces) walnuts, lightly toasted and coarsely chopped (see page 20)

Prepare to bake.

Preheat the oven to 350°F. Lightly grease and flour two 9 by 5-inch loaf pans.

Combine the dry ingredients.

Measure the flour, baking soda, baking powder, and salt into a bowl and whisk to combine.

Beat the sugar, oil, and bananas.

Using a stand mixer with the paddle attachment, beat the sugar, oil, and banana puree on medium-high speed until the mixture is lighter in color, about 3 minutes.

Add the eggs and vanilla.

Crack the eggs into a liquid measuring cup, add the vanilla, and whisk together. With the mixer on low speed, slowly pour in the eggs. Continue to mix until the eggs are fully incorporated.

Alternate additions of the dry and wet ingredients.

Add one-third of the dry ingredients and mix briefly on low speed, then add half of the buttermilk. Mix well and repeat, using half of the remaining dry ingredients and the rest of the buttermilk. Add the remaining dry ingredients and mix just until combined.

Add the nuts.

Use a large spatula to scrape the sides of the bowl and fold in 1 cup of the walnuts. Scrape the bowl one more time, then divide the batter between the prepared pans. Sprinkle the loaves with the remaining ¹/₂ cup walnuts.

Bake.

Bake for 30 minutes, then rotate the pans and bake for 30 minutes more. Lower the temperature to 325°F, rotate again, and bake for 30 minutes more. The loaves should be golden brown with cracked tops, and a skewer inserted in the center should come out clean.

Pumpkin Bread

My nephew Sam was born the same year we opened the first Grand Central Bakery in Portland. This pumpkin bread was one of his early solid foods—he would toddle into the bakery and ask for it by name. Today, he is a strapping 14-year-old, and despite the extensive display of delicious treats he can choose from when he visits his dad at work, he goes for pumpkin bread 99 percent of the time. This sweet, fragrant bread stays moist for days.

SERVES 6 TO 8 PER LOAF; MAKES 2 LOAVES

3^1/$_4$ cups (1 pound, .25 ounce) all-purpose flour

1^1/$_2$ teaspoons baking soda

1 teaspoon salt

1 tablespoon pumpkin pie spice (see sidebar)

^{1}/$_3$ cup (2.75 fluid ounces) vegetable oil or canola oil

1^2/$_3$ cups (11.75 ounces) granulated sugar

1^1/$_3$ cups (9.25 ounces) packed light brown sugar

2 cups (15 ounces) pumpkin puree

4 eggs

^{1}/$_3$ cup (2.75 fluid ounces) water

^{1}/$_3$ cup (2.75 fluid ounces) buttermilk

Prepare to bake.

Preheat the oven to 350°F. Lightly grease and flour two 9 by 5-inch loaf pans.

Combine the dry ingredients.

Measure the flour, baking soda, salt, and pumpkin pie spice into a bowl and whisk to combine.

Combine the oil, sugar, and pumpkin.

Using a stand mixer with the paddle attachment, mix the oil, granulated and brown sugars, and pumpkin puree on medium-low speed until well blended, about 2 minutes.

Add the eggs.

Crack the eggs into a liquid measuring cup and whisk together. With the mixer on low speed, slowly pour in the eggs, incorporating each addition completely before adding the next. Scrape the bottom and sides of the bowl.

Alternate additions of the dry and wet ingredients.

Add one-third of the dry ingredients and mix briefly on low speed, then add the water. Mix well and repeat, using half of the remaining dry ingredients and all of the buttermilk. Add the remaining dry ingredients and mix just until combined. Scrape the sides of the bowl and then divide batter between the prepared pans.

Bake.

Bake for 60 to 75 minutes, rotating the pans every 20 minutes or so. The loaves should be dark golden brown with cracked tops, and a skewer inserted in the center should come out clean.

Pumpkin Pie Spice

^{1}/$_4$ cup ground cinnamon

2 tablespoons ground ginger

1 tablespoon ground nutmeg

1 tablespoon ground cloves

1 tablespoon ground allspice

Combine all of the ingredients in a small bowl and stir with a fork until well combined. Store in a cool, dry place for up to 3 months.

Cranberry Orange Pecan Bread

I grew up baking a version of this Christmastime classic with canned orange juice concentrate. When it came time to develop a recipe for the bakery, we updated the family favorite by replacing the concentrate with freshly squeezed orange juice and plenty of zest. The result is a more subtle orange flavor that allows the tartness of the cranberries to shine through.

SERVES 6 TO 8 PER LOAF; MAKES 2 LOAVES

3^1/$_2$ cups (1 pound, 1.5 ounces) all-purpose flour

1^1/$_2$ teaspoons salt

^{3}/$_4$ teaspoon baking soda

2^1/$_4$ cups (15.75 ounces) granulated sugar

^{3}/$_4$ cup (6 fluid ounces) vegetable oil or canola oil

3 eggs

1^1/$_4$ cups (10 fluid ounces) buttermilk

Zest and juice from one large orange
    (about 1^1/$_2$ tablespoons zest plus ^{1}/$_4$ cup juice)

^{1}/$_2$ teaspoon vanilla extract

1^3/$_4$ cups cranberries, fresh or frozen

^{1}/$_2$ cup (1.75 ounces) pecans, lightly toasted and
    coarsely chopped (see page 20)

Prepare to bake.

Preheat the oven to 350°F. Lightly grease and flour two 9 by 5-inch loaf pans.

Combine the dry ingredients.

Measure the flour, salt, and baking soda into a bowl and whisk to combine.

Beat the sugar and oil.

Using a stand mixer with the paddle attachment, beat the sugar and oil on medium-high speed until thoroughly combined; the mixture will look sandy.

Crack the eggs into a liquid measuring cup and whisk together. With the mixer on low speed, slowly pour in the eggs. Increase to medium speed and continue to mix for 2 minutes more.

Mix the wet ingredients, then alternate additions of the dry ingredients and the wet ingredients.

Whisk together the buttermilk, orange zest and juice, and vanilla. Add one-third of the dry ingredients and incorporate on low speed, then increase the speed to medium. Mix for 1 minute. Add half of the buttermilk mixture and mix briefly to incorporate, then turn the speed down to low. Add half of the remaining dry ingredients, and incorporate before increasing the speed to medium for 1 minute. Repeat with the remaining buttermilk mixture and the remaining dry ingredients. Scrape the bottom and sides of the bowl.

Add the cranberries and nuts.

Fold the cranberries and pecans into the batter by hand, scrape the sides of the bowl, and then divide the batter evenly between the prepared pans. Each should be slightly more than half full.

Bake.

Bake the loaves for 60 to 75 minutes, rotating the pans every 20 minutes or so. The loaves will be golden brown with cracked tops, and a skewer inserted in the center should come out clean.

PANCAKES
AND THEIR EGGY COUSINS

My mother has always integrated some element of farming into her daily life; even as a city resident she embraced animal husbandry. As a result, throughout my childhood we always had a few laying hens—if not 50! (This really happened, when we lived in Seattle.) Although I took it for granted at the time, I realize now how lucky we were to have a ready supply of good eggs, and I understand how they shaped my mother's repertoire. Growing up, we ate lots of pancakes and baked goods that benefited from the bright, protein-rich eggs that were in constant supply. Good eggs are an important ingredient in the scratch baker's pantry, but especially in the following items.

Making Crepes:
Tricks for Making the Cook's Job Quick and Easy

* It won't harm the batter to let it rest for up to 20 minutes before making the crepes.

* Use the best eggs you can find. Farm-fresh eggs make a huge difference in the flavor, texture, and color of crepes.

* Peel half of the wrapper off a stick of cold butter. Use it like a glue stick to lightly coat the pan between crepes. Start with the sides of the pan, where most sticking occurs, and spiral in to the center of the skillet. Quickly add the batter before the butter burns.

* Keep your crepes thin! They should be slightly translucent when held up to a window.

* If you get too much batter in the pan, pour the excess right back into the blender.

* As with pancakes, the second or third crepe will be better than the first. Continue to adjust the level of hydration as needed until the batter is gone.

* Add your filling of choice after the next crepe is in the skillet. Cook a crepe, remove to a plate, butter the skillet, add batter, then fill (and eat) the crepe on the plate—then repeat. I get my next crepe going right away so that the skillet doesn't get too hot from sitting empty.

* To roll crepes, add your favorite condiment in a thin layer, fold the left and right sides over an inch or so, and roll it up from the bottom, like a burrito.

* Some favorite fillings include jam, honey, butter (use the butter stick) and powdered malted chocolate milk flavoring (try Ovaltine), and confectioners' sugar lightly drizzled with freshly squeezed lemon juice.

* Get a sugar shaker. Jam-filled crepes dusted with confectioners' sugar make a nice presentation.

* Our family eats crepes (and pancakes) as they come out of the skillet, but you can keep them warm in a 200°F oven and enjoy them all at once, as a group. Still, I think they're best straight from the pan.

Breakfast Crepes à la Ben

My brother Ben has been making crepes for his three kids for over twelve years. They eat them every other day before school and insist that the crepes appear on schedule. He figures he's made over eighteen thousand crepes now and can complete an entire batch, start to finish, in just fifteen minutes.

Ben thinks crepes are a great way to sneak some protein into kids who hate eggs. Sam, his oldest son, likes to fill his crepes with raspberry jam or chocolate, so Ben uses Ovaltine powder in the hope that it has some added nutritional benefits. Theo is more of a purist and eats his with confectioners' sugar, while Ana drizzles her crepes with honey before rolling them up.

The crepes are tossed on plates, filled, rolled, and eaten out of hand—no forks for this crew. Also, Ben's crepes are eaten as they are made, so it's important to remember who got the last crepe or an argument is likely to ensue about who gets the next one— they're that tasty. This recipe makes enough crepes for three growing kids and their dad.

MAKES 12 TO 14 TEN-INCH CREPES

3 eggs
1 1/2 cups (12 fluid ounces) whole milk
1 1/4 cups (6.25 ounces) all-purpose flour
1 tablespoon granulated sugar
1/2 teaspoon salt

Make the crepe batter.

Add the eggs, milk, flour, sugar, and salt to a blender. Mix on low speed for 20 seconds. Stop, scrape the sides of the blender, then mix for an additional 10 seconds. There should be a vortex the size of a nickel in the batter when the blender is on low speed.

Adjust and test the batter.

Depending on the size of the eggs and humidity of the flour, the batter may need to be adjusted. Thick batter makes thick crepes and crepes made with overly thin batter have lots of holes and are difficult to flip without tearing. Make a test crepe and adjust the batter as needed, adding a few tablespoons of milk for a wetter batter, or a few tablespoons of flour for a stiffer batter. The batter should pour off a spoon easily, leaving enough behind to coat the spoon. Eventually you'll develop an eye for what proportions work for you.

Cook the crepes.

Melt a bit of butter in a heavy 10- to 12-inch nonstick (or well-seasoned) skillet over medium-high heat until just before the butter burns. Be sure there's enough butter to cover the surface of the pan.

Pour in a pool of batter half the diameter of the skillet. Lift the pan off the heat and angle, jiggle, and rotate it in a circle to distribute the batter evenly. When the skillet temperature is just right, a crepe will be ready to flip in 30 seconds. Flip it with a spatula and cook the other side for 15 seconds. It should be blond to light brown in color.

Cook the crepes without stopping until the batter is gone. Cooking them back-to-back will help you judge the timing. Once you get the rhythm, 12 crepes will take under 12 minutes. You can hold them in a warm oven (200°F) until you gather everyone together.

Popovers

My mother remembers eating popovers with butter and jam as a child, with Sunday supper. Her mother, Dorothy Piper, born in 1902, was a devotee of the 1923 edition of Fannie Farmer's Boston Cooking School Cookbook. *I'm told my grandmother followed Fannie's advice to a T and insisted on pouring her popover batter into the recommended "hissing-hot cast iron gem pan." This predecessor to the muffin tin was a popular piece of kitchen equipment at the turn of the century that was used to bake all sorts of small cakes.*

My grandmother had a deep cast-iron pan tapered specifically for popovers. I encourage any baker lucky enough to stumble upon one of these pans to buy it. If you can't find one at an antique store or flea market, Chicago Metallic's deep popover pan also turns out a dramatic popover, and a simple heavy-gauge muffin tin will do the trick too. Regardless of the pan you use, I am in complete agreement with Ms. Farmer that the best popovers start in a "hissing-hot" pan.

Some popover recipes call for using a blender to mix the batter, but I like to use a whisk simply because I'd rather wash a whisk than a blender. Whether you serve popovers for breakfast or alongside a roast with gravy, plan to have them ready just as you sit down. Popovers are never better than when they're served steaming hot, straight from the oven.

MAKES 6 POPOVERS IN A POPOVER PAN,
OR 10 IN A STANDARD MUFFIN TIN

1 cup (8 fluid ounces) whole milk

3 eggs

$1/_2$ teaspoon salt

1 cup (5 ounces) all-purpose flour

Mix the batter.

Whisk the milk, eggs, and salt together in a bowl with high sides until the mixture is uniform in color and slightly foamy. Sift the flour (this will help reduce the number of lumps), then add it slowly, whisking until the batter is uniform and has the texture of heavy cream. (If it's lumpy, run the batter through a fine-mesh sieve.)

Let the batter rest.

Cover the batter with plastic wrap and allow it to rest on the counter for 20 to 30 minutes. (Resting isn't essential, but it improves the height and finished texture of the popovers.) Preheat the oven to 450°F. Once the oven is hot, put the pan in to heat until it's "hissing hot."

Bake.

Put some softened butter and a small pastry brush next to the oven. Pull the hot pan from the oven and, working quickly, brush each cup with butter, then fill it halfway with batter. Return the pan to the oven and bake for 15 minutes, then lower the oven temperature to 350°F and continue baking for 10 more minutes, or until the popovers are golden brown and have "popped," that is, puffed up and begun to lean over the edges of each cup. Serve immediately.

Dutch Babies

When I was six years old, Sunset *magazine featured a Dutch baby on its cover. Although that was back in 1971, I feel like I remember the arrival of that particular issue. (More likely, the tattered copy lying around our house for years is what lingers in my memory.) What I do remember for sure is the introduction of the Dutch baby into our family's life. Credited to Seattle restaurateur Viktor Manka, Dutch babies taste like giant popovers, and we loved them.*

For a sweet breakfast, finish Dutch babies with a squeeze of lemon juice and a dusting of confectioners' sugar, maple syrup, or good jam. But don't reserve this eggy treat just for mornings. For a simple dinner, my mother sometimes added ground beef, Cheddar cheese, and green onions (it was the 1970s after all), and I like to use this recipe to make Yorkshire pudding to go with roast beef, substituting pan drippings for some of the butter.

Make a little Dutch baby for yourself, or a large one for a crowd. A cast-iron skillet works the best. In fact, my most well-seasoned cast-iron skillet is a result of making endless Dutch babies. If you're making an eight-serving Dutch baby, use a Dutch oven with the lid off.

Prepare to bake.

Put the appropriate size cast-iron skillet in the oven and preheat it to 350°F.

Make the batter.

Combine the eggs, milk, flour, and salt in a bowl with high sides, a food processor, or a blender. Whisk by hand or briefly blend until the batter is smooth and lump free.

Bake.

When the oven is hot, quickly remove the skillet and close the door. Add the butter and, as soon as it melts, pour in the batter. Return the skillet to the oven, set a timer, and don't open the oven door until the timer goes off. The Dutch baby should be deep golden brown, and the sides should be puffed up.

SERVES	SKILLET	EGGS	MILK	FLOUR	SALT	BUTTER	BAKING TIME
2	8-inch	2	$1/2$ cup (4 fluid ounces)	$1/2$ cup (2.5 ounces)	$1/4$ teaspoon	2 tablespoons	20 minutes
4	10-inch	4	1 cup (8 fluid ounces)	1 cup (5 ounces)	$1/2$ teaspoon	$1/4$ cup (2 ounces, or $1/2$ stick)	25 minutes
6	12-inch	6	$1^1/2$ cups (12 fluid ounces)	$1^1/2$ cups (7.5 ounces)	$3/4$ teaspoon	6 tablespoons (3 ounces, or $3/4$ stick)	30 minutes
8	12-inch	8	2 cups (16 fluid ounces)	2 cups (10 ounces)	1 teaspoon	$1/2$ cup (4 ounces, or 1 stick)	35 minutes

LEAVENED WITH YEAST

Although yeast is most often associated with bread-making, it can be used to leaven a variety of baked goods. I like the substantial texture and hearty flavor that comes from using yeast and longer periods of fermentation. You won't find these breakfast treats to be light and flaky, but you will find them delicious.

Basics of Leavening with Yeast

The behavior of yeast can be baffling to an inexperienced baker, but with a basic understanding of its chemistry, you can take control of the leavening process.

Humans have been leavening baked goods with yeast for thousands of years. It probably happened inadvertently at first: a crude mixture of wheat flour and water left outside began to collect yeast spores naturally, which resulted in a lighter, better-tasting loaf. While leavening bread with a natural starter is a worthy goal for the serious baker, practical home bakers are well served by commercially produced active dry yeast.

The leavening process begins when yeast enzymes break the starch from flour down into simple sugars, which are easy for yeast to metabolize. Carbon dioxide and ethyl alcohol, the by-products of all this metabolic activity (fermentation), fill the elastic bubbles created by development of the flour's gluten, encouraging the dough to rise.

The most challenging aspect of leavening with yeast is calculating the time it will take. The rate of fermentation depends on two variables: temperature and the amount of sugar accessible to fuel the yeast. You can experiment with different sugar levels, but I encourage novice bakers to focus on a single variable, and temperature is the variable with the most impact. To move the dough along, keep it in a warm place. Yeast is extremely active above 80°F. Or to slow the rising process, put the dough in a cool place; yeast gets sleepy and goes dormant below about 50°F. I use my refrigerator, which runs about 45°F, to slow the rising process, or find a warm spot to hurry something along, typically the top of my stove or a window with the sun streaming in. For the final rise of shaped dough (sometimes called proofing), I think a warm room temperature (between 70°F and 75°F) works best.

Baked goods leavened with yeast usually come together in several stages. Use the following guidelines to decide when it's time to move on to the next stage.

HOW TO JUDGE FERMENTATION

STAGE OF DOUGH OR BATTER	SIGNS OF TOO LITTLE FERMENTATION	SIGNS OF TOO MUCH FERMENTATION	SIGNS THAT IT'S JUST RIGHT
Pre-ferment or sponge	No bubbles, odor, or increase in volume	Stringy, collapsed, or separated Smells strongly of alcohol or acidity	Bubbly with increased volume Sweet, light, yeasty odor
Final dough	Hasn't doubled in size Stiff, not stretchy	Collapsed in the bowl Has a strong odor	Nicely domed and springs back slowly after light pressure Lightly alcoholic tang
Final formed product	Small, stiff, and dense Unusually dark color when baked	Big, pillowy, and more than doubled in size Collapses when poked or scored Ashen, light color when baked	Increases 30% to 50% in size Elastic when poked with a finger; indentation quickly disappears Rich golden color when baked

The Bakery Cinnamon Rolls

My earliest memories of the bakery revolve around these cinnamon rolls. A Grand Central favorite since day one, they're the only item we've never taken off the menu. The hearty whole grain dough combined with the sugary cinnamon goo sets these cinnamon rolls apart from the rest. No frosting needed.

Cinnamon rolls are the perfect answer to breakfast occasions that call for a special treat. Or offer them instead of toast, as a sweet complement to scrambled eggs and bacon that feels a bit decadent, like having dessert with breakfast.

Beginning the fermentation with a sponge (or pre-ferment) improves the texture and flavor of this whole grain dough. I recommend mixing the dough and forming the rolls the day before you plan to serve them. Store them in the refrigerator overnight,. When you wake up, put them out to warm up while you're preheating the oven.

MAKES 12 ROLLS

SPONGE

2^1/$_2$ cups (20 fluid ounces) tepid water (about 80°F)

2 teaspoons active dry yeast

3 tablespoons molasses

^{1}/$_2$ cup (2.5 ounces) whole wheat flour

^{1}/$_2$ cup (3 ounces) eight-grain cereal (with cracked—not rolled—grains)

2 cups (10 ounces) unbleached white or bread flour

FINAL DOUGH

2^1/$_2$ to 3 cups (12.5 to 15 ounces) unbleached white or bread flour

^{1}/$_4$ cup (2 ounces, or ^{1}/$_2$ stick) unsalted butter, melted and slightly cooled

1 tablespoon plus 1 teaspoon salt

FILLING

^{1}/$_2$ cup (4 ounces, or 1 stick) unsalted butter, at room temperature

^{3}/$_4$ cup (5.25 ounces) granulated sugar

^{3}/$_4$ cup (5.25 ounces) packed light brown sugar

1 teaspoon ground cinnamon

^{1}/$_4$ cup (1.5 ounces) currants

Make the sponge.

Measure the water, yeast, molasses, whole wheat flour, cereal, and white flour into a bowl with high sides and whisk or beat until smooth. Cover tightly with plastic wrap and let the sponge sit at room temperature for 2 hours, or in the refrigerator for about 12 hours, until it shows signs of active fermentation. It should be bubbly and a bit stringy when you stir it.

Mix the final dough.

Combine the active sponge with the flour, butter, and salt in the bowl of a stand mixer fitted with the dough hook attachment or a bowl with high sides. If using a stand mixer, mix on low speed until the dry ingredients are fully incorporated, 2 to 3 minutes, then increase the speed to medium and mix for 3 to 4 minutes more. The dough should be smooth and pull away from the sides of the bowl. If the dough seems too wet or sticky, add a bit more flour. If mixing by hand, stir the ingredients together with a wooden spoon until evenly incorporated, then turn the dough out onto a lightly floured surface and knead until it is a smooth, cohesive mass.

Let the dough rise.

Lightly brush a clean, large bowl with oil or butter, then put the dough in the bowl, cover with plastic wrap, and let rise until doubled in size. When you poke the dough gently, the indentation should spring back slowly. You can speed the process along by putting the dough in a warm spot (about 80°F), or slow it down in a cooler spot (about 60°F), or refrigerate to stretch the process out over an entire day.

(continued)

At the bakery, we chill the dough for an hour after it has risen to the desired height. During this time, the activity of the yeast slows down, and the dough becomes slightly stiffer, making it easier to form.

Prepare the baking pan and filling, roll, and fill the dough.

Grease a 9 by 13-inch baking pan with 2 tablespoons of the butter.

Combine the granulated and brown sugars with the cinnamon. Reserve $1/3$ cup of the mixture to sprinkle on top of the rolls. Since you'll be using the reserved mixture the next day, it's best to store it in an airtight container.

Turn the dough out onto a lightly floured surface. Use a combination of gentle stretching and light rolling to shape it into a 20 by 12-inch rectangle. Spread the remaining 6 tablespoons butter over the entire rectangle of dough and sprinkle the cinnamon sugar and currants on top.

Tuck and Goose

The characteristic perky, conical shape of our cinnamon rolls is achieved by gently stretching the loose end of the dough, wrapping it around itself, and tucking the tail under and into the center of the bottom of each roll. Push up slightly at the same time to make the center pop out.

Shape and cut the dough.

With a long side of the dough facing you, begin rolling from the bottom, using a good amount of pressure and wrist action as you push the dough forward and then pull it back toward you. This creates a nice tight roll. The log should be 20 to 24 inches long and 2 to 3 inches in diameter.

Cut the rolls.

Using a serrated knife, slice the log in half. Score each half into six 2-inch-thick rolls, then gently cut the rolls. Arrange them in the prepared pan so that they're evenly spaced, 3 by 4. As you place the rolls in the buttered pan, "tuck and goose" each one (see sidebar).

Let the rolls rise.

Cover the pan loosely with plastic wrap and let the rolls sit in a warm spot (at least 75°F) for 30 to 60 minutes before refrigerating overnight; this time will vary depending on the temperature. Look for signs that the yeast is active: the rolls expanding and swelling slightly; the sides coming close to touching one another; or moisture forming inside the plastic wrap.

Bake.

Preheat the oven to 350°F when you wake up. Take the rolls from the refrigerator and set them in a warm spot (75°F to 80°F) to come to room temperature and rise; the top of your oven as it preheats is a perfect spot. Don't remove the plastic wrap. You'll know the rolls have risen properly when they touch one another and the dough is soft enough that it springs back leisurely when lightly poked.

Remove the plastic wrap, sprinkle the reserved $1/3$ cup cinnamon sugar on top of the rolls, and bake for 35 to 45 minutes, rotating the pan halfway through the baking time. The rolls should be a dark golden brown. If the rolls begin to color too much, lower the oven temperature to 325°F after the first 30 minutes.

Pecan Sticky Buns

For delicious sticky buns, add toasted pecans and gooey caramel to the bottom of the baking pan when making The Bakery Cinnamon Rolls (page 42). Follow the directions for The Bakery Cinnamon Rolls, but leave out the currants, and don't grease the pan with the 2 tablespoons of butter. And rather than reserving part of the sugar mixture for the top of the rolls, put it all inside.

MAKES 12 BUNS

GOOEY CARAMEL

$1/2$ cup (4 ounces, or 1 stick) unsalted butter, at room temperature

1 cup (7 ounces) packed light brown sugar

$1/2$ cup (6 ounces) honey

$1/2$ cup (5.75 ounces) corn syrup

1 teaspoon salt

1 teaspoon vanilla extract

1 cup (3.5 ounces) pecan halves or pieces, lightly toasted (see page 20)

Make the caramel.

Put the butter in a small bowl or the bowl of a stand mixer and add the brown sugar, honey, corn syrup, salt, and vanilla. Using the paddle attachment, blend until smooth.

Pan the buns.

Smear the caramel over the bottom of the pan and sprinkle the pecans on top of the caramel. Then place the rolls on top so that they're evenly spaced, 3 by 4.

Let the buns rise.

Cover the pan loosely with plastic wrap and let the rolls sit in a warm spot (at least 75°F) for 30 to 60 minutes before refrigerating overnight; this time will vary depending on the temperature of your kitchen. Look for signs that the yeast is active: the rolls expanding and swelling slightly; the sides coming close to touching one another; or moisture forming inside the plastic wrap.

Bake.

Preheat the oven to 350°F when you wake up. Take the buns from the refrigerator and set them in a warm spot (75°F to 80°F) to come to room temperature and rise; the top of your oven as it preheats is a perfect spot. Don't remove the plastic wrap. You'll know the rolls have risen properly when they touch one another and the dough is soft enough that it springs back leisurely when lightly poked.

Remove the plastic wrap. Place a baking sheet under the pan to catch any gooey drips and bake the buns for 35 to 40 minutes, rotating the pan halfway through the baking time. The buns should be dark golden brown. If they begin to color too much, lower the oven temperature to 325°F after the first 30 minutes.

Let the buns cool for a few minutes, until the caramel has stopped bubbling. Run a knife or cake server around the edge of the pan, then carefully invert the buns onto a large platter or a clean baking sheet.

Gaufres Bruxelloises (Belgian Waffles)

This recipe comes from Odile Buchannan. Odile and her family were our neighbors both on Lopez Island and in Seattle, where they lived across the street. From her crepes cooked on top of a wood-fired stove to her bouillabaisse made from scraps the local fisherman would have thrown out (called by-catch), to these waffles, Odile left an indelible mark on our family's gastronomic progress.

My mother threw a memorable brunch party once after a particularly successful trip to the U-pick fields in Redmond. She served Odile's waffles, piled with freshly picked strawberries and smothered in whipped cream, with Irish coffee. Unlike most waffles, Odile's are leavened with yeast, giving them the structure to stand up to any topping. My family still enjoys these waffles, usually topped with whipped cream, fresh berries, and maple syrup.

When you're dealing with yeast, remember to use time and temperature to your advantage and make these yummy waffles fit your schedule. (See Basics of Leavening with Yeast, on page 41.) Mix the batter the night before and add the egg whites right before you cook the waffles.

MAKES 6 WAFFLES

$2^1/_4$ teaspoons (1 package) active dry yeast

$1/_4$ cup (1.75 ounces) granulated sugar

$2^1/_2$ cups (20 fluid ounces) lukewarm whole milk
   (110°F to 115°F)

3 cups (15 ounces) all-purpose flour

1 teaspoon salt

2 eggs, separated

$1/_2$ cup (4 ounces, or 1 cup stick) unsalted butter,
   melted and slightly cooled

1 teaspoon vanilla extract

Confectioners' sugar, for dusting

Lightly sweetened whipped cream (page 137)

Fresh strawberries, sliced and lightly sweetened,
   for topping

Proof the yeast.

The evening before you make the waffles, combine the yeast and sugar in a bowl, then pour in the milk and let the mixture stand for 5 minutes. The yeast should produce bubbles and give the appearance of expanding; both are signs that sufficient fermentation has taken place to add the flour.

Add the flour and salt.

Stir in the flour and salt with a wooden spoon, mixing until the batter is smooth. Put the dough in a warm spot (70°F to 75°F) for 1 hour to develop.

Add the egg yolks, butter, and vanilla.

Beat the egg yolks slightly, then stir them into the dough, along with the butter and vanilla. Cover with plastic wrap and refrigerate overnight. Store the egg whites in an airtight container in the refrigerator overnight, as well.

Make the waffles.

In the morning, preheat a waffle iron (approximately 6 by 11 inches) until moderately hot.

Using a wire whisk, rotary beater, or stand mixer with the whisk attachment, whip the egg whites until they're stiff enough to hold unwavering peaks on the whisk when it's lifted from the bowl. Gently fold the egg whites into the batter, and stop mixing as soon as they're thoroughly incorporated.

Ladle about $1^1/_2$ cups of batter into the center of the hot waffle iron. Lower the heat to medium-low and close the lid. Bake for 5 minutes, until the steaming stops. The waffle should be golden brown on both sides. (You can peek to check the waffle color after 3 minutes or so, but don't lift the cover any earlier or the waffle may stick to the grid.)

Sprinkle with the confectioners' sugar and serve at once, accompanied by bowls of whipped cream and strawberries.

Black Cherry and Raspberry Kuchen

Over the years, Grand Central has topped this simple yeasted breakfast cake with every fruit and berry imaginable. I'm partial to the beautiful and fragrant combination of black cherries and raspberries, fresh in the summer or from the freezer in the winter. This cake is equally delicious with lemon glaze or vanilla glaze, so I've included recipes for both.

Because it relies on yeast for leavening, timing kuchen so that it can be served for breakfast straight from the oven can be tricky. Don't let that discourage you; remember that manipulating the temperature puts you in control of the timing of the yeast, not the other way around! (See Basics of Leavening with Yeast, on page 41.)

SERVES 12

BATTER

1¹/₂ cups (12 fluid ounces) whole milk

¹/₂ cup (3.5 ounces) packed light brown sugar

10 tablespoons (5 ounces, or ³/₄ stick) unsalted butter

1 tablespoon active dry yeast

3 eggs

3¹/₂ cups (1 pound, 1.5 ounces) all-purpose flour

1¹/₂ teaspoons salt

TOPPING

1 cup pitted black cherries, fresh or frozen

2 cups raspberries, fresh or frozen

¹/₄ cup (1.75 ounces) turbinado or brown sugar

4 tablespoons (2 ounces, or ¹/₂ stick) unsalted butter

LEMON GLAZE

1 cup (4 ounces) confectioners' sugar, sifted

2 tablespoons freshly squeezed lemon juice

VANILLA GLAZE

1 cup (4 ounces) confectioners' sugar, sifted

2 tablespoons heavy cream or half-and-half

1 teaspoon vanilla extract

Prepare the pan.

Lightly grease and flour a 9 by 13-inch baking pan.

Proof the yeast.

Gently heat the milk, brown sugar, and 10 tablespoons of the butter in a small saucepan; it should feel warm to the touch. When the butter has almost melted, add the yeast and let the mixture stand. The yeast should produce bubbles and give the appearance of expanding; both are signs that sufficient fermentation has taken place to proceed with the recipe.

Make the batter.

Whisk the eggs lightly to break them up. Measure the flour and salt into a bowl with high sides and whisk to combine. Pour the eggs and the milk mixture over the flour and gently stir with a wooden spoon or rubber spatula, mixing just until the wet ingredients are incorporated. Spread the batter in the prepared pan and cover with plastic wrap.

Let the batter rise.

If you want to bake the kuchen right away, put the dough in a warm spot (80°F to 90°F); it will be ready in about 1 hour. (I like to turn my oven on to preheat and leave the kuchen to rise on the top of the stove.) If you'll be baking the kuchen later, put the dough in a cool spot, or refrigerate it for up to 8 hours.

(continued)

Bake.

Preheat the oven to 350°F. When the dough has doubled in height, evenly distribute the fruit over it, then sprinkle with the turbinado sugar. Melt the 4 tablespoons butter and drizzle it over the top. Bake the kuchen for 30 minutes, then rotate the pan and lower the temperature to 325°F and bake for 10 to 15 minutes more. The top should be golden brown and the cake should begin to pull away from the sides of the pan.

Make the glaze.

While the kuchen is baking, make the glaze of your choice by whisking all of the ingredients together until smooth. Drizzle the glaze over the warm kuchen and serve immediately.

GRANOLA

Megan's Apricot Almond Granola

My older sister, Megan, remembers beginning to make granola with our mother when she was eleven or twelve. At the time, our family spent summers and most weekends at our farm on Lopez Island in Washington's San Juan Islands. This is where my mother explored her latent bohemianism and first capitalized on her irrepressible entrepreneurial spirit by selling fresh bread, homemade jam, crunchy granola, home-canned pickles, and fresh vegetables from our abundant garden at a funky serve-yourself roadside stand.

Over the years, Megan has made granola for hungry fishermen, friends, family, and bakery customers. She professes, "I never go camping or to a horse show without a big bag; my friends say they're addicted." She always makes a big batch and often puts some in cellophane bags or Mason jars with hand-printed labels to give as gifts. Megan's granola will keep for up to a month in an airtight container at room temperature.

Megan uses whole dried apricots, sliced into a thin julienne, and roughly chopped almonds, but this granola is delicious with any mixture of fruits and nuts. Just be sure to wait until the granola is completely cool before adding the dried fruit.

MAKES ABOUT 10 CUPS

1 cup (12 ounces) honey

$^1/_4$ cup (2 ounces, or $^1/_2$ stick) unsalted butter

$^1/_4$ cup (2 fluid ounces) vegetable oil or canola oil

5 cups (1 pound, 14 ounces) five-grain cereal
   (with rolled grains), or 2$^1/_2$ cups (15 ounces)
   each of rolled oats and rolled barley

$^1/_2$ cup (1.5 ounces) wheat bran

$^1/_2$ cup (3 ounces) flaxseeds

$^1/_2$ cup (4 ounces) sunflower seeds

1$^1/_4$ cups (6 ounces) almonds, coarsely chopped

1 cup (6 ounces) dried apricots, julienned or
   coarsely chopped

Prepare to bake.

Preheat the oven to 325°F. Line 2 baking sheets with parchment paper.

Combine the wet ingredients.

Put the honey, butter, and oil in a small saucepan over low heat and stir occasionally until melted and evenly combined.

Combine the dry ingredients.

Measure the five-grain cereal, wheat bran, flaxseeds, sunflower seeds, and almonds into a large bowl with high sides.

Add the wet ingredients to the dry ingredients.

Pour the warm honey mixture over the dry ingredients and stir until the dry ingredients are evenly coated.

Bake.

Divide the granola between the prepared pans, spreading the mixture evenly over the pans; it shouldn't be too deep. Bake for about 35 minutes, stirring every 10 minutes. The granola should be golden brown.

Finish the granola.

Let the granola cool completely before adding the apricots. Store in an airtight container.

3

Keeping the Cookie Jar Full

Although my mother fed us well, her kitchen was closed between meals. She wasn't much of a believer in snacks, but the cookie jar was usually full of her homemade cookies, giving us something to steal as we passed through.

I developed a serious interest in baking in my early teens, sometimes as a means of escaping chores, other times to satisfy my craving for a treat in our snackless household. I made pan after pan of Toll House chocolate chip cookies, molasses cookies, and oatmeal raisin cookies. (Had my sister not been allergic to peanuts, peanut butter cookies would have been included in the mix.) These classic cookies were the backbone of my repertoire. They seem to be everyone's preferred choices, and when my mother opened the bakery, she made versions of all three, plus peanut butter cookies.

We've sold those same cookies at Grand Central Bakery since day one, and I've yet to hear anyone complain. Over the years they've been supplemented by special holiday cookies, other bakers' picks, and a multitude of experiments and new ideas.

In addition to these well-loved, large, chewy cookies, there are recipes for tasty little shortbread tea cookies, sandwich cookies, macaroons, and a few other family favorites, as well as our plain, buttery shortbread dough, which makes the best-tasting decorated cookie I have ever eaten.

Grand Central Classics **54**

Oatmeal Chocolate Chip Cookies 56

Peanut Butter Cookies 58

Oatmeal Raisin Cookies 59

Ginger Molasses Cookies 60

Triple-Chocolate Cookies 61

Almond Anise Biscotti 62

Shortbread Tea Cookies **64**

Vanilla Almond Cookies 66

Ginger Oat Cookies 67

Cocoa Nib Cookies 69

Orange Nutmeg Cookies 70

Pistachio Cranberry Cookies 72

Hazelnut Poppy Seed Cookies 73

Salty Peanut Cookies 74

Sesame Cookies............................ 75

**COOKIE DECORATING
WORKSHOP** **76**

Classic Buttery Shortbread
and Royal Icing 78

Sandwich Cookies **81**

Peanut Butter
Sandwich Cookies.......................... 82

Chocolate Mint
Sandwich Cookies.......................... 83

Graham Cracker
Sandwich Cookies.......................... 84

Lemon Cream
Sandwich Cookies.......................... 85

Macaroons..................................... **86**

Pink Almond Macaroons 87

Hazelnut Macaroons 88

Coconut Macaroons 89

Family Favorites **90**

Lacy Oatmeal Cookies 90

Favorite Lemon Bars 91

GRAND CENTRAL CLASSICS

Long-time regulars of Grand Central will recognize the Almond Anise Biscotti, Triple-Chocolate Cookies, and the four big cookies as classic Grand Central treats. We've been making all six since the mid-1980s. At the bakery, we call the oatmeal chocolate chip, oatmeal raisin, ginger molasses, and peanut butter cookies "the big cookies." They weigh in at 3 ounces and measure over 5 inches across, which is significantly larger than the cookies you're likely to make at home. In fact, they probably wouldn't even fit in your average cookie jar. To accommodate slightly smaller appetites (and cookie jars), in this book the recipes have been written to yield a cookie half that size, 1.5 ounces with a 2- to 3-inch diameter.

People fall into two camps when it comes to cookies: crisp cookie fans and soft cookie fans. At Grand Central, we sit firmly on the soft cookie side of the debate with these classics, which should bend before breaking. If you happen to prefer a crisp cookie, just add a few minutes to the baking time. I promise not to hold it against you.

Big Cookie Method

For the perfect shape and texture, scoop the dough into $1^1/_2$-ounce balls (about the size of ping-pong balls), and press them into $^1/_2$-inch-thick disks prior to baking. Use your hands and a tablespoon if you don't have a scoop. Here's the most efficient method I've found: Portion all of the dough with a scoop, line the chunks up on a sheet pan, then moisten your palms lightly (to prevent the dough from sticking to them) and roll the dough into balls before pressing into disks.

Butter for Cookies

Creaming the butter and sugar properly is crucial to getting the big cookies right. The goal is to beat the butter and sugar to the point that the sugar granules begin to dissolve. Starting with soft butter is essential; I leave my butter at room temperature for several hours or even overnight so that the texture is consistent all the way through. However, butter can get too soft. If it appears greasy, it's too warm and will be overly soft. This rarely happens unless the room temperature is above 78°F.

For the best results, take the butter out of the refrigerator and leave it in a cool spot where the temperature is consistent, away from sunny windows or a hot oven.

If you haven't softened the butter ahead of time, don't despair. Put the butter in the bowl of a stand mixer with the paddle attachment, and beat it. Begin on low speed and slowly increase to medium speed. When the texture of the butter is creamy soft, add the sugar and proceed with the recipe.

Use Your Freezer

My brother-in-law, Clint, a contractor, is a lucky man. One morning when I was visiting, I got up early with my sister, Megan. As I sat at the kitchen island counter, chatting over a cup of hot coffee, she mixed pancake batter, fried bacon, and made Clint's lunch. After taking sandwich makings from the refrigerator, she pulled a bagful of frozen balls of cookie dough from the freezer, removed four, and returned the bag to the freezer. By the time breakfast was ready and the sandwiches had been made, there were freshly baked chocolate chip cookies for Clint's lunch.

Freezing ready-to-bake cookie dough is a great trick. If there's space in your freezer for a baking sheet, you can put a tray of just-scooped cookies in and transfer them to freezer bags when they're frozen and firm. If you're short on freezer space, chill the dough balls in the refrigerator for an hour before packing them loosely in freezer bags. In a pinch, scooped cookie dough can go straight from the freezer to the oven, but I think the best results are achieved when the dough balls soften enough at room temperature to be flattened into disks prior to baking.

Oatmeal Chocolate Chip Cookies

New bakery customers often request a "plain" choco-late chip cookie, hoping to find the ubiquitous and more familiar Toll House–type cookie. But once they've tried the Grand Central version, with bittersweet and milk chocolate chips and the perfect amount of oat-meal, they're hooked. Buy the best chocolate chips you can find or, for a less uniform look, chop a bar of good chocolate into small chunks.

MAKES ABOUT 3 DOZEN COOKIES

2 cups (10 ounces) all-purpose flour

1 teaspoon baking soda

3/4 teaspoon baking powder

1 teaspoon salt

1 cup (8 ounces, or 2 sticks) unsalted butter,
    at room temperature

1 cup (7 ounces) granulated sugar

1 cup (7 ounces) packed light brown sugar

2 eggs, at room temperature

2 teaspoons vanilla extract

2 3/4 cups (9 ounces) rolled oats

1 cup (6 ounces) bittersweet chocolate chips
    or chunks

1 cup (6 ounces) milk chocolate chips or chunks

Prepare to bake.

Preheat the oven to 350°F. Line 2 baking sheets with parchment paper.

Combine the dry ingredients.

Measure the flour, baking soda, baking powder, and salt into a bowl and whisk to combine. (Put the dry ingredients through a fine-mesh sieve if the flour or baking soda is clumpy.)

Cream the butter and sugar.

Using a stand mixer with the paddle attachment, beat the butter, granulated sugar, and brown sugar on medium speed for 3 to 5 minutes, until lighter in color and fluffy. Scrape the bottom and sides of the bowl several times during the process.

Incorporate the eggs and vanilla.

While the mixer is running, crack the eggs into a liquid measuring cup and add the vanilla. Reduce the speed to low, then slowly pour in the eggs, letting them fall in one at a time and incorporating the first egg completely before adding the next. Scrape the bottom and sides of the bowl once during the process.

Add the dry ingredients and finish the dough.

Gradually add the dry ingredients (in 2 to 3 additions) with the mixer on low speed. Scrape the bottom and sides of the bowl once, to fully incorporate the butter and sugar. Combine the oats and chocolate in the same bowl used for the dry ingredients, then add them to the dough with the mixer on low speed, mixing just until everything is well distributed. Often it's easier to fin-ish mixing by hand using a stiff rubber spatula.

Shape the cookies.

Use the Big Cookie Method (see page 55) to scoop the dough into balls the size of ping-pong balls (about 1.5 ounces). Arrange the dough balls on the prepared pans, 6 per pan, then press into 1/2-inch-thick disks.

Bake.

Bake for 10 minutes, rotating the pans halfway through the baking time. The edges of the cookies should be golden brown, while the centers will appear blond and slightly underdone. Let the cookies cool on the baking sheets.

Peanut Butter Cookies

This cookie is exactly what you'd expect from a classic peanut butter cookie: nutty, sweet, and soft in the middle, complete with emblematic fork crisscross on top. Unlike some peanut butter cookie recipes, this one is equally successful and delicious whether you use natural peanut butter or an everyday brand name. Be sure to stir natural peanut butter thoroughly before measuring it to distribute the oil.

MAKES ABOUT 3 DOZEN COOKIES

3 cups (15 ounces) all-purpose flour

2 teaspoons baking soda

1 teaspoon salt (2 teaspoons if you use
    unsalted peanut butter)

1 cup (8 ounces, or 2 sticks) unsalted butter,
    at room temperature

1 cup (7 ounces) granulated sugar, plus extra
    for dusting

1 cup (7 ounces) packed light brown sugar

1 cup (9.5 ounces) peanut butter, at room
    temperature

2 eggs, at room temperature

2 teaspoons vanilla extract

Prepare to bake.

Preheat the oven to 350°F. Line 2 baking sheets with parchment paper.

Combine the dry ingredients.

Measure the flour, baking soda, and salt into a bowl and whisk to combine. (Put the dry ingredients through a fine-mesh sieve if the flour or baking soda is clumpy.)

Cream the butter, sugar, and peanut butter.

Using a stand mixer with the paddle attachment, beat the butter, granulated sugar, and brown sugar on medium speed for 3 to 5 minutes, until mixture is lighter in color and fluffy. Add the peanut butter and cream for another minute. Scrape the bottom and sides of the bowl several times during the process.

Incorporate the eggs and vanilla.

While the mixer is running, crack the eggs into a liquid measuring cup and add the vanilla. Reduce the speed to low, then slowly pour in the eggs, letting them fall in one at a time and incorporating the first egg completely before adding the next. Scrape the bottom and sides of the bowl once during the process.

Add the dry ingredients.

Gradually add the dry ingredients (in 2 to 3 additions) with the mixer on low speed. Scrape the bottom and sides of the bowl once, to fully incorporate the butter and sugar.

Shape the cookies.

Use the Big Cookie Method (see page 55) to scoop the dough into balls the size of ping-pong balls (about 1.5 ounces). Arrange the dough balls on the prepared pans, 6 per pan. Lightly dust with granulated sugar before pressing with a fork to make a crisscross pattern and then press the cookies into 1/2-inch-thick disks.

Bake.

Bake for 10 minutes, rotating the pans halfway through the baking time. The tops of the fork marks and the edges of the cookies should be brown and crisp and the middle should be soft. Let the cookies cool on the baking sheets.

Oatmeal Raisin Cookies

Oatmeal raisin is my favorite big cookie. I love the caramely flavor and gooey, soft texture of these cookies when they're pulled from the oven, their edges toasty brown and their centers appearing underdone. (They finish baking on the hot pan.).

MAKES ABOUT 2$1/2$ DOZEN COOKIES

1$3/4$ cups (8.75 ounces) all-purpose flour

1 teaspoon baking soda

1 teaspoon salt

1 cup (8 ounces, or 2 sticks) unsalted butter,
    at room temperature

1 cup (7 ounces) granulated sugar

1 cup (7 ounces) packed light brown sugar

2 eggs, at room temperature

2 teaspoons vanilla extract

3$1/4$ cups (11.5 ounces) rolled oats

1 cup (4.25 ounces) golden raisins

Prepare to bake.

Preheat the oven to 350°F. Line 2 baking sheets with parchment paper.

Combine the dry ingredients.

Measure the flour, baking soda, and salt into a bowl and whisk to combine. (Put the dry ingredients through a fine-mesh sieve if the flour or baking soda is clumpy.)

Cream the butter and sugar.

Using a stand mixer with the paddle attachment, beat the butter, granulated sugar, and brown sugar on medium speed for 3 to 5 minutes, until the mixture is lighter in color and fluffy. Scrape the bottom and sides of the bowl several times during the process.

Incorporate the eggs and vanilla.

While the mixer is running, crack the eggs into a liquid measuring cup and add the vanilla. Reduce the speed to low, then slowly pour in the eggs, allowing them to fall in one at a time and incorporating the first egg completely before adding the next. Scrape down the bottom and sides of the bowl several times during the process.

Add the dry ingredients and finish the dough.

Gradually add the dry ingredients (in 2 to 3 additions) with the mixer on low speed. Scrape the bottom and sides of the bowl once, to fully incorporate the butter and sugar. Combine the oats and raisins in the same bowl used for the dry ingredients, then add them to the dough with the mixer on low speed, mixing just until everything is well distributed. Often it's easier to finish mixing by hand using a stiff rubber spatula.

Shape the cookies.

Use the Big Cookie Method (see page 55) to scoop the dough into balls the size of ping-pong balls (about 1.5 ounces). Arrange the dough balls on the prepared pans, 6 per pan, then press into $1/2$-inch-thick disks.

Bake.

Bake for 8 minutes, rotating the pans halfway through the baking time. The cookies should be golden brown around the edges and appear slightly underdone and blond in the centers. Let the cookies cool on the baking sheets.

Ginger Molasses Cookies

This cookie has crispy edges and a soft center, with a crackly sugar crust. Because the freshly made dough is sticky and a bit difficult to scoop, I recommend chilling it for 30 minutes before scooping, or dipping your scoop in hot water or sugar so the dough doesn't stick.

MAKES ABOUT 2¹/₂ DOZEN COOKIES

3 cups (15 ounces) all-purpose flour

1 ¹/₂ teaspoons baking soda

³/₄ teaspoon salt

1 tablespoon ground ginger

¹/₄ teaspoon ground cloves

³/₄ cup (6 ounces, or 1¹/₂ sticks) unsalted butter,
    at room temperature

2 cups (14 ounces) granulated sugar, plus extra
    for rolling

¹/₂ cup (6 ounces) unsulfured molasses
    (not blackstrap)

2 eggs, at room temperature

1¹/₂ teaspoons white vinegar

Prepare to bake.

Preheat the oven to 350°F. Line 2 baking sheets with parchment paper.

Combine the dry ingredients.

Measure the flour, baking soda, salt, ginger, and cloves into a bowl and whisk to combine. (Put the dry ingredients through a fine-mesh sieve if the flour or baking soda is clumpy.)

Cream the butter, sugar, and molasses.

Using a stand mixer with the paddle attachment, beat the butter, sugar, and molasses on medium speed for 3 to 5 minutes, until the mixture is lighter in color and fluffy. Scrape the bottom and sides of the bowl several times during the process.

Incorporate the eggs and vinegar.

While the mixer is running, crack the eggs into a liquid measuring cup and add the vinegar. Reduce the speed to low, then slowly pour in the eggs, letting them fall in one at a time and incorporating the first egg completely before adding the next. Scrape the bottom and sides of the bowl once during the process.

Add the dry ingredients.

Gradually add the dry ingredients (in 2 to 3 additions) with the mixer on low speed. Scrape the bottom and sides of the bowl once, to fully incorporate the butter and sugar.

Shape the cookies.

Use the Big Cookie Method (see page 55) to scoop the dough into balls the size of ping-pong balls (about 1.5 ounces). Roll the balls in sugar, then arrange them on the prepared pans, 6 per pan. Press each ball into a ³/₄-inch disk.

Bake.

Bake for 10 minutes, rotating the pans halfway through the baking time. The cookies should be rich brown in color, with crackly tops. Let the cookies cool on the baking sheets.

Triple-Chocolate Cookies

These intensely chocolate cookies are a bit tricky, but worth the effort. When perfectly made, they are slightly shiny, with crinkly tops and soft centers almost like mousse. Buy the best chocolate you can find; these cookies deserve it!

New bakers at Grand Central usually come to us with experience. That experience can range from formal training to a string of baking jobs that led to one with us. But they seem to have certain traits in common, like persistence and a desire for perfection, which means they like to do things their own way first. Most of them make these cookies several times before getting them just right, and they all have their own secret to achieving perfection. Don't let that discourage you. Follow the instructions, and they'll be flawless. It's especially important to begin with all ingredients at room temperature.

MAKES ABOUT 2 DOZEN COOKIES

$2/3$ cup (4 ounces) unsweetened baking chocolate

10 ounces bittersweet chocolate
   ($1^2/3$ cups chips or chunks)

1 cup (8 ounces, or 2 sticks) unsalted butter,
   at room temperature

4 eggs, at room temperature

2 cups plus 2 tablespoons (14.75 ounces)
   granulated sugar

$2/3$ cup (3.25 ounces) all-purpose flour

$1/2$ teaspoon baking powder

Pinch of salt

$2/3$ cup (4 ounces) milk chocolate chips

$1^1/2$ teaspoons freshly brewed espresso
   or strong coffee

$1^1/2$ teaspoons vanilla extract

Melt the chocolate and butter.

Put the unsweetened chocolate, bittersweet chocolate, and butter in a double boiler or a metal bowl sus-

pended over a pot of barely simmering water for 5 to 7 minutes. Turn off the heat and allow the ingredients to continue to melt; it may take as much as 20 minutes for the chocolate to slowly melt. Stir until smooth and evenly combined. If you don't use the mixture right away at this point, keep it at 80°F to 85°F, on the warm side of cool. (You can do this by leaving the bowl suspended over the pot of warm water, or leaving it on the oven as it preheats.)

Whip the eggs and sugar and combine the dry ingredients.

Using a stand mixer with the paddle attachment, beat the eggs and sugar on high speed for 14 minutes, until the mixture is extremely fluffy and white, and the volume has increased substantially. Add the espresso and vanilla, reduce the speed to medium-high, and continue mixing for 2 minutes.

Add the dry ingredients.

Reduce the mixer speed to low, add the dry ingredients, and mix briefly—less than 30 seconds, or just long enough to incorporate the flour.

Finish the batter.

Add the melted chocolate mixture (it should be just barely warm) and mix on medium-low speed for 1 minute, or until the color is uniformly brown. Fold in the milk chocolate chips by hand and let the batter sit at room temperature for 30 to 45 minutes so it can set up.

Bake.

Preheat the oven to 350°F and line 2 baking sheets with parchment paper.

Portion the cookie dough using a small ($1^1/2$-ounce) scoop or mounded teaspoon. Gently spoon the batter onto the prepared pans so that each spoonful retains as much roundness and volume as possible.

Bake for 10 to 12 minutes, rotating the pans halfway through the baking time. The cookies should be slightly shiny, with crinkly tops and soft centers.

Almond Anise Biscotti

Angela Owens, a Seattle neighbor, introduced my family to biscotti. Angela is the daughter of renowned food writer and cook Angelo Pellegrini, author of The Unprejudiced Palate, Wine and the Good Life, *and* The Food Lover's Garden, *among others. Angela and her father, Pelli, were two of the many important influences who expanded our family's culinary horizons, infusing daily life with their Italian heritage.*

Angela doesn't share her recipes, but her biscotti inspired my mother to make dozens before landing on this version, which we've used at Grand Central Bakery for many years. We use vegetable oil at the bakery, but this recipe is delicious made with olive oil. I know Pelli would approve. Stored in an airtight container, the biscotti will keep at room temperature for up to a month.

MAKES ABOUT 3 DOZEN BISCOTTI

3 1/2 cups (1 pound, 1.5 ounces) all-purpose flour

1 1/2 teaspoon baking powder

1/2 teaspoon salt

1 1/2 cups (10.5 ounces) granulated sugar

1 cup (8 fluid ounces) olive oil

2 eggs

1 teaspoon vanilla extract

3/4 teaspoon almond extract

1 1/2 cups (4 ounces) sliced almonds

2 tablespoons anise seeds

Prepare to bake.

Preheat the oven to 350°F. Line 2 baking sheets with parchment paper.

Combine the dry ingredients.

Measure the flour, baking powder, and salt into a bowl and whisk to combine.

Combine the sugar and olive oil.

Using a stand mixer with the paddle attachment, beat the sugar and olive oil on medium speed for 3 minutes, until the sugar has dissolved and the mixture is lighter in color.

Add the eggs, vanilla, and almond extract.

While the mixer is running, crack the eggs into a liquid measuring cup and add the vanilla extract and almond extract. Reduce the speed to slow, then slowly pour in the eggs, letting them fall in one at a time and incorporating the first egg completely before adding the next. Scrape the bottom and sides of the bowl once during the process.

Add the dry ingredients, almonds, and anise seeds.

Gradually add the dry ingredients with the mixer on low speed. Scrape the bottom and sides of the bowl and mix for about 30 seconds, until the dough is homogenous. Add the almonds and anise seeds and mix just until incorporated.

Shape the dough.

Turn the dough out onto a lightly floured work surface and divide it into 4 equal pieces, each about 12 ounces. Roll each piece into a 10-inch log and place the logs lengthwise on the prepared pans, 2 logs per pan. Pat each log into a long, skinny rectangle measuring about 10 by 3 inches and about 1 inch thick.

Bake.

Bake the logs for 25 minutes, until firm and golden brown, rotating the pans once, halfway through the baking time. Let cool completely, preferably for at least an hour.

Slice the biscotti.

Preheat the oven to 250°F. Slice the logs at a 45-degree angle into $1/2$-inch-thick biscotti. This will generate a lot of crumbs, but a sharp serrated knife and an hour of cooling after the first bake will make a big difference. Save the ends for snacking or put them in the freezer for crumbling under the fruit in your next rustic fruit tart.

Bake again.

Place the biscotti on the parchment-lined baking sheets, flat side down, and bake for 45 minutes, until completely dry. Let the biscotti cool on the baking sheets.

SHORTBREAD TEA COOKIES

Many bakers have left a mark on Grand Central's product line, but few are as indelible as Laura Ohm's. She is my right hand, consistently bringing amazing, tasty ideas to the table, both literally and figuratively. Before Laura turned a creative hand to our selection of shortbread tea cookies, we served just two: Orange Nutmeg and Hazelnut Poppy Seed. Today our little cookies are in continuous, delicious rotation throughout the year.

At the bakery, these little cookies are sold individually from big glass jars and by the dozen in cellophane bags tied with pretty ribbons. Packed in a cute box or tin, they make a lovely hostess or holiday gift. Logs of frozen dough, wrapped and packaged with baking instructions, are an even better present. By stocking your freezer ahead of time, you can produce a great variety of cookies amidst the frenzy that surrounds the holidays.

These cookies should be mixed ahead; they're best when the dough has chilled for at least three hours, but it can remain in the refrigerator up to three days or in the freezer for several months. At the bakery, we mix thirty- to forty-pound batches of dough, form it into two-pound logs, and bake several dozen at a time to fill the café cookie jars. At home, I make a slightly smaller amount. If I have last-minute guests and need to produce a treat on short notice, I defrost a log from the freezer, slice it up, and voilà, freshly baked cookies in minutes!

Shortbread Tea Cookie Method

Each shortbread tea cookie has its own unique flavor and character, but the method for making them is essentially the same. Mix the ingredients for the dough, form it into logs, chill, slice, bake, and eat. Follow the instructions for mixing in individual recipes, making sure to cream the butter and sugar well, until the mixture is light and fluffy. Here are some tips on how to proceed once you've mixed the dough:

FORM THE DOUGH INTO LOGS AND CHILL.

Use a bench knife or sturdy spatula to divide the dough in half. Place each half on a 12- to 14-inch length of parchment paper, waxed paper, or plastic wrap. Smooth and pat the dough into a rectangle by flattening the top and sides with your hands. Then use the paper to help roll and shape the dough into logs 2 inches in diameter and about 10 inches long. Twist the ends of the paper to seal the log, then refrigerate the dough until firm, at least 2 hours and up to 3 days (or freeze for up to 3 months). If you're baking previously frozen dough, defrost it overnight in the refrigerator.

FINISH AND BAKE THE COOKIES.

Preheat the oven to 350°F and line two baking sheets with parchment paper. Pull the chilled log from the refrigerator and allow it to soften slightly. Unwrap the log and cut off the portion you'll be baking. If the recipe calls for encrusting the outside with sugar or seeds to give the cookies a decorated edge, brush the log with egg wash first (see page 20). This gives the sugar or seeds something to adhere to and provides a nice glossy, brown finish. Put the item in which the log will be rolled on a large plate or a flat pan with sides and roll the log until completely coated.

Use a sharp or serrated knife to slice the dough into $1/4$- to $1/2$-inch-thick squares. Cookies containing large amounts of fruit or nuts will be more difficult to slice; use a serrated knife and be patient. If the slices crumble, gently push them back together and double-check that the dough has softened enough.

BRUSH WITH EGG WASH

SPRINKLE WITH SUGAR

SLICE

Place the cookies 1 inch apart, in 3 by 4 rows, on the prepared pans. You might need to bake in batches. Bake for 20 to 25 minutes, rotating the pans halfway through the baking time. They should be firm to the touch. Enjoy the cookies warm, or let them cool completely before storing in an airtight container at room temperature for up to 1 week.

Vanilla Almond Cookies

Essentially Viennese vanilla crescents, these vanilla almond shortbread cookies are typically made at Christmastime, but we think they're too delicious to relegate just to the holidays. This dough is also good for drop cookies.

MAKES ABOUT 4 DOZEN COOKIES

2 cups (10 ounces) all-purpose flour

1 cup (4 ounces) freshly ground almonds (not almond meal)

2/3 cup (2.75 ounces) confectioners' sugar

1/2 teaspoon salt

1 cup (8 ounces, or 2 sticks) unsalted butter, at room temperature

1 teaspoon vanilla extract

Combine the dry ingredients.

Measure the flour, almonds, confectioners' sugar, and salt into a bowl and whisk to combine.

Beat the butter.

Using a stand mixer with the paddle attachment, beat the butter on medium speed until smooth and creamy, about 3 minutes.

Add the vanilla and dry ingredients.

Reduce the mixer speed to low, then add the vanilla and the dry ingredients and mix just until the dry ingredients disappear into the dough.

Shape and chill the dough.

Use the Shortbread Tea Cookie Method (see page 65) to shape the dough into 2 logs 2 inches in diameter, then chill for at least 2 hours and up to 3 days (or freeze for up to 3 months).

Bake.

Preheat the oven to 325°F. Line 2 baking sheets with parchment paper.

Slice the cookies 1/4 to 1/2 inch thick and place them about 1 inch apart, in 3 by 4 rows, on the prepared pans. Bake for 20 to 25 minutes, rotating the pans halfway through the baking time. The cookies are ready when they begin to brown around the edges.

Ginger Oat Cookies

This buttery oatmeal shortbread is studded with nuggets of candied ginger, which are the yang to the brown sugar's yin. The result is a truly perfect balance of sweet and spicy that's great for dunking in a cup of hot tea.

MAKES ABOUT 4 DOZEN COOKIES

1²/₃ cups (8.25 ounces) all-purpose flour

1 teaspoon salt

1 teaspoon ground ginger

1²/₃ cups (5.75 ounces) rolled oats

1 cup (8 ounces, or 2 sticks) unsalted butter,
  at room temperature

²/₃ cup (5.25 ounces) packed light brown sugar

2 tablespoons coarsely chopped candied ginger

Egg wash (see page 20)

Turbinado sugar, for rolling

Combine the dry ingredients.

Measure the flour, salt, and ground ginger into a bowl and whisk to combine. Stir in the oats.

Cream the butter and sugar.

Using a stand mixer with the paddle attachment, beat the butter and brown sugar together on medium speed until light and fluffy, about 5 minutes.

Add the dry ingredients and candied ginger.

Add the dry ingredients and mix just until evenly incorporated. Fold in the candied ginger with a sturdy spatula.

Shape and chill the dough.

Use the Shortbread Tea Cookie Method (see page 65) to shape the dough into 2 logs 2 inches in diameter, then chill for at least 2 hours and up to 3 days (or freeze for up to 3 months).

Slice and bake the cookies.

Preheat the oven to 325°F. Line 2 baking sheets with parchment paper.

Lightly brush each log of dough with the egg wash, then roll it in the turbinado sugar, using some pressure so that the sugar adheres to it.

Slice the cookies ¹/₄ to ¹/₂ inch thick and place them about 1 inch apart, in 3 by 4 rows, on the prepared pans. Bake for 16 to 20 minutes, rotating the pans halfway through the baking time. The cookies are ready when they begin to brown around the edges and the centers are blond.

Cocoa Nib Cookies

Inspired by our friends at Bread Farm in Edison, Washington, these cookies are for real bittersweet chocolate lovers. Cocoa nibs are toasted cocoa beans that have been crushed into tiny crunchy bits; they impart wonderful texture and a bitter, nutty chocolate flavor to these cookies.

MAKES ABOUT 4 DOZEN COOKIES

1¹/₄ cups (6.25 ounces) all-purpose flour

¹/₂ cup (1.5 ounces) unsweetened cocoa powder

¹/₂ teaspoon salt

¹/₂ teaspoon baking soda

12 tablespoons (6 ounces, or 1¹/₂ sticks) unsalted butter, at room temperature

¹/₄ cup (1.75 ounces) granulated sugar

³/₄ cup (5.25 ounces) packed light brown sugar

1 teaspoon vanilla extract

¹/₃ cup (2 ounces) cocoa nibs

¹/₂ cup (3 ounces) semisweet chocolate chips

Combine the dry ingredients.

Measure the flour, cocoa powder, salt, and baking soda into a bowl and whisk to combine. (Put the mixture through a fine mesh sieve if the cocoa powder is lumpy.)

Cream the butter and sugar and add the vanilla.

Using a stand mixer with the paddle attachment, beat the butter, granulated sugar, and brown sugar on medium speed until very smooth, about 3 minutes. Add the vanilla, then reduce the mixer speed to low.

Add the dry ingredients and chocolate.

Add the dry ingredients and mix just until they disappear into the dough. Fold in the cocoa nibs and chocolate chips with a sturdy spatula.

Shape and chill the dough.

Use the Shortbread Tea Cookie Method (see page 65) to shape the dough into 2 logs 2 inches in diameter, then chill for at least 2 hours and up to 3 days (or freeze for up to 3 months).

Slice and bake the cookies.

Preheat the oven to 325°F. Line 2 baking sheets with parchment paper.

Slice the cookies ¹/₄ to ¹/₂ inch thick and place them about 1 inch apart, in 3 by 4 rows, on the prepared pans. Bake for 15 to 20 minutes, rotating the pans halfway through the baking time. The cookies should be firm to the touch.

Orange Nutmeg Cookies

One of the first two little tea cookies sold at Grand Central Bakery, this tender shortbread is richly perfumed with freshly grated nutmeg and loads of fresh orange zest. The log of dough is brushed with egg wash and rolled in turbinado sugar before slicing and baking, which gives the cookies shimmering, crunchy edges.

MAKES ABOUT 4 DOZEN COOKIES

2 cups (10 ounces) all-purpose flour

1/2 teaspoon salt

1 1/2 teaspoons ground nutmeg, preferably
    freshly grated

1 cup (8 ounces, or 2 sticks) unsalted butter,
    at room temperature

3/4 cup (5.25 ounces) granulated sugar

1 egg, at room temperature

2 tablespoons finely chopped orange zest

Egg wash (see page 20)

Turbinado sugar, for rolling

Combine the dry ingredients.

Measure the flour, salt, and nutmeg into a bowl and whisk to combine.

Cream the butter and sugar.

Using a stand mixer with the paddle attachment, beat the butter and granulated sugar together on medium speed until very smooth and fluffy, about 5 minutes.

Add the egg and orange zest.

Add the egg and orange zest and reduce the mixer speed to low.

Add the dry ingredients.

Add the dry ingredients and mix just until they disappear into the dough. Chill the dough for approximately 30 minutes so it will be easier to handle.

Shape and chill the dough.

Use the Shortbread Tea Cookie Method (see page 65) to shape the dough into 2 logs 2 inches in diameter, then chill for at least 2 hours and up to 3 days (or freeze for up to 3 months).

Slice and bake the cookies.

Preheat the oven to 350°F. Line 2 baking sheets with parchment paper.

Lightly brush each log of dough with the egg wash, then roll it in the turbinado sugar, using some pressure so that the sugar adheres to it.

Slice the cookies 1/4 to 1/2 inch thick and place them about 1 inch apart, in 3 by 4 rows, on the prepared pans. Bake for 20 to 25 minutes, rotating the pans halfway through the baking time. The cookies are ready when the edges have browned slightly and the centers are light golden brown.

ORANGE NUTMEG COOKIES
AND COCOA NIB COOKIES, PAGE 69

Pistachio Cranberry Cookies

Green pistachios and bright red cranberries make this the perfect Christmas cookie, but once you sample one, you will want to eat them year-round. I recommend using unsalted, natural pistachios, an ingredient I have been pleasantly surprised to find in the bulk aisle of many grocery stores.

MAKES ABOUT 4 DOZEN COOKIES

2 1/3 cups (11.5 ounces) all-purpose flour

1 teaspoon salt

1 cup (8 ounces, or 2 sticks) unsalted butter,
   at room temperature

2/3 cup (4.75 ounces) granulated sugar

1 teaspoon vanilla extract

1 cup (4 ounces) pistachios, lightly toasted
   (see page 20)

1 1/4 cups (6.5 ounces) dried cranberries

Combine the dry ingredients.

Measure the flour and salt into a bowl and whisk to combine.

Cream the butter and sugar and add the vanilla.

Using a stand mixer with the paddle attachment, beat the butter and sugar together on medium speed until very smooth and creamy, about 5 minutes. Add the vanilla, then reduce the mixer speed to low.

Add the dry ingredients and pistachios and cranberries.

Add the dry ingredients and mix just until they disappear into the dough. Fold in the pistachios and cranberries with a sturdy spatula. Make sure the pistachios and cranberries are well distributed; this will make it easier to form and slice the log.

Shape and chill the dough.

Use the Shortbread Tea Cookie Method (see page 65) to shape the dough into 2 logs 2 inches in diameter, then chill for at least 2 hours and up to 3 days (or freeze for up to 3 months).

Slice and bake the cookies.

Preheat the oven to 325°F. Line 2 baking sheets with parchment paper.

Slice the cookies 1/4 to 1/2 inch thick and place them about 1 inch apart, in 3 by 4 rows, on the prepared pans. Bake for 16 to 20 minutes, rotating the pans halfway through the baking time. The cookies are ready when they begin to brown around the edges.

Hazelnut Poppy Seed Cookies

Oregon's beloved hazelnut pairs beautifully with poppy seeds in this not-too-sweet cookie that is the perfect complement to vanilla ice cream.

MAKES ABOUT 4 DOZEN COOKIES

3 cups plus 3 tablespoons (1 pound) all-purpose flour

1/4 cup (1.25 ounces) poppy seeds

1 teaspoon salt

1 1/2 cups (12 ounces, or 3 sticks) unsalted butter, at room temperature

1 cup (7 ounces) granulated sugar

2 teaspoons vanilla extract

1 cup (4 ounces) hazelnuts, lightly toasted and skinned (see page 89)

Combine the dry ingredients.

Measure the flour, poppy seeds, and salt into a bowl and whisk to combine.

Cream the butter and sugar and add the vanilla.

Using a stand mixer with the paddle attachment, beat the butter and sugar together on medium speed until very smooth, about 3 minutes. Add the vanilla, then reduce the mixer speed to low.

Add the dry ingredients and hazelnuts.

Add the dry ingredients and mix just until they disappear into the dough. Fold in the hazelnuts with a sturdy spatula.

Shape and chill the dough.

Use the Shortbread Tea Cookie Method (see page 65) to shape the dough into 2 logs 2 inches in diameter, then chill for at least 2 hours and up to 3 days (or freeze for up to 3 months).

Slice and bake the cookies.

Preheat the oven to 325°F. Line two baking sheets with parchment paper.

Slice the cookies 1/4 to 1/2 inch thick and place them about 1 inch apart, in 3 by 4 rows, on the prepared pans. Bake for 15 to 20 minutes, rotating the pans halfway through the baking time. The cookies should be firm to the touch.

Salty Peanut Cookies

When Laura Ohm first developed this recipe, she and I were training for an endurance cycling event. We'd often bring along a stash of these brown sugar-y shortbread cookies, chock-a-block with salty peanuts. Instead of choking down one more energy bar at the 50-mile mark of our long rides, we'd refuel with a couple of these power-packed cookies. But don't feel like you have to ride 50 miles to earn one of these—they'll get you through a grueling day at work just as successfully, especially when accompanied by hot coffee. Biting into one of these is like nibbling on a buttery piece of peanut brittle. At the bakery we start with natural, skin-on peanuts, but salted cocktail peanuts taste great too.

MAKES ABOUT 4 DOZEN COOKIES

$2\frac{1}{2}$ cups (10 ounces) peanuts (with or without skins on)

$1\frac{1}{2}$ teaspoons vegetable oil or canola oil

$1\frac{1}{4}$ teaspoon salt

2 cups (10 ounces) all-purpose flour

1 cup (8 ounces, or 2 sticks) unsalted butter, at room temperature

$\frac{1}{3}$ cup (2.25 ounces) granulated sugar

$\frac{2}{3}$ cup (4.25 ounces) packed light brown sugar

$\frac{1}{4}$ teaspoon vanilla extract

Make the salted peanuts.

Preheat the oven to 350°F.

Toss the peanuts in the oil and $\frac{3}{4}$ teaspoon of the salt, then spread them on a baking sheet and toast until lightly golden, about 20 minutes.

Combine the dry ingredients.

Measure the flour and the remaining $\frac{1}{2}$ teaspoon salt into a bowl and whisk to combine.

Cream the butter and sugar and add the vanilla.

Using a stand mixer with the paddle attachment, beat the butter, granulated sugar, and brown sugar on medium speed until light and fluffy, about 5 minutes. Add the vanilla, then reduce the mixer speed to low.

Add the dry ingredients and salted peanuts.

Add the dry ingredients and mix just until they disappear into the dough. Work in the whole peanuts with a sturdy spatula.

Shape and chill the dough.

Use the Shortbread Tea Cookie Method (see page 65) to shape the dough into 2 logs 2 inches in diameter. The peanuts will make forming the logs difficult; be patient and persistent. Chill the dough for at least 2 hours and up to 3 days (or freeze for up to 3 months).

Slice and bake the cookies.

Preheat the oven to 325°F. Line 2 baking sheets with parchment paper.

Slice the cookies $\frac{1}{4}$ to $\frac{1}{2}$ inch thick and place them about 1 inch apart, in 3 by 4 rows, on the prepared pans. Bake for 20 to 25 minutes, rotating the pans halfway through the baking time. The cookies should be golden caramel brown and slightly firm to the touch.

Sesame Cookies

While it it somewhat unusual to see sesame oil listed as an ingredient in a cookie recipe, when combined with butter, the oil gives these cookies an indescribably delicate quality. The wonderfully nutty flavor and tender texture combine to create a cookie that practically melts in your mouth. Use hulled sesame seeds and keep them refrigerated—along with the sesame oil—to prevent them from turning rancid before you use them up.

MAKES ABOUT 4 DOZEN COOKIES

2 cups (10 ounces) all-purpose flour

½ teaspoon salt

**1 cup (8 ounces, or 2 sticks) unsalted butter,
    at room temperature**

⅓ cup (2.25 ounces) granulated sugar

¼ teaspoon vanilla extract

½ teaspoon toasted sesame oil

Egg wash (see page 20)

Sesame seeds, for rolling

Combine the dry ingredients.

Measure the flour and salt into a bowl and whisk to combine.

Cream the butter and sugar and add the vanilla and sesame oil.

Using a stand mixer with the paddle attachment, beat the butter and sugar together on medium speed until very smooth and creamy, about 5 minutes. Reduce the mixer speed to low, then add the vanilla and sesame oil.

Add the dry ingredients.

Add the dry ingredients and mix just until they disappear into the dough.

Shape and chill the dough.

Use the Shortbread Tea Cookie Method (see page 65) to shape the dough into 2 logs 2 inches in diameter, then chill for at least 2 hours and up to 3 days (or freeze for up to 3 months).

Slice and bake the cookies.

Preheat the oven to 325°F. Line 2 baking sheets with parchment paper.

Lightly brush each log of dough with egg wash, then roll it in the sesame seeds, using some pressure so that the seeds adhere to it.

Slice the cookies ¼ to ½ inch thick and place them about 1 inch apart, in 3 by 4 rows, on the prepared pans. Bake for 20 to 25 minutes, rotating the pans halfway through the baking time. The cookies are ready when the edges begin to brown.

Decorated shortbread cookies are a bright accent within Grand Central Bakery's generally rustic palette. In celebration of "minor" holidays, like St. Patrick's Day, Halloween, and Valentine's Day, we think nothing's more festive than a beautifully decorated cookie.

About ten years ago, I started a holiday tradition that I love. In lieu of giving Christmas presents to my nieces and nephews, I invite them to my house for a night of cookie decorating. The scene is chaotic and the kids are hopped up on sugar, but at the end of the night each one of them leaves with boxes of beautiful holiday cookies. Many are eaten right away, others are shared with neighbors and friends, and certain special cookies are set aside for Santa. Despite the fact that many of the cookies are weighted down by silver dragées and thick icing, I insist that what's underneath tastes good. I always use Grand Central's classic vanilla shortbread recipe and royal icing with a touch of lemon.

I firmly believe that home baking shouldn't require a bunch of special equipment, but a trip to a specialty kitchen or cake-decorating store really pays off when it comes to these cookies.

Equipment

COOKIE CUTTERS

Having a large collection of cookie cutters is just plain fun. Look for cutters that aren't too big and avoid shapes with lots of skinny parts. A simple sturdy cutter between 2 and 3 inches in diameter is easy to use, especially for young kids. In my experience, some of the best cutters for the job include mittens, trees, and a little log cabin, which is especially fun to decorate.

PASTRY BAGS

If you are seriously committed to cookie decorating, I recommend buying several 12- or 14-inch cloth-coated or plastic pastry bags, and gaskets for the tips. Both are reusable and highly functional. If you aren't ready to make the investment or you'll be working with very young kids, disposable plastic triangles are great. Aside from being easy to use, the transparent bags make it possible to identify the frosting by color.

TIPS

A #3 or #4 tip is the perfect size for cookie decorating. Disposable plastic triangles don't require tips; just clip the end with scissors.

SMALL BOWLS

Have three or four small glass or stainless steel bowls handy for mixing different colors and keeping them separate with a minimum of dish washing.

SMALL OFFSET SPATULA

A small offset spatula isn't 100 percent necessary, but it is 100 percent handy for smoothing the icing. An offset spatula is a small metal spreading tool with a narrow 4-inch blade and an offset wooden handle, allowing you to use the full surface of the blade when frosting cookies or a cake.

FOOD COLOR

Gel or paste food colors offer the most vibrant color choices, but food color from the grocery store works too. In addition to being available in a greater variety of color choices, higher-end food color offers greater nuance because it's easy to blend and introduce in small increments.

COLORED DECORATING SUGAR

Some grocery stores carry colored decorating sugar, but it's worth the effort to make your own. Not only will you spend less money, you'll be able to create a wide palette of custom colors using gel or paste food color with clear crystal sugar purchased at a baking specialty store.

To make decorating sugar, put 1 cup of granulated or crystal sugar in a small stainless steel bowl. Use a toothpick to get a very small amount of color, about the size of half of a pea. Add it to the sugar, using a spoon to toss and distribute the color throughout. Suddenly the sugar will take on an even, intense color that can be made more vibrant by repeating the process.

BAKING SHEETS

Every year, I seem to add another baking sheet to my collection. There's no tool more easily acquired, or more essential to success in baking cookies on a large scale. Having at least three pans really helps me to be efficient, as I use the pans not only for baking, but also for cooling, storing, and chilling (before baking), and for individual decorating trays.

The Game Plan

Decorating cookies is a big project. Since I'm usually doing it with kids, I like to have the dough mixed, chilled, and ready for rolling before they arrive. As they've gotten older, my nieces and nephews have increasingly enjoyed helping mix, roll, cut, and bake the cookies. No matter how—or by whom—these steps must be completed before you can focus on making royal icing and explaining decorating techniques.

Older kids love to cut the cookies, maybe because they feel very accomplished after extracting a perfect cookie shape from a sheet of shortbread dough. Younger children tend to tire of this part quickly, anxious to get to the decorating.

My solution for accommodating all ages and attention spans? Bake the majority of the cookies ahead of time. I'd rather do this methodically and leisurely over the course of a couple hours and a couple cups of coffee when I'm alone. Roll, cut, chill, and bake—if you take the time, you can slip into this easy routine without even noticing. To get the best-looking, best-tasting cookies, chill the cookies before putting them in the oven.

Prepare the ingredients and equipment.

Measure the flour and salt into a small bowl and whisk to combine.

Cream the butter and sugar.

Using a stand mixer with the paddle attachment, beat the butter and sugar on medium-high speed for at least 6 minutes. It is sufficiently combined when the mixture is lighter in color and fluffy, a result of the sugar dissolving into the softened butter. Scrape the bottom and sides of the bowl several times during the process.

Add the vanilla and dry ingredients.

Add the vanilla and dry ingredients and mix on low speed just until the dough begins to come together.

Chill the dough.

Divide the dough into 2 pieces, shape them into flat disks, and wrap in plastic wrap. At this stage, the dough can be refrigerated for up to 1 week or frozen for up to 6 months.

Roll out the dough.

Many beginning bakers struggle with rolling dough out to a consistent thickness. The key is to begin with a flattened disk of dough at room temperature. When it's too cold, dough is nearly impossible to roll, and when it's too warm, it gets sticky. Take well-chilled, firm dough from the refrigerator and let it sit out for 30 minutes before rolling. It should still be cool and firm, but will also be pliable when pressure is applied.

Sprinkle no more than 1 tablespoon of flour on your work surface. Move the dough around the surface, then flip it over once or twice to coat it with a light dusting of flour and keep it from sticking. Roll the dough starting from the center and working out to achieve an overall even thickness. Use a bench knife or bowl scraper to keep the dough from sticking to

(continued)

Classic Buttery Shortbread and Royal Icing

Referring to a baked good as being "short" means that its characteristic flavor and texture come from shortening or—don't cringe—fat, in this case butter. Butter keeps the texture delicate by coating the flour's gluten strands and preventing them from becoming long and chewy, therefore "shortening" them.

This universally adaptable cookie dough can be used for multiple applications, from colorful, decorated cookies to scrumptious little tea cookies to a flawless tart crust. Be sure to plan ahead when you make this dough; it must be chilled for 1 to 2 hours before rolling. And before you start mixing the dough, make some room in the refrigerator or freezer for a baking sheet, so you can chill the cookies before baking them.

For the icing, use dehydrated meringue powder in place of egg whites if salmonella is a concern. You can also purchase pasteurized egg whites in most grocery stores. Two tablespoons is the equivalent of one egg white.

ROYAL ICING (MAKES SLIGHTLY MORE THAN 1 CUP)

1 egg white

1¹/₂ tablespoons freshly squeezed lemon juice

2 cups (8 ounces) confectioners' sugar, sifted, or more for thickening icing

YIELD	About 1¹/₂ pounds	About 2¹/₄ pounds	About 3 pounds
ALL-PURPOSE FLOUR	2¹/₃ cups (11.5 ounces)	3¹/₂ cups (1 pound, 1.5 ounces)	4²/₃ cups (1 pound, 7 ounces)
SALT	1 teaspoon	1¹/₂ teaspoons	2 teaspoons
BUTTER, AT ROOM TEMPERATURE	1 cup (8 ounces, or 2 sticks)	1¹/₂ cups (12 ounces, or 3 sticks)	2 cups (1 pound, or 4 sticks)
GRANULATED SUGAR	²/₃ cup (4.75 ounces)	1 cup (7 ounces)	1¹/₃ cups (9.5 ounces)
VANILLA EXTRACT	1 teaspoon	1¹/₂ teaspoons	2 teaspoons

the work surface. At the bakery, we roll most dough between sheets of parchment paper or plastic wrap, which helps avoid adding too much flour. Consider trying this at home.

Cut out the cookies.

Dip a cookie cutter in flour and cut as many cookies as you can from the sheet of dough. (Dough scraps can be reworked, but try to handle them as little as possible.) The most efficient strategy for me involves using the same cutter for several cookies at a time, cutting them out in a symmetrical pattern. Evenly space the cookies on a parchment-lined baking sheet and chill for 5 to 10 minutes before baking. You can skip this step, but the cookies won't hold their shape or sharp edges as well.

If you're using decorating sugar, sprinkle it onto the cookies before baking. During the winter holidays, we sell thousands of snowflake cookies dusted with decorating sugar and outlined with royal icing to highlight the shimmer. The spectacle of hundreds of pans of pale pink hearts on Valentine's Day is also lovely.

Bake the cookies.

Preheat the oven to 350°F and arrange 2 racks near the middle of the oven. Bake 1 or 2 pans at a time. Baking time will vary according to the size of the cookies and how long they've been chilling. To start, bake for 5 minutes, then rotate the pan(s) and bake for 5 minutes more. The cookies are ready when the edges begin to turn golden. The centers should remain fairly light, almost without color. Let the cookies cool on the baking sheet(s).

Make the icing.

When it comes to the perfect consistency for royal icing, every baker has an opinion or a preference; it also depends on how you're planning to use it. Here's a place where you need to put your instincts to work—the moisture of the sugar, the consistency of the color, and the size of the egg whites all will affect the final consistency of the icing. Before you fill a bag, test your icing with a spoon; for detail work, it should pause slightly before it streams off the tip of a spoon. For covering the whole cookie, you'll want it slightly thinner, which will cause it to stream off the spoon immediately.

Lightly whisk the egg white and lemon juice with a fork. Add 1$\frac{1}{2}$ cups of the sugar and whisk until smooth. If the icing is too thick, add more lemon juice; if it's too thin, add more confectioners' sugar. You may store the icing in an airtight container in the refrigerator for up to 3 days. If you store it before use, whisk it together before pouring into small bowls to add color.

(continued)

Add the color.

Intensity is the main difference between gel or paste food color and the kind you find at the grocery store. A very small amount of gel or paste adds a lot of color, so go slowly. Begin with a tiny dab of coloring on the end of a toothpick. Incorporate it thoroughly, then add more icing or color until you achieve the desired intensity.

Fill the pastry bag.

Spoon 1 cup of each icing color into a 12- or 14-inch pastry sleeve fitted with a gasket and a #4 tip. Be sure to leave some icing in the bowl for spreading.

There are a few painless ways to get the icing in a pastry bag. If there's someone else around, ask your helper to hold the bag wide open, then plop the icing down into the center. If you're alone, put the tip of the bag at the bottom of a pint glass or cylindrical jar, with the end of the bag folded so the tip points up. Fold the top edge of the bag over the rim of the glass to support the cone while you fill it.

Decorate the cookies.

Flooding is the name of the technique used to cover a cookie with thinned royal icing. Use a #3 or #4 tip held about $1/4$ inch above the cookie. First ice the outline of the cookie, leaving space along the edge for spillage, then fill in the rest when the outline has dried. Close any empty spaces by pushing the icing in place with a toothpick. For raised designs or a three-dimensional effect, dry the flooding layer for at least 2 hours, then pipe new icing on top of the dry icing.

You can achieve a sparkly effect with decorating sugar, which is processed into round grains four to six times larger than the grains of granulated sugar. To apply it, place the iced cookies on parchment paper and sprinkle decorating sugar over the tops. Let the cookies sit for about 15 minutes, then tip them upside down to remove excess sugar.

Handling a Pastry Bag

It takes a little bit of experience to wield a pastry bag, and practice will definitely pay off. Use two hands to start. I place my right (dominant) hand at the top of the bag and use my left hand to guide the tip. Try it both ways to find which feels more natural to you. Use a piece of parchment paper as a canvas and draw some lines and shapes. If you're decorating cookies with kids, have them practice too.

Try lining sugared cookies with royal icing in a variety of colors using a tip. Pipe icing onto the cookies and sprinkle with decorating sugar for a sparkling effect called sugaring. Tip the cookie to remove excess sugar.

SANDWICH COOKIES

There's something irresistible about crisp cookies held together with creamy filling. While sandwich cookies aren't a bakery staple, regular customers will recognize the peanut butter and chocolate mint sandwich cookies, which appear throughout the year. Because I've grown fond of them, we've added two other sandwich cookies—graham cracker and lemon cream—for the home baker.

Peanut Butter Sandwich Cookies

On the rare occasions when my mother treated us to store-bought cookies, Nutter Butters were our favorite. Besides being enticed by the catchy jingle, we thought they were just plain yummy. Today I prefer this homemade, all-butter peanut butter sandwich cookie. Once you've had one, you won't be able to resist a nutter.

Because this recipe uses refrigerator-style cookies, you'll need to chill the dough before slicing and baking, so plan accordingly.

MAKES ABOUT 2 DOZEN SANDWICH COOKIES

COOKIES

2 cups (10 ounces) all-purpose flour

1/2 teaspoon baking soda

1/4 teaspoon salt

12 tablespoons (6 ounces, or 11/2 sticks) unsalted butter, at room temperature

1/2 cup (3.5 ounces) granulated sugar

1/2 cup (3.5 ounces) packed light brown sugar

2/3 cup (6.25 ounces) peanut butter, at room temperature

1 egg, at room temperature

1 teaspoon vanilla extract

FILLING

2 tablespoons unsalted butter, at room temperature

1/2 cup (4.75 ounces) peanut butter, at room temperature

1/4 cup (1 ounce) confectioners' sugar

1/2 teaspoon salt

2 tablespoons heavy cream, or more as needed

Combine the dry ingredients.

Measure the flour, baking soda, and salt into a bowl and whisk to combine.

Cream the butter, sugar, and peanut butter.

Using a stand mixer with the paddle attachment, beat the butter, granulated sugar, and brown sugar on medium speed for 3 to 5 minutes, until well combined. Add the peanut butter and continue to beat for another minute.

Add the egg, vanilla, and dry ingredients.

Reduce the mixer speed to low, add the egg and vanilla, and mix just until combined. Add the dry ingredients and mix just until they disappear into the dough. Chill the dough for 30 minutes so it will be easier to handle.

Shape and chill the dough.

Divide the dough into 2 equal pieces and roll each into an oblong log 8 to 10 inches long; aim for a cross between the shape of a biscotti and a peanut. Wrap the logs in plastic wrap and refrigerate for at least 2 hours and up to 3 days (or freeze for up to 3 months).

Slice and bake the cookies.

Preheat the oven to 325°F. Line 2 baking sheets with parchment paper.

Slice the cookies 1/4 to 1/2 inch thick and place them about 1 inch apart, in 3 by 4 rows, on the prepared pans. Bake for 15 to 20 minutes, rotating the pans halfway through the baking time. The cookies should be dry, firm to the touch, and deep golden brown. Let the cookies cool completely while you make the filling.

Make the filling.

Using a stand mixer with the paddle attachment, mix the butter, peanut butter, sugar, and salt on low speed until evenly combined. Add the cream, increase the speed to medium, and beat for 1 minute, adding more cream if needed to make a spreadable consistency.

Fill and assemble the sandwich cookies.

Turn half of the cookies upside down, then use a small teaspoon to put a dollop of filling about the size of a nickel on the inverted cookies. Cover with the remaining cookies and press together gently so the filling spreads to the edges of the sandwich.

Chocolate Mint Sandwich Cookies

We developed this cookie for the winter holidays, a window that's much too short for the true lover of the combination of chocolate and mint. If they last, these cookies actually improve with age; the mint flavor permeates the entire cookie after a few days.

The cookies for this sandwich are made in the style of the Cocoa Nib Cookies (page 69). You need to chill the dough for at least 2 hours before slicing and baking, so plan ahead.

MAKES ABOUT 2 DOZEN SANDWICH COOKIES

COOKIES

2 cups (10 ounces) all-purpose flour

$1/2$ cup (1.5 ounces) unsweetened cocoa powder

$1/4$ teaspoon salt

1 cup (8 ounces, or 2 sticks) unsalted butter,
   at room temperature

1 cup (7 ounces) granulated sugar

1 teaspoon vanilla extract

FILLING

6 ounces semisweet chocolate
   (1 cup of chips or chunks)

$1/2$ cup (4 fluid ounces) heavy cream

$1/2$ teaspoon peppermint extract

Combine the dry ingredients.

Measure the flour, cocoa powder, and salt into a bowl and whisk to combine. (Put the mixture through a fine mesh sieve if the cocoa powder is lumpy.)

Cream the butter and sugar and add the vanilla.

Using a stand mixer with the paddle attachment, beat the butter and sugar on medium speed until very smooth, about 3 minutes. Add the vanilla, then reduce the speed to low.

Add the dry ingredients.

Add the dry ingredients and mix just until they disappear into the dough.

Shape and chill the dough.

Use the Shortbread Tea Cookie Method (see page 65) to shape the dough into 2 logs 2 inches in diameter, then chill for at least 2 hours and up to 3 days (or freeze for up to 3 months).

Slice and bake the cookies.

Preheat the oven to 325°F. Line 2 baking sheets with parchment paper.

Slice the cookies $1/4$ to $1/2$ inch thick and place them about 1 inch apart, in 3 by 4 rows, on the prepared pans. Bake for 15 to 20 minutes, rotating the pans halfway through the baking time. The cookies should be dry, firm to the touch, and deep golden brown. Let the cookies cool completely while you make the filling.

Make the filling.

Put the chocolate in a small bowl. Put the cream in a small saucepan over medium heat and bring to a boil. Immediately pour the cream over the chocolate. Let the chocolate sit for a few minutes, then add the peppermint extract and stir until smooth. Let the ganache cool until it's creamy and spreadable, about 30 minutes.

Fill and assemble the sandwich cookies.

Turn half of the cookies upside down, then use a small teaspoon to put a mound of filling about the size of a nickel on the inverted cookies. Cover with the remaining cookies and press together gently so the filling spreads to the edges of the sandwich.

Graham Cracker Sandwich Cookies

When I was very little, sandwiching frosting between graham crackers was one of my specialties. This grown-up version features an almost savory home-made graham cracker paired with sweet vanilla frosting. This filling is moist, so if you're after a crisp cookie, bake ahead and store them in an airtight container for up to 4 days, then fill them just before serving.

MAKES ABOUT 2 DOZEN SANDWICH COOKIES

GRAHAM CRACKERS

2 cups (10 ounces) all-purpose flour

1/2 cup (2.5 ounces) whole wheat flour

1/2 teaspoon baking soda

1/2 teaspoon salt

1/2 teaspoon ground cinnamon

1 cup (8 ounces, or 2 sticks) unsalted butter, at room temperature

1/4 cup (1.75 ounces) granulated sugar

1/4 cup (1.75 ounces) packed light brown sugar

1/4 cup (3 ounces) honey

FROSTING

1/2 cup (4 ounces, or 1 stick) unsalted butter, at room temperature

2 cups (8 ounces) confectioners' sugar

1/2 teaspoons vanilla extract

1 to 2 tablespoons heavy cream, half and half, or whole milk

Combine the dry ingredients.

Measure the flours, baking soda, salt, and cinnamon into a bowl and whisk to combine.

Cream the butter, sugar, and honey.

Using a stand mixer with the paddle attachment, beat the butter, granulated sugar, brown sugar, and honey on medium speed until lighter in color and fluffy, 3 to 5 minutes. Stop the mixer to scrape the bottom and sides of the bowl.

Add the dry ingredients and chill the dough.

With the mixer on low speed, add the dry ingredients all at once and mix just until combined. Wrap the dough in plastic wrap and refrigerate for 1 hour or up to 3 days.

Shape the cookies.

Preheat the oven to 350°F. Line 2 baking sheets with parchment paper.

Lightly dust a work surface with flour and coat a rolling pin with additional flour. Roll the dough out to a thickness of 1/8 inch, then use a sharp chef's knife to cut the dough into rectangles. For a completely authentic look, dock the dough by pricking it with a fork. Place the rectangles 1 inch apart, in 3 by 4 rows, on the prepared pans.

Bake.

Bake for 15 to 20 minutes, rotating the pans halfway through the baking time. The cookies should be dry, firm to the touch, and deep golden brown. Let them cool completely on the baking sheets while you make the frosting.

Make the frosting.

Using a stand mixer with the paddle attachment, mix the butter and 2 cups of the confectioners' sugar on low speed until well blended, then increase to medium speed and beat for 3 minutes. Add the vanilla and 1 tablespoon of the cream and continue to beat on medium speed for 1 minute, adding up to 1 additional tablespoon of cream if needed to achieve a spreadable consistency.

Fill and assemble the sandwich cookies.

Turn half of the cookies upside down, then use a small butter knife or offset spatula to spread a layer of frosting on the inverted cookies, leaving the edges uncovered. Cover with the remaining cookies and press together gently so the filling spreads to the edges of the sandwich.

Lemon Cream Sandwich Cookies

This delicate lemon cookie is filled with tangy cream cheese frosting for the perfect balance of tart and sweet, crispy and creamy. Zest a whole lemon, squeeze out the juice, and in the end, you will have used the whole lemon.

Allow this sticky dough plenty of time to set up in the refrigerator before rolling and cutting it for cookies. A simple 2-inch round cutter is wonderfully easy to use, but don't hesitate to experiment with any solid shape with a 2-inch diameter—hearts, stars, squares, and hand-cut rectangles all look lovely.

MAKES ABOUT 1 DOZEN SANDWICH COOKIES

COOKIES

1½ cups (7.5 ounces) all-purpose flour

1 teaspoon baking powder

½ teaspoon salt

½ cup (4 ounces, or 1 stick) unsalted butter,
    at room temperature

1 cup (7 ounces) granulated sugar

2 egg yolks, at room temperature

3 tablespoons freshly squeezed lemon juice

2 tablespoons finely chopped lemon zest

FILLING

4 ounces cream cheese, at room temperature

1 cup (4 ounces) confectioners' sugar

1 tablespoon freshly squeezed lemon juice

1 tablespoon finely chopped lemon zest

Combine the dry ingredients.

Measure the flour, baking powder, and salt into a bowl and whisk to combine.

Cream the butter and sugar, then add the egg yolks and lemon juice and zest.

Using a stand mixer with the paddle attachment, beat the butter and sugar together on medium speed for 2 to 3 minutes, until the mixture is lighter in color and fluffy.

Add the egg yolks, lemon juice, and lemon zest and mix until thoroughly incorporated. Scrape the bottom and sides of the bowl.

Add the dry ingredients.

With the mixer on low speed, add the dry ingredients and mix just until they disappear into the dough.

Shape and chill the dough.

Line a sheet pan with parchment paper or plastic wrap, transfer the dough to the prepared pan, and form it into a 1-inch-thick disk by patting it into shape. Wrap the dough and refrigerate for at least 1 hour or up to 3 days. If you don't use it after 1 hour, allow the dough to warm up slightly, until it becomes pliable and easy to roll.

Cut out and bake the cookies.

Preheat the oven to 350°F. Line 2 baking sheets with parchment paper.

Lightly dust a work surface with flour and coat a rolling pin with additional flour. Roll the dough out to a thickness of ⅛ inch. Cut out the cookies with a cutter or knife dipped in flour and place them 1 inch apart, in 3 by 4 rows, on the prepared pans. Bake for about 15 minutes, rotating the pans halfway through the baking time. Let them cool completely while you make the filling.

Make the filling.

Using a stand mixer with the paddle attachment, mix the cream cheese and confectioners' sugar on low speed until smooth and well combined. Add the lemon juice and zest, increase the speed to medium, and beat for 1 minute.

Fill and assemble the sandwich cookies.

Turn half of the cookies upside down, then use a small butter knife or offset spatula to spread a layer of filling on the inverted cookies, leaving the edges uncovered. Cover with the remaining cookies and press together gently so the filling spreads to the edges of the sandwich.

MACAROONS

To be completely honest, I'd never made a Parisian macaroon before testing this recipe. Laura Ohm, our resident Francophile, manages the Grand Central Bakery pastry commissary and kitchen. She developed our take on these pretty little French gems when I no longer worked regular production shifts.

I've made my share of simple coconut macaroons, but I always felt like Parisian macaroons sat too solidly on the fussy side of the pastry spectrum to find a place in my home baking regime. I couldn't have been more wrong. While macaroons do require a certain amount of attention, they're really just simple nut meringues, filled with jam, chocolate ganache, or buttercream. Typically made by stirring ground almonds into a basic sugar and egg white meringue, perfect Parisian macaroons have a crust that can be smooth or craggy and is thinner and more fragile than an eggshell. Their chewy interior is light and moist and melts almost the instant it hits the tongue.

They've long been popular in French sweet shops, and now macaroon madness has erupted on this side of the pond, with these little cookies serving as a nutty vehicle for pastry chefs to strut their culinary chops. Lately I've noticed flavors beyond comprehension: olive oil, curry, tarragon, white truffle and hazelnut, rose-lychee raspberry, and chocolate–passion fruit, to name but a few. At Grand Central Bakery, we stick to our version of the classics: pale pink almond raspberry and caramel-colored hazelnut mocha, both of which, along with coconut macaroons, are appropriate for Passover.

Pink Almond Macaroons

I never mind having a few extra egg yolks around to enrich custard, but macaroons call for so many egg whites that it's especially convenient to buy a carton of egg whites when making them. They're available in the dairy section of most grocery stores. Leftover egg whites can be frozen for up to 3 months.

**MAKES ABOUT 1¹/₂ DOZEN FILLED MACAROONS,
OR 3 DOZEN PLAIN COOKIES**

1¹/₄ cups (5 ounces) confectioners' sugar
1¹/₂ cups (5 ounces) almond meal
3 egg whites, at room temperature
¹/₈ teaspoon salt
¹/₄ cup (1.75 ounces) granulated sugar
Pink food color
¹/₄ cup best-quality raspberry jam (optional)

Combine the dry ingredients.

Sift the confectioners' sugar into a bowl and whisk it with the almond meal.

Make the meringue.

Using a stand mixer with the whisk attachment, whip the egg whites and salt in an impeccably clean, dry bowl on medium speed until the whites begin to foam and turn opaque. Increase the speed to medium-high, gradually adding the granulated sugar, 1 tablespoon at a time, until the whites gain volume and hold creamy, medium-firm peaks; they shouldn't be glossy, but should look more like whipped cream.

Fold the meringue into the dry ingredients.

Scrape the meringue into the dry ingredients and gently fold together just until the dry ingredients have been absorbed and the mixture appears smooth and creamy. Add the food color, one drop at a time, until you reach the desired shade. Be careful not to work the batter so much that it becomes runny.

Form the cookies.

Preheat the oven to 325°F. Line a baking sheet with parchment paper.

You can use a pastry bag to pipe the cookies, or make free-form cookies with a spatula. To use a pastry bag, fold down the top of the bag to make a 4-inch cuff. (You can use the bag without a tip.) Scrape the batter into the bag, then unfold the cuff and twist the top of the bag closed, squeezing the batter downward. Pipe 1¹/₂-inch disks of batter onto the prepared pan. Or, for pretty, free-form meringues, lightly flick a heaping tablespoon of batter onto the baking sheet with a quick motion of your wrist. You should be able to fit 6 rows of 6 to 7 cookies on a large baking sheet. Let the macaroons stand at room temperature until a soft, dry skin forms, 15 to 20 minutes.

Bake.

Bake the macaroons for 15 to 20 minutes, rotating the pan at least once during baking. The macaroons will puff, become shiny, and fall very slightly, and should be dry when fully baked. Let the cookies cool and dry completely, then make sandwich cookies using the raspberry jam.

Hazelnut Macaroons

*A real Oregonian will tell you that a hazelnut is actu-
ally called a filbert. At Grand Central, we're proud of
Oregon's filbert crop and try to squeeze them into as
many items as possible.*

MAKES ABOUT 1$^1/_2$ DOZEN FILLED MACAROONS,
OR 3 DOZEN PLAIN COOKIES

MACAROONS

1 cup (5 ounces) hazelnut meal, or 1 cup (4 ounces)
    lightly toasted, skinned whole hazelnuts
    (see sidebar, opposite)

1$^1/_4$ cups (5 ounces) confectioners' sugar

3 egg whites, at room temperature

$^1/_8$ teaspoon salt

$^1/_4$ cup (1.75 ounces) granulated sugar

FILLING (OPTIONAL)

$^1/_3$ cup (3 fluid ounces) freshly brewed hot coffee

1 cup (6 ounces) semisweet chocolate chips
    or chunks

Grind Your Own Nut Meal

It's easy to make nut meal by grinding whole nuts.
The result is likely to be slightly more coarse than
commercially produced nut flours—but it's every bit
as delicious.

To make your own nut meal, add about half of
the confectioners' sugar called for in the recipe to
help absorb the oil released when grinding the nuts.
(If you're making nut meal for a recipe that doesn't
call for sugar, it helps to freeze the nuts before
grinding.) Put the toasted nuts and confectioners'
sugar in the bowl of a food processor with the steel
blade and pulse several times, until the texture resembles cornmeal. Be sure to use the pulse setting
to avoid making nut butter! Store nut meal in the
refrigerator or freezer, and use it soon after buying
or making it.

Combine the dry ingredients.

Combine the hazelnut meal and 1 cup of the confectioners' sugar in a nut grinder or the bowl of a food processor. Grind to a fine powder, stopping the machine
once or twice to scrape the corners and sides of the
bowl. Transfer the mixture to a bowl, add the remaining $^1/_4$ cup confectioners' sugar, and whisk until evenly
combined.

Make the meringue.

Using a stand mixer with the whisk attachment, whip
the egg whites and salt in an impeccably clean, dry bowl
on medium speed until the whites begin to foam and
turn opaque. Increase the speed to medium-high and
gradually add the granulated sugar, 1 tablespoon at a
time, until the whites gain volume and hold creamy,
medium-firm peaks; they shouldn't be glossy, but should
look more like whipped cream.

Fold the meringue into the dry ingredients.

Scrape the meringue into the dry ingredients and gently fold together just until the dry ingredients have
been absorbed and the mixture appears smooth and
creamy.

Form the cookies.

Preheat the oven to 325°F. Line a baking sheet with
parchment paper.

You can use a pastry bag to pipe the cookies or make
free-form cookies with a spatula. To use a pastry bag,
fold down the top of the bag to make a 4-inch cuff. (You
can use the bag without a tip.) Scrape the batter into the
bag, then unfold the cuff and twist the top of the bag
closed, squeezing the batter downward. Pipe 1$^1/_2$-inch
disks of batter onto the prepared pan. Or, for pretty,
free-form meringues, lightly flick a heaping tablespoon
of batter onto the baking sheet with a quick motion
of your wrist. You should be able to fit 6 rows of 6 to
7 cookies on a large baking sheet. Let the macaroons
stand at room temperature until a soft, dry skin forms,
15 to 20 minutes.

Bake.

Bake macaroons for 15 to 20 minutes, rotating the pan at least once during baking. The macaroons will puff, become shiny, and fall very slightly, and should be dry when fully baked. Let the cookies cool and dry completely.

Make the filling.

To make the mocha ganache filling, pour the hot coffee over the chocolate and let it sit for several minutes to melt the chocolate, then stir until smooth. When the ganache has cooled slightly and is creamy and spreadable, use it to fill the macaroons.

Toasting and Skinning Hazelnuts

Preheat the oven to 275°F. Place shelled hazelnuts on a baking sheet in a single layer, then toast for 20 to 30 minutes, until the skins crack and the nuts begin to turn light golden brown. (You can also toast them at 350°F for 10 to 15 minutes, but stay close to the oven and check them periodically to be sure they don't burn.)

Hazelnut skins are especially tight, but toasting loosens them considerably. To remove the skins, put the toasted nuts in a colander with large holes and place the colander in the sink. Use a clean dish towel to rub the nuts; this will peel off most of the skins. Shake the colander occasionally to let the skins fall into the sink. Alternatively, you can put the freshly toasted hazelnuts in a clean cloth towel and gather it closed. Let the nuts steam for 4 to 5 minutes, then rub vigorously, through the towel, for 1 to 3 minutes. You can either pick out the skinned nuts, or shake them in a colander to separate them from the skins.

Coconut Macaroons

In Grand Central's early days, we offered simple chewy almond macaroons for Passover. Soon after they were added to the lineup, an anonymous message was posted on the kitchen bulletin board: "Almond macaroons, yuck! Macaroons should be all about the coconut." I was a bit bent out of shape at the time, but the comment motivated me to come up with this recipe for coconut macaroons.

These rich and chewy macaroons were an instant hit. I know cream of coconut isn't among the most politically correct ingredients, but it works like a charm.

MAKES ABOUT 2 DOZEN COOKIES

½ cup (4 fluid ounces) cream of coconut

¼ cup (3 ounces) corn syrup

3 egg whites, at room temperature

¾ teaspoon vanilla extract

¼ teaspoon salt

1 cup plus 2 tablespoons (4.5 ounces) unsweetened macaroon-cut coconut

1½ cups (4.5 ounces) sweetened flake coconut

Prepare to bake.

Preheat the oven to 325°F. Line 2 sheet pans with parchment paper.

Make the batter.

Whisk the cream of coconut, corn syrup, egg whites, vanilla, and salt together until well combined. Fold in the macaroon and flake coconuts, then use your hands to shape the batter into tightly packed rounds the size of ping-pong balls.

Bake.

Place the macaroons on the prepared pans, leaving 1 inch between cookies. Bake for 20 to 25 minutes, rotating the pans halfway through the baking time. The macaroons should be deep golden brown on top and dark brown around the edges.

FAMILY FAVORITES

Amidst the assortment of typical American cookies we made as kids—Toll House chocolate chip cookies from the recipe on the bag, and oatmeal raisin from *The Joy of Cooking*—these two cookies worked their way into our family repertoire. Put a plate of Lacy Oatmeal Cookies or Favorite Lemon Bars in front of either of my brothers and they'll disappear quickly. I still love both of these recipes.

Lacy Oatmeal Cookies

I thought these cookies were super fancy when I was a little girl. When I took over as the cookie baker in our household, I turned to this butter-stained card in my mother's red recipe box often. Essentially a simplified florentine, these are a wonderful and easy treat.

While testing this recipe, I discovered that these make delicious sandwich cookies. Use the filling for the Hazelnut Macaroons (see page 88) or the filling for the Chocolate Mint Sandwich Cookies (see page 83), substituting vanilla extract for the peppermint extract.

MAKES ABOUT 3 DOZEN COOKIES

$1/2$ cup (2.5 ounces) all-purpose flour

$1/4$ teaspoon baking powder

$1/2$ teaspoon salt

$1/2$ cup (1.75 ounces) quick oats

$1/3$ cup (2.75 ounces, or $2/3$ stick) unsalted butter, at room temperature

$1/2$ cup (3.5 ounces) granulated sugar

2 tablespoons heavy cream

2 tablespoons corn syrup or brown rice syrup

1 teaspoon vanilla extract

Prepare to bake.

Preheat the oven to 350°F. Line 2 baking sheets with parchment paper.

Combine the dry ingredients.

Measure the flour, baking powder, and salt into a bowl and whisk to combine. Stir in the oats.

Melt the butter, then add the remaining ingredients.

Melt the butter in a saucepan over medium-low heat. Remove from the heat and add the sugar, cream, corn syrup, and vanilla. Using a heatproof rubber spatula or wooden spoon, stir everything together until homogenous and smooth.

Add the dry ingredients.

Fold in the dry ingredients and let the mixture sit for 5 minutes.

Bake.

Drop marble-size balls of dough (about 1 teaspoon each) onto the prepared pans, about 12 per pan, in 3 by 4 rows; they need room to spread. Bake for 5 minutes total, rotating the pans halfway through the baking time. The cookies should be thin and flat, with lightly browned edges. Allow the cookies to cool slightly before eating or sandwiching. They will become crispy as they cool.

Favorite Lemon Bars

I don't know when I developed my deep and abiding affection for shortbread crust and lemon custard, but it was when I was very young. And because I was a novice when I began baking lemon bars, they were always imperfect, with awkward, lopsided crusts and unevenly distributed filling. Still, they always tasted good.

Over the years, different lemon bars have appeared in Grand Central's lineup. This is Ellen's version, and even though Grand Central Bakery has never sold them, they might be my favorite so far. They are tangy and bright, with a delicate, buttery crust and, if you use good-quality farm-fresh eggs, a beautiful, intense color.

**MAKES 1 DOZEN LARGE BARS
OR 2 DOZEN SMALL BARS**

CRUST

2 1/2 cups (12.5 ounces) all-purpose flour

3/4 teaspoon salt

1 cup (8 ounces, or 2 sticks) unsalted butter,
   at room temperature

3/4 cup (5.25 ounces) granulated sugar

1 teaspoon vanilla extract

FILLING

6 eggs, lightly beaten

2 cups (14 ounces) granulated sugar

1/4 cup plus 1 tablespoon (1.5 ounces)
   all-purpose flour

1 cup (8 fluid ounces) freshly squeezed lemon juice

1 tablespoon finely chopped lemon zest

1/2 cup (4 fluid ounces) whole milk

1/2 teaspoon salt

Confectioners' sugar, for dusting

Prepare to bake.

Preheat the oven to 350°F. Generously coat a 9 by 13-inch pan with pan spray or melted butter.

Make the crust.

Measure the flour and salt into a bowl and whisk to combine. Using a stand mixer with the paddle attachment, beat the butter and sugar together on medium speed for about 3 minutes, until the mixture is lighter in color and fluffy. Add the vanilla and mix to incorporate. Reduce the speed to low and add the dry ingredients, scraping the bottom and sides of the bowl several times. Stop mixing when the ingredients are fully incorporated but the dough is still crumbly. This happens quickly; the mixture will look dry and floury, then little clumps will suddenly appear. Don't overmix or the crust will be difficult to distribute in the pan.

Bake the crust.

Transfer the dough to the prepared pan and use your fingers to evenly distribute it over the bottom. It isn't necessary to press it in, but do bring the dough up the sides of the pan slightly to contain the filling. Press lightly to hold the crust in place, then bake for 25 minutes, until toasty brown.

Make the filling.

While the crust is baking, whisk the eggs with the sugar and flour. Stir in the lemon juice and zest, milk, and salt. Lower the oven temperature to 325°F and whisk the filling to reblend it just before you pour it over the warm crust.

Bake the bars.

Bake the bars until the filling feels firm when touched lightly, about 20 minutes. Let cool to room temperature on a wire rack, which will take about 30 minutes, before cutting into bars. Cut into twelve large 3-inch squares if you're eating the lemon bars by themselves, or twenty-four small 1 1/2- to 2-inch squares if they're accompanying something else. Dust generously with confectioners' sugar before serving.

4
Mealtime

If I had to choose between a life of savory or sweet, I'd take savory. Give me fried trout over blueberry pancakes for breakfast any day. Of course, there's a certain irony in that; my family has built a small empire around baked goods and pastry, something most people associate with double-crust pies, Danish, and chocolate croissants. Even though flaky pastry—mostly the sweet kind—is my livelihood, I've always insisted that Grand Central Bakery's cafés offer several savory pastry options.

Home baking is about much more than satisfying the sweet tooth. This chapter is an eclectic collection of recipes for savory baked goods from snacks and side dishes to robust items around which you can build a satisfying breakfast, lunch, or dinner. You'll find detailed directions for tailoring a rustic tart to make use of seasonal ingredients, a foolproof recipe for homemade pizza, and potpie recipes guaranteed to please any palate. Like their fruity cousins, many of these recipes lend themselves to experimentation and improvisation with each change of season.

The Bread Basket **94**

Clover Rolls 95

Buttermilk Biscuits 96

Cornbread 97

Savory Casseroles **98**

Corn Pudding 99

Rosemary Bread Pudding 100

Seasonal Strata 101

Savory Pies **102**

Seasonal Rustic Savory Tarts 103

Classic Leek and
Cheese Quiche 105

Savory Hand Pies 106

Spicy Potato Hand Pie Filling 108

Steak and Onion
Hand Pie Filling 108

Improv Pizza **110**

Artisan Pizza 111

Ben's Pan Pizza 113

Potpies **114**

Chicken Potpie 115

Salmon and Leek Potpie 116

THE BREAD BASKET

Despite the fact that I am able bring a different loaf of artisan bread home from the bakery every day of the week, sometimes nothing tastes better than biscuits or cornbread straight from my oven. Homemade bread items such as these elevate a special meal or complete a hearty soup or stew. What's chili without the cornbread?

Clover Rolls

Our family is relatively low-key when it comes to major holidays, but Thanksgiving at my mother's table is not to be missed. Dedicated to giving thanks for our good fortune, the bounty of the harvest, and the sheer pleasure of eating, no holiday is more sacred to us. We forgo rustic artisan bread from the bakery for this feast in favor of light and buttery clover rolls fresh from the oven. They were made to sop up gravy.

This recipe is written in such a way that the rolls go straight from the oven to the table. If that schedule doesn't jibe with yours, consult the Basics of Leavening with Yeast (page 41) to adjust the time and temperature to fit your needs.

MAKES ABOUT 1 DOZEN ROLLS

SPONGE

1¾ cups (14 fluid ounces) tepid water
   (about 80°F)
2 teaspoons active dry yeast
1 tablespoon honey
2 cups (10 ounces) bread flour or unbleached
   all-purpose flour

FINAL DOUGH

3 cups (15 ounces) bread flour or unbleached
   all-purpose flour
2 tablespoons unsalted butter, melted, plus more
   for brushing and dipping
2 teaspoons salt
1 teaspoon active dry yeast

Make the sponge.

About 3 to 4 hours before the meal you plan to serve the rolls with, combine the water, yeast, and honey in a bowl with high sides or the bowl of a stand mixer. Add the flour and mix vigorously with a wooden spoon or the paddle attachment on low speed for about 1 minute. Cover tightly with plastic wrap and let the sponge sit in a warm spot for 30 to 45 minutes, until bubbly.

Mix the final dough.

Add the flour, 2 tablespoons of the butter, the salt, and yeast to the sponge. Using a stand mixer with the paddle attachment, mix on low speed for 2 minutes, then on medium speed for 3 minutes, until the dough is stretchy and glossy and pulls away from the sides of the bowl.

Let the dough rise.

Use a plastic bowl scraper to release the dough from the bowl onto a floured work surface. Gather and round the dough, then place it in a clean, lightly greased bowl large enough that the dough can double in size. Because this dough is kept warm and contains quite a bit of yeast, it should rise quickly. Cover with plastic wrap and let the dough rise until doubled in size, about 1 hour at room temperature.

Shape the rolls.

Brush a standard-size muffin tin with melted butter. About 1 hour before baking, or when the dough has doubled in size, turn it out of the bowl onto the work surface. Divide it into 12 even pieces with a bench knife or a chef's knife, then divide each into 3 smaller pieces. Round each small piece, dip one side into the melted butter, then arrange 3 balls in each muffin cup with the buttered sides touching.

Let the rolls rise.

Lightly brush the tops of the rolls with melted butter, then cover with plastic wrap. Preheat the oven to 400°F and let the rolls rise nearby, in a warm spot, for about 30 minutes. When they've risen properly, the rolls should dent easily when poked, and the dough should spring back slightly.

Bake.

Bake for about 25 minutes, rotating the tin halfway through the baking time, or until the rolls are golden brown. Serve them hot from the oven with plenty of fresh butter.

Buttermilk Biscuits

Buttermilk biscuits had a regular place on our family's dinner table. Nothing stretches a roast chicken like a pile of hot, buttery biscuits. They were my mother's secret weapon for sating the appetites of four hungry teenagers. We'd drench the first one in gravy and eat a second for dessert, with butter and jam.

Because I was always eager to help cook dinner, I took my lessons in biscuit-making seriously. The importance of using cold ingredients and a light hand when making biscuits and short dough were the first guiding principles of baking I committed to memory. Read the Short Dough Workshop (page 16) for more detailed instructions on mixing perfect biscuits.

MAKES ABOUT 1 DOZEN BISCUITS

3 cups (15 ounces) all-purpose flour

2 tablespoons granulated sugar

1 1/2 teaspoons baking powder

1 teaspoon salt

3/4 teaspoon baking soda

3/4 cup (6 ounces, or 1 1/2 sticks) cold
    unsalted butter

1 1/4 cups (10 fluid ounces) buttermilk,
    or more as needed

Prepare to bake.

Preheat the oven to 350°F. Line a baking sheet with parchment paper.

Combine the dry ingredients.

Measure the flour, sugar, baking powder, salt, and baking soda into a mixing bowl with high sides or the bowl of a stand mixer and whisk to combine.

Cut in the butter.

Dice the butter into 1/2-inch cubes. Use your hands or the paddle attachment of the stand mixer to blend the butter into the dry ingredients until the texture of the flour changes from silky to mealy. There should still be dime- to quarter-size pieces of butter remaining.

Add the buttermilk.

Make a well in the flour mixture and pour in 1 cup of the buttermilk in one addition. Gently mix the dough just until it comes together; it will look rough. Scrape the dough from the sides and bottom of the bowl, then add the remaining 1/4 cup buttermilk and mix again to incorporate any floury scraps. The majority of the dough will come together on the paddle if using a stand mixer. Stop mixing while there are still visible chunks of butter and floury patches. The dough should come out of the bowl in 2 to 3 large, messy clumps, leaving only some small scraps and flour around the sides of the bowl. If the dough is visibly dry and crumbly, add extra buttermilk, 1 tablespoon at a time, mixing no more than one rotation after each addition.

Form and cut the dough.

Turn the dough out onto a lightly floured work surface and knead it a few times, just until it forms a cohesive mass. Use a rolling pin or the palms of your hands to gather the dough and gently pat it into an oblong shape 1 1/2 to 2 inches thick. It won't look smooth or particularly cohesive; that's okay.

Cut biscuits at least 2 1/2 inches in diameter. (If you don't have a biscuit cutter, see the sidebar on page 24.) Layer the leftover scraps on top of one another and gently pat them out to a thickness of 1 1/2 to 2 inches and again cut into biscuits. Place the biscuits on the prepared pan in 3 by 4 rows.

Bake.

Bake for 25 to 30 minutes, rotating the pan halfway through the baking time. The biscuits should be toasty golden brown. Serve immediately.

Cornbread

When I was little and asked to help with making dinner, my mother often told me—rather nonchalantly—to make cornbread from the recipe on the side of the cornmeal box. It didn't take long for me to tweak it in my usual fashion: substituting butter for the oil and adding an extra egg. This version, a longtime family favorite, is quick, tasty, and filling; it's also delicious when served right out of the oven, with butter and honey.

SERVES 6 TO 8

1³/₄ cups (7.5 ounces) cornmeal

1¹/₄ cups (6.25 ounces) all-purpose flour

¹/₃ cup (2.25 ounces) granulated sugar

1 tablespoon baking powder

2 teaspoons salt

3 eggs

1³/₄ cups (14 fluid ounces) whole milk

¹/₂ cup (4 ounces, or 1 stick) unsalted butter, melted and slightly cooled

South of the Border Cornbread

For a Mexican flair, add the chiles and cheese before baking.

1 cup chopped roasted chiles

2 ounces (about ¹/₂ cup) Cheddar cheese, grated

1 cup corn kernels, preferably fresh off the cob

Prepare to bake.

Preheat the oven to 350°F. Grease and flour a 10-inch cast-iron skillet or an 8-inch square baking pan.

Combine the dry ingredients.

Measure the cornmeal, flour, sugar, baking powder, and salt into a bowl with high sides and whisk to combine.

Combine the wet ingredients and add to the dry ingredients.

Crack the eggs into a small bowl, add the milk, and whisk to combine. Stir in the butter.

Pour the wet ingredients over the dry ingredients, and mix by hand just until combined.

Bake.

Pour the batter into the prepared pan and bake for 25 minutes, rotating the pan halfway through the baking time. The cornbread should be golden brown around the edges, which will pull away slightly from the side of the pan. Serve warm from the oven.

SAVORY CASSEROLES

Working in a bakery, I'm surrounded by good bread, and I bring a fresh loaf of crusty artisan bread home for dinner almost every day. Of course, the unused heels and half loaves pile up over time, so I'm always looking for ways to use up stale bread. I eat lots of toast. I make bread crumbs. I store partial loaves in my freezer—and when they threaten to overtake the freezer, I make a savory bread casserole.

Two simple recipes follow that share the same philosophy: Start with stale bread. Season it, then soak in custard or stock, add vegetables (or not), and bake. I'm almost hesitant to provide a recipe; once you get the general idea, you'll be able to wing it. These casseroles should be assembled well ahead of the time you intend to bake them; the bread needs time to absorb the flavorful liquids.

Corn Pudding

This is one of those pudding cake–type recipes that magically reorients itself in the oven. When it comes time to serve it, what appears to be a pan of ordinary cornbread reveals a custard-filled center that always manages to baffle and delight.

This dish is a sophisticated take on eggs and toast, and is perfect for brunch or a simple supper when served with a big green salad. Use the suggestions for Seasonal Strata (page 101) and Seasonal Rustic Savory Tarts (page 103) as guidelines for transforming this delicious, basic recipe by adding seasonal vegetables. Fresh corn in season is especially good.

SERVES 6 TO 8

3 slices bacon, cut into $^1/_4$-inch pieces

1 cup (5 ounces) all-purpose flour

1$^1/_2$ teaspoons salt

1 teaspoon baking powder

$^1/_2$ teaspoon baking soda

$^1/_2$ teaspoon chile flakes

$^2/_3$ cup (3 ounces) cornmeal

2 eggs, beaten

2 cups (16 fluid ounces) whole milk

1 tablespoon granulated sugar

1 tablespoon white wine vinegar

3 ounces Cheddar cheese, grated (about $^3/_4$ cup)

3 tablespoons finely chopped fresh chives

1 cup (8 fluid ounces) heavy cream

Prepare to bake.

Preheat the oven to 350°F. Butter an 8-inch square baking pan and put the pan in the oven to heat while you prepare the pudding.

Fry the bacon.

Fry the bacon until crisp, then transfer it, along with 2 tablespoons of drippings, to a large bowl. If need be, add melted butter so that the total amount of fat equals 2 tablespoons.

Combine the dry ingredients.

Measure the flour, salt, baking powder, baking soda, and chile flakes into a bowl and whisk to combine. Stir in the cornmeal.

Combine the wet ingredients and add the dry ingredients.

Crack the eggs into the bowl with the drippings, then add the milk, sugar, and vinegar and beat until smooth. Add the dry ingredients and whisk until smooth; the batter will be quite thin. Stir in the cheese and chives.

Add the cream and bake.

Pour the batter into the heated pan, then pour the cream into the center without stirring. Bake for 50 to 60 minutes. The pudding should quiver slightly when gently shaken, but the edges should be set and lightly browned. Let stand for 15 to 20 minutes before serving.

Rosemary Bread Pudding

Roast chicken couldn't ask for a better sidekick. Because it's more about the bread and less about the custard-y pudding, this simple side dish is designed to soak up gravy and pan drippings. If you prefer more emphasis on the custard, add another egg and another cup of cream or half-and-half.

SERVES 10 TO 12

12 ounces chewy rustic bread

2 tablespoons olive oil

1 large onion, diced into 1/2-inch cubes (about 2 cups)

Salt

1 large clove garlic, finely chopped

2 tablespoons dry sherry

1 tablespoon finely chopped fresh rosemary

3 eggs

1 cup (8 fluid ounces) heavy cream or half-and-half

1 cup (8 fluid ounces) chicken stock or milk

Freshly ground black pepper

2 tablespoons unsalted butter, at room temperature

Prepare the bread.

Slice the bread and cut it into 1-inch cubes. There should be about 6 to 7 cups. If the bread is fresh, toast the cubes or leave them to dry out overnight on the counter.

Sauté the onion and garlic.

Heat the oil in a sauté pan or skillet over medium heat, add the onion and a generous pinch of salt, and sauté over medium heat for 5 to 10 minutes, until the onion softens and starts to become translucent. Add the garlic, and cook for a few more minutes, then pour in the sherry and cook, stirring occasionally, until the liquid is reduced by half. Let cool slightly before proceeding.

Assemble the pudding.

Add the bread cubes to the onion mixture and gently stir to combine, then sprinkle with the rosemary.

Whisk the eggs, cream, and stock together in a bowl until smooth, then stir in a pinch of salt and freshly ground black pepper.

Smear a 9 by 13-inch baking pan or roasting pan with the butter, cover the bottom of the pan with the bread and onion mixture, then pour the custard over the bread. It should come up to the top of the bread; if not, add a splash of stock or cream. Cover with plastic wrap and refrigerate for at least 3 hours and up to overnight.

Bake.

Preheat the oven to 325°F. Remove the pudding from the refrigerator and let it come to room temperature while the oven preheats. Bake for 1 hour, rotating the pan halfway through the baking time. The top of the pudding should be golden brown.

Seasonal Strata

Strata are ingenious vehicles for using up what's on hand. Whether it's an unusual vegetable from the farmers' market, a bunch of greens languishing in the refrigerator, or a random selection of cheese scraps that have been piling up, this layered bread casserole is intended to encourage improvisation. If you begin with good ingredients and use the suggestions for inspiration, you can't go wrong.

Eggier than its bread pudding sibling, strata can be served as a main course at brunch or a casual supper. The seasonal suggestions listed below are vegetarian and perfectly delicious, but like most things, they're even better with crumbled bacon!

SERVES 10 TO 12

1 pound, 8 ounces crusty artisan bread, sliced
   $1/4$ inch thick

1 tablespoon olive oil

1 onion, diced into $1/2$-inch cubes (about $1/2$ cup)

Salt

1 large clove garlic, finely chopped

$1/4$ cup (2 fluid ounces) white wine

$1^1/2$ cups (10 to 12 ounces) prepared vegetables
   (see chart)

8 ounces Gruyère cheese, grated (about 2 cups),
   or any firm, flavorful cheese

5 eggs

2 cups (16 fluid ounces) half-and-half

Freshly ground black pepper

Line the baking pan with bread.

Butter a 9 by 13-inch baking pan and line it with half of the sliced bread, fitting the pieces together as snugly as possible. (My mother insists on cutting off the crusts for a more refined strata, but I skip this step.)

Sauté the vegetables.

Heat the oil in a sauté pan or skillet over medium heat, add the onion and a generous pinch of salt, and sauté until the onion is soft and beginning to brown, 8 to 10 minutes. Add the garlic, cook for a few more minutes, then pour in the wine and cook, stirring occasionally, until the liquid is reduced by half. Prepare additional vegetables as described in the chart.

Assemble the strata.

Spread the onion mixture and prepared vegetables over the bread and sprinkle with half of the cheese.

Crack the eggs into a bowl, add the half-and-half, a pinch of salt and freshly ground black pepper, and whisk until smooth.

Arrange a second layer of bread over the cheese, then pour the custard over the bread. Sprinkle the remaining cheese over the custard. Cover with plastic wrap and weight the top with a slightly smaller pan or plate. Refrigerate for at least 4 hours and up to overnight.

Bake.

Preheat the oven to 325°F. Let the strata come to room temperature while the oven preheats. Bake for 60 to 75 minutes, rotating the pan halfway through the baking time. The filling should be set, and the top should be a deep golden brown.

SPRING: LEEK AND ASPARAGUS (OR ARTICHOKE)	SUMMER: ROASTED ZUCCHINI (OR EGGPLANT) WITH TOMATOES AND RED PEPPERS	FALL: CREAMY WINTER SQUASH WITH MUSHROOMS	WINTER: HEARTY GREENS
When sautéing the onion, add $1/2$ cup sliced leeks (white part with some of the green), then add $1^1/2$ cups diced asparagus (or baby artichokes), trimmed and steamed.	Slice 1 zucchini (or small eggplant) lengthwise and cut 1 red bell pepper into strips. Roast or grill the vegetables with olive oil and salt, then layer them with thick slices of fresh tomato when assembling the strata.	Roast a whole winter squash, then scoop out the flesh and puree it. Mix about 1 cup of squash puree into the custard. When sautéing the onion, add about 2 cups mushrooms.	Wash and coarsely chop 2 large bunches of hearty greens, such as kale, chard, mustard greens, or spinach. (You'll be amazed how much they cook down.) Cook and stir the greens in a wide skillet until tender.

SAVORY PIES

Whether sweet or savory, making a pie can seem like an ambitious project. One of the many good reasons to have a block of pie dough or a fully formed pie shell in the freezer is the ease with which it can be transformed into a special lunch or a light supper. Refer to the Flaky Pastry Workshop on page 174 for tips and tricks for building a meal around a disk of buttery dough.

Seasonal Rustic Savory Tarts

If you have a disk of pie dough and some onion base in your freezer, you can easily and quickly whip up a delicious savory tart for supper. The onion base in this recipe is a terrific jumping-off point for a range of flavors and textures.

This free-form rustic tart, or galette, is a delicious way to showcase seasonal vegetables. The following chart offers suggestions for tailoring your tart to each season and its plenty. Use the chart for inspiration and don't be afraid to experiment.

SERVES 8 TO 10

1 disk All-Butter Flaky Pie Dough (page 173)

2 tablespoons olive oil

2 tablespoons unsalted butter

2 to 3 onions (about 1 pound), thinly sliced

2 teaspoons kosher salt

$1/4$ cup (2 fluid ounces) heavy cream

1 egg

1 ounce Parmesan cheese, grated (about $1/3$ cup)

Egg wash (see page 20)

Caramelize the onions.

Heat the olive oil and butter in a large, heavy sauté pan or skillet over medium-high heat, add the onions, sprinkle with the salt, and sauté until the onions release some liquid and begin to develop a few dark spots, about 10 minutes. Turn the heat down to medium-low and continue cooking until the onions are soft and toasty brown, 35 to 45 minutes. Try not to stir them too often during the caramelizing process; instead, give the pan a good shake every 5 minutes or so to redistribute the contents. Let the onions cool, check the seasoning, and add more salt if necessary.

Add the cream and egg.

Whisk the cream and egg together, then gently stir the mixture into the onions. Fold in the grated Parmesan cheese and add any seasonal ingredients you like.

Roll out the dough and form the tart.

Line a baking sheet with parchment paper. On a lightly floured work surface, roll the dough out to a circle 14 to 16 inches in diameter and about $1/8$ inch thick. Fold the dough in half and then in half again, then transfer it to the prepared pan, centering the point in the middle of the pan. Carefully unfold the dough.

(continued)

SEASONAL SUGGESTIONS FOR RUSTIC TART FILLINGS

SPRING	SUMMER	FALL	WINTER
Asparagus Trim away the ends of 8 ounces of asparagus. Dice the spears into 2-inch pieces, saving a few whole spears to garnish the finished galette.	**Zucchini** Grate 1 zucchini, toss it with 1 teaspoon salt, and let sit in a colander for 20 minutes. Squeeze the liquid from the zucchini before folding it into the onion base along with a pinch of finely chopped fresh marjoram.	**Mushroom** Sauté about 8 ounces of mixed wild mushrooms or some nice, dark creminis. Add a splash of sherry or Marsala, then fold the mushrooms into the onion base.	**Bacon and Blue Cheese** Crumble 8 slices of crisply cooked bacon and 4 ounces of blue cheese into the onion base. Slightly unattractive, but oh-so-delicious on a cold winter day.
Leek Gruyère Sauté 1 cup of diced leeks and replace the Parmesan cheese with Gruyère.	**Roasted Corn with Chiles** Roast 2 ears of corn and 1 Anaheim pepper. Cut the corn kernels off the cob, seed and dice the pepper, and fold both into the onion base with some crumbled Cotija cheese.	**Roasted Squash** Add 1 cup of roasted squash puree (see page 194) to the onion base, along with 4 to 6 slices of crisply cooked and crumbled bacon.	**Garlic Mashed Potato** This is the perfect way to use up leftover mashed potatoes. Add 1 to 2 finely chopped cloves of garlic to the onion base, then fold in 1 cup of mashed potatoes.
Sautéed Greens Sauté several large handfuls of spinach, kale, chard, or arugula. Let the greens cool, squeeze out the excess liquid, then coarsely chop the greens and fold them into the onion base.			

THE **GRAND CENTRAL** BAKING BOOK

Spread the filling (there should be about 2 cups) over the pastry, leaving a 3-inch border all the way around. Carefully lift and fold the border up over the filling, letting the dough pleat each time you lift and fold it. It should pleat about 8 to 10 times as you work your way around. If you have time, chill the tart for 20 minutes before baking. Preheat the oven to 375°F.

Bake.

Brush the tart with the egg wash and bake for 40 to 45 minutes, rotating the pan halfway through the baking time. The crust should be a deep golden brown and the filling should be bubbly.

Classic Leek and Cheese Quiche

In the 1970s, when I was a little girl, quiche was the epitome of fancy luncheon fare, and every groovy café had one on their menu. Though it went out of vogue some time ago, I never stopped making quiche. A classic and delicious dish such as this is worthy of a place in your baking repertoire.

What follows is a basic recipe to which you can add everything from crumbled bacon to sautéed greens to steamed asparagus. Because I like the way it looks, I use an 8-inch springform pan for quiche; it ends up being quite tall, with deep custard filling. A deep-dish pie pan will create the same rustic appearance.

SERVES 6 TO 8

1 disk All-Butter Flaky Pie Dough (page 173)
2 tablespoons olive oil
1/2 large white onion, diced into 1/4-inch cubes
    (about 1/3 cup)
Salt

8 ounces sliced leeks (1 large or 2 small leeks),
    whites and 2 to 3 inches of green
2 shallots, finely chopped (about 1 1/2 tablespoons)
1 clove garlic, finely chopped
5 eggs
1 cup (8 fluid ounces) whole milk or half-and-half
Freshly ground black pepper
3 ounces Gruyère, Swiss, or Parmesan cheese,
    or a mixture, grated (about 3/4 cup)
4 to 6 ounces chopped cooked vegetables (optional)
4 slices bacon, crisply cooked and crumbled
    (optional)

Blind bake the crust.

Roll out the pie dough (see page 175) and use it to line an 8-inch springform pan. Blind bake the crust as described on page 188.

Sauté the vegetables.

Heat the oil in a sauté pan or skillet over medium heat, add the onion and a generous pinch of salt, and sauté for 5 to 7 minutes. Add the leeks, shallots, and garlic and continue sautéing until the onion is lightly caramelized and the leeks are tender, about 10 minutes. Let the mixture cool, then spread it evenly over the crust. Preheat the oven to 325°F.

Make the custard.

Whisk the eggs and milk together with a pinch of salt and freshly ground pepper. Fold in the grated cheese then pour the custard over the leeks, sautéed vegetables, and bacon.

Bake.

Bake until the custard is set, about 35 minutes, rotating the pan halfway through the baking time.

Savory Hand Pies

From Cornish pasties and Latin American empanadas to Indian samosas and all-American Hot Pockets, there's no mystery as to why so many cultures have a tradition of baking savory fillings into handheld pies; they're flavorful, satisfying, and portable. I've included recipes for two favorite fillings, Steak and Onion and Spicy Potato. Once you get the idea, experiment and come up with your own versions. Try filling hand pies with leftover pot roast and potatoes; sautéed greens and onions with Parmesan cheese; or thick bolognese sauce. Whatever you use, you'll need 1 1/2 to 2 cups of filling for this recipe. You can make small hand pies to serve as appetizers, or full-size for supper with a salad.

The quality of the crust is as important as the filling it encases. I encourage you to try making the Rough Puff Pastry, which can be put together in advance and kept in the freezer until you need it. Of course, the final product will also be plenty tasty if you purchase a high-quality commercial puff pastry; look for all-butter puff pastry in upscale markets. Whichever route you go, both the pastry and the filling can be stored in the refrigerator for up to 2 days. When you're ready to assemble the hand pies, the final product can be put together in just a few minutes. Hand pies are possibly the best prepared item to have in your freezer, as they can go straight into the oven without defrosting.

MAKES 6 LARGE OR 12 SMALL HAND PIES

2 pounds Rough Puff Pastry (page 176)

1 egg white

1 tablespoon water

Pinch of salt

1 1/2 to 2 cups filling (see recipes on page 108)

Roll out the puff pastry.

Rolling the dough out into a large, even rectangle is the greatest challenge in making hand pies. The goal is to end up with a rectangle measuring about 14 by 16 inches. When it's properly rolled, you'll be able to cut smaller, evenly sized rectangles of dough.

Begin with a 2-pound rectangle of Rough Puff Pastry, a good rolling pin, and plenty of counter space. Take the dough out of the refrigerator and dust a large work surface with a small amount of flour. (Unless you have a tile counter, roll the pastry directly on the countertop.)

Position the puff pastry rectangle so that the seam (the long side) is facing you, and begin rolling from the center of the rectangle, away from you and then toward you. Focus on pushing out, not down, with the rolling pin. Use your energy to elongate the dough rather than flatten it.

Flip the dough over and continue rolling in the same way. If the dough begins to stick, use a bench knife to release it, dust the work surface with a bit more flour, and then continue to roll the dough.

As you roll, you'll find that the dough has a tendency to retract slightly, like a rubber band. That means it needs to rest, which will give the gluten time to relax. Put the dough on a sheet pan or fold it loosely and put it on a plate and let it rest in the refrigerator for at least 20 minutes.

Take the dough out of the refrigerator and continue to roll up and down until it measures 15 or 16 inches in length. Turn the dough and roll it out to 14 inches. You may need to go back and forth in each direction several times to reach the eventual goal of a 14 by 16-inch rectangle.

Cut dough rectangles.

Use a sharp chef's knife to cut individual rectangles. For 6 large hand pies, split the rectangle in half lengthwise to make two wide vertical strips. (See photograph, opposite.) Cut each strip horizontally into three equal pieces to yield approximately six 4 1/2 by 7-inch rectangles. For 12 smaller hand pies split the vertical strips again for a total of 4 vertical strips.

Preheat the oven to 350°F. Line a sheet pan with parchment paper.

CUT

BRUSH WITH EGG WASH

ADD FILLING

reinforce the seal. Trim the edges with a sharp chef's knife. Slice small steam vents in the top of each hand pie, then transfer to the sheet pan and bake immediately. Alternatively, you can refrigerate the pies for up to 2 days before baking, or freeze them for up to 3 months.

Bake.

Bake for 1 hour, rotating the pan halfway through the baking time. The pastry should be golden brown.

PRESS TO SEAL EDGES

CRIMP WITH FORK

TRIM EDGES AND SLIT VENTS

Fill and form the hand pies.

Put the egg white, water, and salt in a small bowl and whisk with a fork to combine. Use a pastry brush to paint a small amount of the egg white mixture around the edges of each rectangle. Put $1/4$ to $1/3$ cup of filling in the center of each rectangle, then fold the top over the filling so that the edges meet. Seal each rectangle using the side of your hand and then use a fork to crimp and

Spicy Potato Hand Pie Filling

I adapted this recipe from one in Julie Sahni's Classic Indian Cooking. *It's the same filling she uses for vegetarian samosas and masala dosas. When it's baked into a hand pie, you get a sort of modern samosa that's good hot from the oven or at room temperature, making it perfect for a picnic.*

MAKES ABOUT 2 CUPS OF FILLING,
TO FILL 8 HAND PIES

1 pound new potatoes, skin on, diced into
$\frac{1}{2}$-inch cubes (about 2 cups)
3 tablespoons vegetable oil or canola oil
1 teaspoon coriander seeds
1 large yellow onion, diced into $\frac{1}{2}$-inch cubes
(about $\frac{3}{4}$ cup)
$\frac{1}{2}$ teaspoon salt
1 teaspoon grated fresh ginger
1 clove garlic, minced
2 jalapeño peppers, seeded and diced
1 teaspoon ground cumin
Salt
$\frac{1}{2}$ cup green peas, fresh or frozen
2 tablespoons freshly squeezed lemon juice

Prepare the potatoes.

Boil the potatoes until they're soft enough to easily insert a knife, about 10 to 15 minutes.

Sauté the onion and spices.

Heat the oil in a large, heavy sauté pan or skillet over medium heat. Add the coriander seeds and fry for about 20 seconds, until the seeds begin to turn brown and become aromatic. Lower the heat to medium, then add the onion. Sprinkle with salt and sauté for 10 minutes, stirring occasionally, until the onion begins to brown. Add the ginger, garlic, jalapeños, and cumin and sauté 5 to 10 minutes, until the mixture begins to lightly brown.

Finish the filling.

Add the potatoes, peas, and lemon juice to the pan and cook, until the potatoes begin to brown and the peas are cooked through, about 10 minutes. Taste the filling and adjust the seasoning if need be, then let it cool completely before making the hand pies.

Steak and Onion Hand Pie Filling

Caramelized onions plus grass-fed beef . . . Yum! Make this with last night's leftovers, or with a freshly grilled New York or rib-eye steak.

MAKES ABOUT 2 CUPS OF FILLING,
TO FILL 8 HAND PIES

4 tablespoons olive oil
2 yellow onions, diced into $\frac{1}{2}$-inch cubes
(about 1 cup)
1 teaspoon salt
1 pound New York or rib-eye steak, diced into
$\frac{1}{4}$-inch cubes (about 2 cups)
2 tablespoons sherry
1 cup (8 fluid ounces) chicken stock
Freshly ground black pepper
1 tablespoon finely chopped fresh tarragon

Sauté the onions and meat.

Heat the oil in a large, heavy sauté pan or skillet over medium-high heat. Add the onions, sprinkle with the salt, and sauté, stirring occasionally, until caramelized, about 20 minutes. When the onions are rich golden brown and soft all the way through, add the steak. If you're using leftovers, add the sherry and chicken stock immediately. For uncooked steak, sprinkle with salt and freshly ground black pepper; sauté for 5 to 10 minutes, until the meat is brown on the outside and pink in the middle, then add the sherry and chicken stock.

Simmer for 20 to 30 minutes, until most of the liquid is gone, then taste and adjust the seasoning if need be. Add the tarragon. Let the filling cool.

IMPROV PIZZA

Few foods lend themselves to improvisation and customization like pizza. Since most people know what they like on it, what they need is a good recipe for crust that they can make at home. When you bite into the average American pizza, it's obvious that the crust is an afterthought—a flavorless platform weighted down with heavy toppings. Contemporary artisan pizzas turn the focus to a tasty crust topped with modest amounts of high-quality, delicious ingredients. The best crust has sizable holes and is crisp, with a great chewy texture.

These are variations on one recipe that can be used to make pizza two completely different ways: three 10- to 12-inch round pizzas baked on a stone or a large pan pizza. The dough for round pizzas is made in the style of artisan bread, with a long, slow fermentation, then baked on a stone for a thin, crispy crust. Some people are of the opinion that pizza baked on a stone has a superior crust, but it requires practice, not to mention a pizza stone and peel.

The single pan pizza is convenient because it doesn't require any special equipment and the dough can be made when you're short on time.

Artisan Pizza

This crust recipe comes compliments of our head bread baker, Mel Darbyshire. When making pizza, Mel likes an artisan technique that calls for minimal yeast and long fermentation. If you're in a hurry, add a scant teaspoon of yeast to both the pre-ferment and the final dough and cut your fermentation (or rising) time in half. If you're new to bread baking, consult the sidebar *How to Judge Fermentation* (page 41).

This dough begins with a poolish, which is a preferment made with equal parts (by weight) of flour and water. By fermenting a small amount of dough before mixing it into the final dough, you will make a crust that has more complex flavor and a better texture. This process takes time, but not a lot of effort. In order to have it ready for dinner, start the pre-ferment ten to twelve hours before you want to make pizza. Unbleached, high-gluten bread flour will yield the best results when making a fermented dough like this one, but unbleached all-purpose will also work.

Key to Pizza Crust

High heat is critical to a good crust, and home ovens don't get as hot as the stone hearth ovens used in most pizzerias, but that doesn't stop me from trying. I don't think I've ever managed to bake pizza at home without setting off the fire alarm! Switch your hood vent on before you start, and do what you can to create good ventilation in your kitchen. Put the pizza stone in the oven, near the bottom or on the floor, and preheat the oven to 450°F—or higher if you dare—for at least 30 minutes.

The dough will be sticky, wet, and hard to handle, but those are the same attributes that make for great texture and flavor. You couldn't use this dough for tossing pies. Think small and rustic and don't worry if your pizza doesn't look perfect.

MAKES THREE 10 TO 12-INCH ROUND PIZZAS

PRE-FERMENT

1^1/$_3$ cups (7 ounces) high-gluten bread flour
1 cup (8 fluid ounces) tepid water (about 70°F)
1 teaspoon dry active yeast

FINAL DOUGH

3 cups (1 pound) high-gluten bread flour
1^1/$_4$ cups (10 fluid ounces) tepid water
1 teaspoon dry active yeast
1 tablespoon salt

Mix the pre-ferment.

Measure the flour, water, and yeast into a bowl with high sides and whisk or beat until smooth. Cover tightly with plastic wrap and let the pre-ferment sit at room temperature for 6 to 8 hours. The mixture should be bubbly, with a slightly stringy texture.

Mix the final dough and let it rise.

Combine the pre-ferment, flour, water, yeast, and salt in the bowl of a stand mixer fitted with the dough hook attachment or a bowl with high sides. If using a stand mixer, mix on low speed for 3 minutes. Stop the mixer and run a plastic bowl scraper or a rubber spatula around the sides of the bowl to loosen the dough and bring it to the center, then switch to medium-high for 3 minutes. It will be sticky and a bit of a challenge to handle.

Let the dough rise.

Generously coat a clean bowl with olive oil, then scrape the dough from the mixer into the oiled bowl using a plastic bowl scraper. Cover with plastic wrap and let the dough rise in a warm place (about 75°F) for 1 to 2 hours, until doubled in size.

Punch down the dough and let it rise again.

Punch down the middle of the dough. Pull the edges out and fold them back on top of the center of the dough. Divide the dough into 3 balls. Place the dough balls on a baking sheet and cover with plastic wrap. Let the dough rise in a warm place until the balls double in size, about 2 hours. At this point, it's ready to be shaped into a pizza.

Preheat the oven to 450°F at least 30 minutes before baking the pizza.

Form the pizzas on parchment paper.

Traditionally, pizza is formed and topped on a peel. The peel is dusted liberally with cornmeal, which allows the dough to slide easily onto the stone in the oven. This step can be tricky with wet dough like this one. The solution? Put a piece of parchment paper on the peel and stretch and form the dough on top of it. The paper acts like the cornmeal, allowing the dough to slide from the peel onto the stone in one easy motion. Parchment paper gets dark in the hot oven, but it won't catch fire.

Some of My Favorite Pizza Toppings

*   Greens, egg, and ham: a béchamel base with Parmesan cheese, prosciutto, fresh spinach, and an egg cracked on the middle of the pie halfway through the baking time
*   Tomato and fresh mozzarella: an olive oil base with Parmesan cheese, slices of tomato and fresh mozzarella, and torn basil leaves
*   Sausage and caramelized onions: an olive oil base with seasoned ground pork, caramelized onions, and Parmesan cheese

Top and bake the pizzas.

This crust is delicious and full of flavor; use a light hand to top it. Less is definitely more. Begin with a thin layer of sauce, or a drizzle of olive oil, followed by a modest scattering of cheese. Finish with the meat and/or vegetables. You should be able to see all of the toppings when you've finished. That is, the sauce should show through the cheese layer, and the cheese shouldn't be covered entirely by the next layer of toppings. Slide the pizza onto the hot stone and quickly close the door to keep the heat in. Bake for 12 to 15 minutes, until the crust is deep brown and crispy and the cheese is bubbling.

Cool and serve the pizza.

As tempting as it is to eat it hot from the oven, pizza needs at least 5 minutes to cool on the counter before it can be cut without making a mess of the toppings. I like to use scissors after brushing the crust edges with olive oil, to soften them slightly.

Ben's Pan Pizza

My brother Ben is the father of three very sporty children. He dutifully hauls them to practices, enthusiastically watches their games, and happily throws end-of-season team pizza parties at his home. In order to fill the bottomless pits of the growing athletes' stomachs, Ben makes pan pizzas ahead and reheats them when it's party time. This is a great trick for making pizza when you're short on time, or cooking for a crowd.

MAKES ONE 8 BY 12-INCH PIZZA

PRE-FERMENT

1⅓ cups (7 ounces) high-gluten bread flour

1 cup (8 fluid ounces) tepid water (about 80°F)

2 teaspoons dry active yeast

FINAL DOUGH

4 cups (1 pound, 5 ounces) high-gluten bread flour

1¼ cups (10 fluid ounces) tepid water (about 80°F)

3 tablespoons olive oil

2 teaspoons dry active yeast

1 tablespoon salt

Mix the pre-ferment.

Measure the flour, water, and yeast into a bowl with high sides and whisk or beat until smooth. Cover tightly with plastic wrap and ferment for one hour before adding ingredients for the final dough.

Mix the final dough and let it rise.

Combine the pre-ferment, flour, water, olive oil, yeast, and salt in the bowl of a stand mixer fitted with the dough hook attachment. Mix on low speed for 3 minutes. Stop the mixer and run a plastic bowl scraper or a rubber spatula around the sides of the bowl to loosen the dough and bring it to the center, then switch to medium-high speed for 5 minutes.

Let the dough rise.

Generously coat a clean bowl with olive oil, then scrape the dough from the mixer into the oiled bowl using a plastic bowl scraper. Cover with plastic wrap and let the dough rise in a warm place (at least 75°F) for 1 hour, until doubled in size.

Preform the dough.

Generously dust a work surface with flour. Scrape the dough out of the bowl onto the work surface and gently tug it into a rectangular shape measuring about 8 by 10 inches. Cover with plastic wrap and let rest for 15 minutes to allow the dough to relax and stretch easily into a large rectangle that fits nicely into the baking sheet.

Fit the dough into the pan.

Liberally oil a 12 by 18-inch rimmed baking sheet. Transfer the dough to the prepared pan, then tug and pull the dough into the corners and up the sides of the pan, stretching it from the middle as well as the sides. It takes some practice to stretch the dough evenly over the large baking sheet. Ideally, you'll be able to cover the entire pan without creating holes or extremely thin spots. If the dough wants to spring back to its original shape, let it rest for 5 to 10 minutes. Be patient—this skill is developed over time, with practice. If you make a hole in the dough, patch it with a small piece of dough from a thicker area. Above all, resist the urge to ball up the dough and start over.

Top and bake the pizza.

Use a light hand to top the pizza. (It's less important with a pan pizza since the crust is a bit thicker.) Begin with a layer of sauce followed by a liberal covering of grated cheese. Finish with the meat and/or vegetables and some additional cheese, if desired. You should still be able to see the various toppings when you've finished. That is, the sauce should show through the cheese layer, and the cheese shouldn't be covered entirely by the next layer of toppings. Bake for 30 to 40 minutes, rotating the pan once, until the crust is brown and crispy and the cheese is bubbling.

POTPIES

The 1950s were no friend to home cooking in America. Industrial food giants enlisted the services of Madison Avenue to convince the American housewife that good food came from the freezer aisle of the grocery store, rather than the local farm stand or the home victory gardens she'd been encouraged to start in the 1940s. During this era, Swanson introduced a prolific crop of frozen vegetables and prepared entrees to the American kitchen and snatched the potpie from the hands of scratch cooks. Perhaps because the Swanson version isn't *that* bad, I've yet to meet someone who doesn't say "yum" at the mention of chicken potpie.

There's no secret to turning out a delicious potpie. After all, when you get right down to it, potpie is little more than leftovers crowned with a crust. Be resourceful: Use what you have in the refrigerator, adjust the quantities based on your preferences, and remember that anything baked in gravy with crust on top is going to taste good!

I've included two recipes for potpie: a classic version using chicken, and a Northwest variation with salmon and leeks. If you want to forgo the meat, there's a variation on the latter using parsnips and mushrooms. But don't feel constrained by these recipes; use your instincts and imagination to create your own versions of these cozy casseroles.

A buttery, flaky crust is the key to really good potpie; I recommend using Rough Puff Pastry (page 176). Making the pastry is a bit of a commitment, but if you make a big batch, you can freeze the unused portion so you'll have a crust ready and waiting the next time you want to make a potpie. If you don't have time to make puff pastry, try the All-Butter Flaky Pie Dough (page 173) or a favorite crust recipe. Or to really streamline the process, purchase the best frozen puff pastry you can find; it's becoming increasingly easy to get all-butter puff pastry in upscale markets.

Chicken Potpie

There are two different methods for preparing the chicken and stock necessary to make a chicken potpie. If you have leftover chicken, you're halfway there. When I don't have leftover chicken, I buy a small fryer (3 to 4 pounds). Count yourself lucky if there's any meat or stock left after making a potpie. But if there is, this chicken makes the best chicken salad, and what could be better than having home-made stock in the freezer?

SERVES 6 TO 8

1 pound Rough Puff Pastry (page 176)

LEFTOVER CHICKEN

1 roast chicken

1 onion, peeled and quartered

2 carrots, chopped

2 celery stalks

5 cups (40 fluid ounces) water

FILLING

¹/₄ cup (2 fluid ounces) olive oil

1 large white onion, diced into ¹/₂-inch cubes (about ³/₄ cup)

Salt

8 ounces cremini mushrooms

12 ounces carrots (about 4 carrots)

1 to 3 cloves garlic, finely chopped

1 teaspoon finely chopped fresh sage

2 teaspoons finely chopped fresh rosemary

Freshly ground black pepper

1 to 1¹/₂ pounds cooked chicken meat, cut into bite-sized pieces

3 tablespoons unsalted butter

3 tablespoons all-purpose flour

3 cups (24 fluid ounces) chicken stock

2 to 3 tablespoons white wine, Marsala, or sherry

Prepare the chicken.

Remove the meat from a leftover roast chicken and set it aside. Put the bones in a 4- to 6-quart stockpot with the onion, carrots, celery stalks, and water. Bring the contents to a boil and simmer for 4 to 6 hours over low heat. Let the stock cool, skim any fat from the top, then strain the stock. You'll want at least 1 pound of chicken meat and 3 cups of stock for a potpie.

Sauté the vegetables.

Heat the olive oil in a Dutch oven or wide sauté pan over medium-high heat, then add the onion, sprinkle with 1 teaspoon of salt, and sauté, stirring occasionally, until the onion is completely caramelized, about 20 minutes. In the meantime, clean, stem, and quarter the mushrooms, then add them to the caramelized onion and continue to sauté until the mushrooms begin to brown, about 10 minutes. Peel the carrots and cut them into coins or 2-inch matchsticks. Stir in the carrots, garlic,

(continued)

Using Fresh Chicken

Small fryer chicken (3 to 4 pounds)

1 onion, peeled and quartered

2 carrots, chopped

2 celery stalks

5 cups (40 fluid ounces) water

To start with fresh chicken, put the whole fryer chicken in a stockpot with the onion, carrots, celery and water. After it has simmered gently for about 90 minutes, pull the chicken out of the broth. Once it's cool enough to handle, remove the skin and meat. Discard the skin, store the meat in the refrigerator, and add the bones back to the stockpot and continue to simmer for 2 hours. Let the stock cool, skim any fat from the top, then strain the stock.

sage, and rosemary, then season with salt and freshly ground black pepper. Cook briefly, taste, and adjust the seasoning if need be. Stir in the chicken. Preheat the oven to 375°F.

Make the gravy.

In a separate saucepan, melt the butter over medium heat, sprinkle in the flour, and cook, stirring constantly, until the roux begins to bubble and is the color of light toast, 3 to 4 minutes. Remove from the heat, whisk in the chicken stock, then add the wine, stirring to combine. Don't be concerned if the gravy looks thin; it will thicken in the oven. Taste the gravy and season to taste. Pour the gravy over the chicken and vegetables before rolling out the crust.

Roll out the dough and assemble the potpie.

On a lightly floured surface, roll the pastry out to a thickness of $1/8$ inch and cut out a circle slightly larger than the pan you're using (see sidebar, opposite). Pour the filling into the baking pan and place the dough on top, tucking the edges down inside the pan. Cut a few steam vents, then put the potpie in the oven immediately.

Bake.

Bake for 25 minutes, then rotate the pan and turn down the oven down to 350°F. Bake for about 30 minutes more, until the crust is a dark golden brown and the filling is bubbling. Let cool for 10 minutes before serving.

Salmon and Leek Potpie

Several factors in my life have conspired to make a place for this potpie in my repertoire. First, I have spent all of my life in the Northwest where salmon is king. Second, I share my life with a man who doesn't eat meat. Once, when making a large chicken potpie for a group, I made a small salmon leek potpie in a separate ramekin for David's dinner. What started as a variation for him was so delicious that I began to make it for everyone. This recipe calls for a salmon fillet, but previously canned salmon is an acceptable substitute.

SERVES 6 TO 8

1 pound Rough Puff Pastry (page 176)

$1/4$ cup (2 fluid ounces) olive oil

1 large white onion, diced into $1/2$-inch cubes (about $3/4$ cup)

Salt

8 ounces leeks (1 large or 2 small leeks)

8 ounces carrots (2 to 3 carrots), diced into $1/4$-inch cubes

1 to 3 cloves of garlic, finely chopped

$1/4$ cup (2 fluid ounces) white wine

Freshly ground black pepper

1 to $1^1/2$ pounds salmon fillet, or 18 ounces high-quality canned salmon

$1/4$ cup (2 ounces, or $1/2$ stick) unsalted butter

3 tablespoons all-purpose flour

2 cups (16 fluid ounces) whole milk

1 tablespoon finely chopped fresh dill

1 tablespoon finely chopped fresh chives

Sauté the vegetables.

Heat the oil in a Dutch oven or wide sauté pan over medium-high heat, then add the onion, sprinkle with a little salt, and sauté, stirring occasionally until the onion begins to caramelize, about 10 minutes. Meanwhile, clean the leeks, making sure to rinse the mud out of the thickest part of the leaves. Dice the leeks, using as much of the green part as you wish.

Add the leeks and carrots to the onion, sprinkle with a little more salt, and continue to sauté for 10 minutes more, stirring only occasionally so the vegetables begin to brown. Stir in the garlic and wine and continue cooking until the leeks and carrots begin to soften, about 5 minutes. Season with pepper, then taste and adjust the seasoning if need be. Chunk the salmon into 2- to 3-inch pieces; they will flake apart as they cook, becoming bite-size pieces. Stir the salmon chunks into the vegetables, and set aside. Preheat the oven to 375°F.

Make the béchamel sauce.

In a separate saucepan, melt the butter over medium heat, sprinkle in the flour, and cook, stirring constantly, until the roux begins to bubble and is the color of light toast, 3 to 4 minutes. Remove from the heat and, while whisking continuously and aggressively to avoid lumps, slowly pour in the milk. Add the dill and chives, then pour the sauce over the vegetables and salmon. Refrigerate the filling while you roll out the crust.

Root Vegetable and Mushroom Variation

Use the Salmon and Leek Potpie recipe and procedure, but don't include the fish. Instead, add 8 ounces each of sliced parsnips and quartered cremini mushrooms when you add the leeks and carrots to the onion. In addition, season the béchamel sauce with sage and rosemary instead of the dill and chives.

Roll out the dough and assemble the potpie.

On a lightly floured surface, roll the pastry out to a thickness of $1/8$ inch and cut out a circle slightly larger than the pan you're using (see sidebar, below). Pour the filling into the baking pan and place the dough on top, tucking the edges down inside the pan. Cut a few steam vents, then put the potpie in the oven immediately.

Bake.

Bake for 25 minutes, then rotate the pan and turn down the oven to 350°F. Bake for 30 minutes more, until the crust is a dark golden brown and the filling is bubbling. Let cool for 10 minutes before serving.

Which Pot for Your Pie?

The pan you choose depends on the style of potpie you'd like to make. A deep-dish pie pan, cast-iron skillet, Dutch oven, or rectangular casserole dish all work just fine. In fact, any heavy baking pan that holds two to three quarts will work. (If your pan isn't labeled, you can determine its volume by filling it with water to about 1 inch from the top, then measuring the amount of water it holds.)

If you prefer more filling than crust, use a tall baking casserole or soufflé dish. I like more crust, so I often use a two-quart Dutch oven or a braising pan that isn't as deep. Less cleanup is one advantage to using a Dutch oven or a cast-iron skillet, since the vegetables can be sautéed in the same pan used to bake the potpie. If you don't have either, sauté the vegetables in a separate pan, let them cool, then build the potpie in a casserole dish.

5

Everyday Fruit Desserts

Because I love to spend time cooking dinner, I'm often left with less time than I'd like to devote to dessert. That's why I favor uncomplicated sweets like tarts, puddings, crisps, and cobblers. They're the perfect way to finish a quick weeknight supper or a leisurely dinner with company.

This chapter is filled with ideas for desserts that begin with ripe fruit. Although each one calls for a specific fruit, these homey recipes are intended to inspire creativity and confidence by providing tips for tailoring the dessert to what's in season. Feel free to come up with your own unique combinations based on what's appealing to you.

Fruit Tarts **120**

Fresh Huckleberry Tart 121

Seasonal Rustic Fruit Tarts 122

Lemon Crumble Tart 126

Raspberry Crumble Tart 128

Crisps and Cobblers **129**

Apple Crisp 130

Fresh Berry Crumble 131

Rhubarb Crisp 132

Peach Cobbler 133

Fresh Fruit, Cake, and Cream **134**

Summer Pudding 135

Raspberry Port Trifle 137

Clafouti 138

Strawberry Shortcake 140

FRUIT TARTS

Fruit tarts are a great way to celebrate seasonality, from the simple rustic free-form galette or crostata, to the artful, sculptural tart made in a fluted pan or the beautifully glazed offerings of a fancy French patisserie. The tart recipes in this book are the epitome of quick and easy: piles of vibrant, fresh fruit encased in buttery, flaky pastry. It's hard to imagine that they could be more delicious.

Beating the Bears to the Berries

My family's farm in Goldendale, Washington, sits in the Klickitat Valley, which stretches out beneath Mt. Adams, famous for its abundant huckleberry fields. A wild cousin to the blueberry, the huckleberry has an intense and complex flavor that's equally wonderful fresh or baked into desserts.

Arlene Schuster, a local farmer's wife, was one of the first neighbors we met in Goldendale. In the late summer, Arlene and her kids moved their camp trailer to the huckleberry fields, where they parked it for a week to amass a winter's worth of the amazing berries. Seduced by the tales of berry-laden bushes, we joined them on their foraging adventure that first summer. We kids were sent off to pick berries, coffee cans in hand, with only this warning:

"Watch out for the bears and don't eat all the berries."

I set to my task enthusiastically, spurred on by visions of berry desserts, when suddenly a growl from a nearby bush sent me running back toward the trailer. In my rush to escape, I dropped my coffee can and looked back to find my brothers laughing as they stuffed my berries into their mouths. Cross with my brothers, I returned to gather the remaining berries. We never saw a bear, and we all returned with purple-stained mouths and heaping cans of berries.

At home, my mother made a simple tart that lingers in my memory to this day. This is my version of her tart, which highlights the huckleberry's firm, flavorful quality.

Fresh Huckleberry Tart

This simple recipe depends entirely on the flavor of the berries. Use huckleberries if you can find them fresh, or blueberries, which make an exceptionally good stand-in. The tart is especially delicious topped with a dollop of of lightly sweetened whipped cream (see page 137) or lemon curd (see page 126) or, if you're ambitious, lemon cream made from equal proportions of whipped cream and lemon curd.

Because the dough contains a large quantity of butter and sugar, it can be tricky to roll with a rolling pin. Instead, press the dough into a tart shell and chill or freeze it before baking. The shell won't look as finished as a rolled crust, but it won't detract from its overall attractive, albeit rustic, appearance. You can bake the crust the same day you serve the tart, or up to two days before you use it. If you bake it in advance, leave it out, unwrapped, at room temperature. Be sure to eat the tart within 8 hours of filling it; otherwise the crust begins to get soggy.

SERVES 8

CRUST

1 cup (8 ounces, or 2 sticks) unsalted butter at room temperature

3/4 cup (5.25 ounces) granulated sugar

1 teaspoon vanilla extract

2 1/2 cups (12.5 ounces) all-purpose flour

3/4 teaspoon salt

FILLING AND GLAZE

3 pints (6 cups) fresh huckleberries or blueberries

1/2 cup (3.5 ounces) granulated sugar

2 tablespoons cornstarch

2 tablespoons freshly squeezed lemon juice or berry liqueur

Mix the dough.

Using a stand mixer with the paddle attachment, beat the butter and sugar on medium speed until lighter in color and fluffy, about 4 minutes. Add the vanilla and continue mixing. While the mixer is running, whisk the flour and salt together, then gradually add the dry ingredients and mix just until the dough comes together.

Press the dough into the pan.

Press the dough into a 12-inch springform pan, making the crust thickness as even as possible. If using a tart pan, press the dough all the way up the sides of the pan; if using a springform pan, press the dough about 2 inches up the sides.

Chill and bake the crust.

Chill or, even better, freeze the crust for 30 minutes so it's completely set up before baking. This will help the crust keep its shape in the oven. Preheat the oven to 350°F.

Bake the tart for 25 minutes, rotating the pan halfway through the baking time, until the crust is golden brown. Let the crust cool slightly before filling it.

Make the glaze.

Combine 2 cups of the berries with the sugar in a heavy saucepan over medium heat and cook, stirring occasionally, until the berries burst and begin to break down. Combine the cornstarch and lemon juice and stir to make a slurry, then add it to the berries and continue cooking and stirring until the mixture is slightly thickened and shiny. Put the glaze through a fine-mesh sieve, pressing the solids with the back of a spoon to extract as much glaze as possible. The glaze should be thick and glossy. Keep the glaze warm until needed.

Fill the tart.

Fill the tart shell with the remaining 4 cups of berries. Pour the glaze over the berries and use a pastry brush to distribute it evenly, making sure each berry has a nice sheen. Chill for at least 1 hour before serving.

Seasonal Rustic Fruit Tarts

Much less fussy than a classic fluted French tart, a rustic fruit tart or galette is the absolute essence of an everyday dessert—easy, delicious, and beautiful. Nothing more than fresh fruit tossed with sugar and baked in a crisp, buttery, free-form crust, this simple tart is extremely appealing and the perfect place to experiment with flavors and fruit combinations. Trust your instincts—anything goes!

Several of the variations that follow add an extra step: cooking the filling to maximize flavor. But that doesn't feel like a chore to me as the weather begins to turn chilly. By the time winter rolls around and the pickings are slim when it comes to fresh fruit, you'll welcome these slightly richer cooked fillings, which highlight seasonal offerings, and the contents of a larder well stocked with plump dried fruit and a variety of nuts.

Consider spreading a thin layer of cookie or cake crumbs on the crust before piling on especially juicy fruit; this adds another layer of flavor and keeps the crust from getting soggy. You'll need about 1 1/2 cups of filling for a 12-inch tart and one 10- to 12-ounce disk of All-Butter Flaky Pie Dough (page 173).

RHUBARB

1 10- to 12-ounce disk of All-Butter Flaky Pie Dough (page 173)

1 pound rhubarb stalks, washed and dried

3/4 to 1 cup granulated sugar

2 teaspoons cornstarch

1/4 teaspoon salt

Scant 1/2 teaspoon vanilla extract

Gingersnap or ginger biscotti crumbs (optional)

Slice the rhubarb diagonally, then toss it with the sugar, cornstarch, salt, and vanilla.

STRAWBERRY RHUBARB

1 10- to 12-ounce disk of All-Butter Flaky Pie Dough (page 173)

12 ounces rhubarb stalks, washed and dried

1 1/4 cups hulled whole strawberries

1/2 cup (3.5 ounces) granulated sugar

1 tablespoon cornstarch

1/8 teaspoon salt

Pinch of ground nutmeg

Shortbread cookie or pound cake crumbs (optional)

Slice the rhubarb diagonally, then toss it with the strawberries, sugar, cornstarch, salt, and nutmeg.

BERRIES

**1 10- to 12-ounce disk of All-Butter Flaky
    Pie Dough (page 173)**

$2/3$ cup (4.75 ounces) granulated sugar, or to taste

2 tablespoons cornstarch

$1/4$ teaspoon finely chopped lemon zest

$1/4$ teaspoon salt

**2 pints (3 cups) fresh berries (blackberries, marion-
    berries, raspberries, or blueberries)**

Shortbread cookie or pound cake crumbs (optional)

Measure the sugar, cornstarch, lemon zest, and salt into a large bowl. Add the berries, toss to coat, and let stand until moist, about 5 minutes.

STONE FRUIT

**1 10- to 12-ounce disk of All-Butter Flaky
    Pie Dough (page 173)**

**$1/4$ to $1/2$ cup (1.75 to 3.5 ounces) granulated sugar,
    depending on the sweetness of the fruit**

2 tablespoons cornstarch

2 teaspoons freshly squeezed lemon juice

1 teaspoon vanilla extract

$1/4$ teaspoon salt

**$1^{1}/2$ pounds stone fruit (apricots, plums, peaches,
    or nectarines), washed, halved, and pitted**

Measure the sugar, cornstarch, lemon juice, vanilla, and salt into a large bowl. Thinly slice the fruit, add it to the bowl, and toss to coat. Let stand until moist, about 5 minutes.

(continued)

Cooked Stone Fruit Filling

There's an appealing simplicity to baking unadorned fresh fruit in a flaky pastry crust, but certain fruits benefit from being cooked briefly first. The result can be a more consistent filling and a more dynamic flavor, particularly with stone fruit. It's the perfect solution for the plum tree heavy with fruit in your backyard or a crate of peaches that came home from the roadside farm stand with you, especially because the filling can be canned for use in rustic tarts during the winter, when a taste of summer is a welcome treat.

To make a cooked fruit filling, combine 3 cups of sliced apricots, peaches, nectarines, or plums with $1/4$ cup honey in a saucepan. Mix $1/3$ cup granulated sugar with 2 tablespoons cornstarch, then add to the fruit and gently toss to combine. Cook over low heat until the mixture begins to simmer, then raise the heat to medium-high and bring to a rolling boil. Boil for 1 minute, then remove from the heat. The filling should be shiny, translucent, and thickened. Stir in 2 teaspoons lemon juice and 1 teaspoon vanilla and let cool completely before using. If you're canning this mixture, follow the instructions for canning high-acid fruit in *The Joy of Cooking* or *The Fannie Farmer Cookbook*.

Fall

APPLE

1 10- to 12-ounce disk of All-Butter Flaky Pie Dough (page 173)

1 cup (7 ounces) packed light brown sugar

1/3 cup (2.25 ounces) granulated sugar

3/4 teaspoon ground cinnamon

1/4 teaspoon freshly grated nutmeg

3/4 teaspoon vanilla extract

1/2 teaspoon salt

1 1/4 pounds apples (3 or 4 apples), peeled, halved, cored, and sliced 1/4 inch thick

3 tablespoons unsalted butter

Measure the brown sugar, granulated sugar, cinnamon, nutmeg, vanilla, and salt together in a bowl. To assemble the tart, arrange the apples on the crust, cover with the sugar mixture, and dab with the butter.

CRANBERRY PEAR

1 10- to 12-ounce disk of All-Butter Flaky Pie Dough (page 173)

1 1/4 pounds pears, peeled, halved, and cored

1 1/3 cups fresh cranberries

1 cup (5 ounces) dried cranberries

2 1/2 tablespoons freshly squeezed orange juice

1 cup (7 ounces) granulated sugar

5 teaspoons cornstarch

1/4 teaspoon ground cinnamon

1/8 teaspoon ground nutmeg

1/2 teaspoon vanilla extract

1/2 teaspoon salt

Slice the pears and combine them with the fresh and dried cranberries and orange juice in a large, heavy saucepan over medium heat. Measure the sugar, cornstarch, cinnamon, and nutmeg together in a small bowl, whisk to combine, then add to the fruit. Bring the mixture to a boil and cook until the fruit is shiny, translucent, and thickened, about 10 minutes. Remove from the heat and stir in the vanilla and salt.

Winter

CARAMEL NUT

1 10- to 12-ounce disk of All-Butter Flaky Pie Dough (page 173)

1 cup (8 fluid ounces) heavy whipping cream

1/2 cup (6 ounces) honey

1/2 cup (3.5 ounces) granulated sugar

1/2 teaspoon salt

1/2 cup (2 ounces) almonds, lightly toasted (see page 20)

1/2 cup (1.75 ounces) pecans, lightly toasted (see page 20)

3/4 cup (3 ounces) walnuts, lightly toasted (see page 20)

Combine the cream, honey, sugar, and salt in a heavy saucepan. Stir to combine and moisten the sugar, then place over medium-high heat and bring to a boil. Cook, stirring occasionally, until the mixture caramelizes to a deep amber brown, about 12 minutes. Let cool to room temperature before folding in the nuts. Hold the filling at room temperature until ready to use.

THE GRAND CENTRAL BAKING BOOK

FIG WALNUT

1 10- to 12-ounce disk of All-Butter Flaky
   Pie Dough (page 173)

1½ cups (6 ounces) walnuts, lightly toasted
   (see page 20)

½ cup plus 1²/₃ cups (8.75 ounces)
   confectioners' sugar

¼ cup plus 2 tablespoons (1.75 ounces)
   all-purpose flour

1½ tablespoons granulated sugar

6 egg whites (³/₄ cup)

³/₄ teaspoon vanilla extract

½ cup (4 ounces, or ½ stick) unsalted butter,
   browned (see sidebar)

1½ cups (8 ounces) dried figs, coarsely chopped

Combine ³/₄ cup of the walnuts and the ¹/₂ cup confectioners' sugar in a nut grinder or the bowl of a food processor. Pulse the mixture until the walnuts are finely chopped but not powdery. Transfer the mixture to a bowl and whisk in the 1²/₃ cups confectioners' sugar and the flour and granulated sugar. Separately, whisk the egg whites and vanilla together, then whisk in the brown butter. Stir the egg white mixture into the dry mixture, then fold in the remaining walnuts and figs.

How to Brown Butter

Brown butter (or *beurre noisette* in French) is butter that's been cooked until its milk solids brown. It has a nutty flavor that gives depth to all kinds of baked goods and especially complements those we associate with fall and winter.

Use a heavy gauge pan to brown butter; the solids will stick to aluminum. Melt the butter over medium heat, swirling the pan occasionally and watching it closely. When it turns golden brown and smells toasty, remove it from the heat and dip the bottom of the pan in a basin of water to stop it from browning further.

FOR ALL TARTS

Prepare to bake.

Preheat the oven to 375°F. Line a baking sheet with parchment paper.

Roll out the dough and form the tart.

On a lightly floured work surface, roll the dough out to a circle 14 to 15 inches in diameter and about ¹/₈ inch thick. Fold the dough in half and then in half again, then transfer it to the prepared pan, centering the point in the middle of the pan. Carefully unfold the dough. Sprinkle liberally with cookie or cake crumbs if using juicy fruit.

Gently spread the fruit or filling (there should be about 1¹/₂ cups) over the pastry, leaving a 3-inch border all the way around. Carefully lift and fold the edge up over the filling, letting the dough pleat each time you lift and fold it. It should pleat about 8 to 10 times as you work your way around. If you have time, chill the tart for 20 minutes before baking.

Bake the tart.

For a shiny, sweet finish, lightly brush the dough with egg wash (see page 20) and sprinkle with sugar. Bake for 45 to 55 minutes, rotating the pan halfway through the baking time. The pastry should be golden brown and the filling should be bubbly.

Lemon Crumble Tart

This pretty little tart is ridiculously simple. Its delicate, crumbly shortbread crust doesn't have to be rolled, and the filling possibilities are innumerable. In winter, use curds made from different citrus fruits; I'm partial to lemon. I've always loved the combination of lemon curd and shortbread, but the balance of filling and crust is usually off. This recipe gets it just right. When summer rolls around, any and every kind of berry is delicious, but raspberries are the standout.

These variations are a good example of how the same technique can yield two entirely different results: raspberries are exquisitely light, while lemon curd makes for a sturdier, more intensely flavored dessert.

You can make this tart two different ways: with dough you've just mixed, or with a chunk of shortbread from the freezer. Both methods are unbelievably quick. Serve with a dollop of lightly sweetened whipped cream or crème fraîche if you must, but this one stands alone just fine.

SERVES 8

CRUST

2 1/2 cups (12.5 ounces) all-purpose flour

3/4 teaspoon salt

1 cup (8 ounces, or 2 sticks) unsalted butter,
   at room temperature

3/4 cup (5.25 ounces) granulated sugar

1 teaspoon vanilla extract

LEMON CURD

3/4 cup (5.25 ounces) granulated sugar

3 tablespoons finely chopped lemon zest

4 egg yolks

6 tablespoons freshly squeezed lemon juice

1/4 cup (2 ounces, or 1/2 stick) unsalted butter

1/4 teaspoon salt

3 to 4 tablespoons confectioners' sugar,
   for dusting

Prepare to bake.

Preheat the oven to 350°F. Assemble a 10-inch springform pan.

Make the dough.

Whisk the flour and salt together. Using a stand mixer with the paddle attachment, beat the butter and sugar together on medium speed for about 5 minutes, until lighter in color and fluffy. Add the vanilla and mix to incorporate. Reduce the speed to low and add the dry ingredients, scraping the bottom and sides of the bowl several times. Stop mixing when the ingredients are fully incorporated but the dough is still crumbly. This happens quickly; the mixture will look dry and floury, then little clumps will suddenly appear. Don't overmix, or you'll end up with a ball of dough, which will be difficult to distribute in the pan.

Line the pan with dough and bake the crust.

Set aside 1 cup of the dough, then sprinkle the rest (about 2 1/2 cups) on the bottom of a 10-inch springform pan. Distribute it evenly, without pressing. (If you use frozen shortbread dough, you'll need slightly more than 1 pound. Use the large holes on a grater to shred 3 to 3 1/2 cups of dough into the baking pan. Take out 1 cup and distribute the rest evenly on the bottom of the pan.) Bring the dough slightly up the sides of the pan to contain the lemon curd, then lightly press the dough to hold it in place. Refrigerate the remaining dough. Bake for 25 minutes, rotating the pan halfway through the baking time. The crust should be toasty brown.

Make the lemon curd.

Combine the sugar, lemon zest, and egg yolks in a bowl or the top of a double boiler and whisk together immediately; if you delay, the mixture will coagulate. Put the bowl over a pan or the bottom of the double boiler with about an inch of lightly simmering water and whisk continuously until the sugar dissolves. Add the lemon juice and, still whisking continuously, cook for about 5 minutes. Add the butter and salt, then use a spatula

(continued)

THE **GRAND CENTRAL BAKING** BOOK

to stir constantly until the mixture is the consistency of sour cream, which will happen at about 170°F.

Strain the curd through a fine-mesh sieve. If you won't be using it right away, cover with plastic wrap, placing it directly on the surface so the custard doesn't form a skin, and refrigerate for up to 1 week.

Assemble and bake the tart.

Spoon the curd into the crust and smooth the top with a spatula. Sprinkle the remaining 1 cup of dough over the curd.

Bake for 40 to 45 minutes, rotating the pan halfway through the baking time. The topping should be slightly brown, and the curd will begin to caramelize on top. Immediately dust the warm tart with the confectioners' sugar, then let cool slightly before popping off the springform pan.

Raspberry Crumble Tart

Any fresh berry in season is delicious in this delicate crumble tart, but raspberry is my favorite.

SERVES 8

CRUST

2¹⁄₂ cups (12.5 ounces) all-purpose flour

³⁄₄ teaspoon salt

1 cup (8 ounces, or 2 sticks) unsalted butter,
    at room temperature

³⁄₄ cup (5.25 ounces) granulated sugar

1 teaspoon vanilla extract

FILLING

1 pint (2 cups) raspberries, fresh or frozen

3 tablespoons granulated sugar

3 to 4 tablespoons confectioners' sugar, for dusting

Prepare to bake.

Preheat the oven to 350°F. Assemble a 10-inch springform pan.

Make the dough.

Whisk the flour and salt together. Using a stand mixer with the paddle attachment, beat the butter and sugar together on medium speed for about 5 minutes, until lighter in color and fluffy. Add the vanilla and mix to incorporate. Reduce the speed to low and add the dry ingredients, scraping the bottom and sides of the bowl several times. Stop mixing when the ingredients are fully incorporated but the dough is still crumbly. This happens quickly; the mixture will look dry and floury, then little clumps will suddenly appear. Don't overmix, or you'll end up with a ball of dough, which will be difficult to distribute in the pan.

Line the pan with dough and bake the crust.

Set aside 1 cup of the dough, then sprinkle the rest (about 2¹⁄₂ cups) on the bottom of a 10-inch springform pan. Distribute it evenly, without pressing. (If you use frozen shortbread dough, you'll need slightly more than 1 pound. Coarsely grate 3 to 3¹⁄₂ cups of dough into the baking pan using the large holes on a grater. Take out 1 cup and distribute the rest evenly on the bottom of the pan.) Bring the dough slightly up the sides of the pan to contain the raspberries, then lightly press the dough to hold it in place. Refrigerate the remaining dough. Bake for 25 minutes, rotating the pan halfway through the baking time. The crust should be toasty brown.

Add the raspberries and bake the tart.

Distribute the berries in a single layer over the warm crust and sprinkle with the granulated sugar. Sprinkle the remaining 1 cup of dough over the raspberries.

Bake for 35 to 40 minutes, rotating the pan halfway through the baking time. The berries should collapse and begin to release their juices, and the topping should be slightly brown. Immediately dust the warm tart with the confectioners' sugar, then let cool slightly before popping off the springform pan.

CRISPS AND COBBLERS

I like crisps and cobblers because they're uncomplicated. In fact, they're so easy I sometimes feel like I'm underachieving when I choose to bake one. But I've never received a complaint when bringing a crisp or a cobbler straight from the oven to the table, accompanied by a bowl of freshly whipped cream or some vanilla ice cream. These humble desserts are a no-brainer in the middle of the summer, when berries and stone fruits are ripe, but I probably make them just as often with apples and pears, and with frozen berries in the winter. If you use frozen berries, don't bother to defrost them before baking.

Apple Crisp

Few desserts are as familiar or comforting as apple crisp, especially when served with vanilla ice cream. If you have streusel topping in the freezer, you can make this dessert in minutes. Granny Smith apples used to be my choice for baking. These days, there are oodles of uniquely delicious varieties available, so you can choose from an impressive selection of tart, firm apples. In addition to the Bassetti apples we grow on the farm, Transparents, Honeycrisp, Braeburn, and Jonathan are some of my favorites. I also like this recipe made with pears, or a combination of the two. If you use pears, good varieties include slightly underripe Bartletts, d'Anjou, and Star Crimsons.

SERVES 8

$^3/_4$ **cup (5.25 ounces) packed light brown sugar**

$^1/_2$ **cup (3.5 ounces) granulated sugar**

$^1/_2$ **cup (1.75 ounces) rolled oats**

$^1/_3$ **cup (1.75 ounces) all-purpose flour**

$^1/_2$ **teaspoon salt**

6 tablespoons (3 ounces, or $^3/_4$ stick) cold unsalted butter

2 pounds apples (about 4 large apples)

Prepare to bake.

Preheat the oven to 350°F. Butter a 9-inch deep-dish pie pan, cast iron skillet, or an 8-inch square pan.

Make the streusel.

Measure the brown sugar, granulated sugar, oats, flour, and salt into a bowl with high sides and stir to combine. Cut the butter into small cubes ($^1/_4$ to $^1/_2$ inch) and toss with the dry ingredients. Rub the butter and dry ingredients between your thumbs and fingertips, blending everything together until the mixture is mealy, with some big chunks of butter remaining. Chill the streusel in the refrigerator or freezer for 10 to 15 minutes before using.

Prepare the apples.

Peel and core the apples and slice them $^1/_4$ inch thick. Arrange them in an even layer on the bottom of the pan, and continue to layer until you've used all of the apples.

Assemble and bake the crisp.

Spread the streusel evenly over the apples. Bake for 1 hour, until the top is dark brown and crispy, and the apples are soft and bubbly. Serve hot from the oven.

Fresh Berry Crumble

I'm very fond of crispy brown sugar streusel baked over apples, rhubarb, and pears, but when it comes to berries, this buttery blond crumble topping is the perfect match. Ground almonds add an unexpected round, nutty flavor that makes this crumble stand out. (See Grind Your Own Nut Meal, page 88.) This topping is also heavenly on marionberries, raspberries, loganberries, tayberries, and blackberries of all kinds, too.

SERVES 8

1 cup (7 ounces) granulated sugar

³/₄ cup (3.75 ounces) all-purpose flour

³/₄ cup (2.75 ounces) rolled oats

¹/₂ cup (2.5 ounces) freshly ground almonds
   (not almond meal)

1 teaspoon salt

¹/₂ cup (4 ounces, or 1 stick) cold unsalted butter

3 pints (6¹/₂ cups) fresh berries

1 teaspoon vanilla extract

Prepare to bake.

Preheat the oven to 350°F. Butter a 9-inch deep-dish pie pan or an 8-inch square pan.

Make the crumble topping.

Measure the sugar, flour, oats, ground almonds, and salt into a bowl with high sides and stir to combine. Cut the butter into small cubes (¹/₄ to ¹/₂ inch) and toss with the dry ingredients. Rub the butter and dry ingredients between your thumbs and fingertips, blending everything together until the mixture is mealy, with some big chunks of butter remaining. Chill in the refrigerator or freezer for 10 to 15 minutes before using.

Assemble and bake the crumble.

Toss the berries and vanilla together, then spread the berries evenly over the bottom of the pan. Sprinkle the crumble topping evenly over the berries; it may seem like too much, but the crumble will sink into the berries.

Bake for 1 hour, or until the topping is golden brown and the fruit is bubbling. If you want a more caramelized top, finish the crumble under the broiler for about 5 minutes. Serve hot from the oven.

Oregon's Marionberry

Popular in Oregon, where they originated, marionberries are a cross between Olallie and Chehalem blackberries. They're named for Marion County, where the hybrid was developed. Marionberries are extra juicy, with a great balance of tart and sweet and not too many seeds, making them one of the favorite berries at Grand Central.

Rhubarb Crisp

Combine the sour tang of rhubarb with the sweet crunch of brown sugar streusel and you get one of my favorite quick desserts. This crisp calls for generous amounts of sweet streusel to offset the lip-puckering tartness of rhubarb.

SERVES 8

1 cup (7 ounces) packed light brown sugar

3/4 cup (5.25 ounces) granulated sugar

3/4 cup (2.75 ounces) rolled oats

1/2 cup (2.5 ounces) all-purpose flour

3/4 teaspoon salt

1/2 cup (4 ounces, or 1 stick) cold unsalted butter

2 pounds rhubarb stalks

Prepare to bake.

Preheat the oven to 350°F. Butter a 9-inch deep-dish pie pan or an 8-inch square pan.

Make the streusel.

Measure the brown sugar, granulated sugar, oats, flour, and salt into a bowl with high sides and stir to combine. Cut the butter into small cubes (1/4 to 1/2 inch) and toss with the dry ingredients. Rub the butter and dry ingredients between your thumbs and fingertips, blending everything together until the mixture is mealy, with some big chunks of butter remaining. Chill the streusel in the refrigerator or freezer for 10 to 15 minutes before using.

Prepare the rhubarb.

Cut the rhubarb diagonally into 1-inch pieces. Arrange the pieces in an even layer on the bottom of the pan.

Assemble and bake the crisp.

Spread the streusel evenly over the top of the rhubarb. Bake for about 1 hour, until the top is dark brown and crispy and the rhubarb is soft and bubbly. Serve warm from the oven.

THE **GRAND CENTRAL BAKING** BOOK

Peach Cobbler

Ellen grew up eating cobblers with this topping, which is unlike any other recipe I've seen. It delivers the balance of crunch and chew that I like in a cobbler crust. Even after making thousands of cobblers and trying new recipes occasionally, Ellen always goes back to her mom's recipe. If the peaches you're using aren't too fuzzy, leave the skins on for a simple and more colorful cobbler.

SERVES 8

1 cup (7 ounces) granulated sugar

1 cup (5 ounces) all-purpose flour

1 teaspoon salt

1/2 teaspoon baking powder

1 egg, lightly beaten

2 pounds peaches (about 4 large peaches),
   pitted and sliced

2 tablespoons packed light brown sugar

1/2 teaspoon freshly grated nutmeg

1/4 cup (2 ounces, or 1/2 stick) unsalted butter,
   melted

Prepare to bake.

Preheat the oven to 350°F. Butter a 9-inch deep-dish pie pan or an 8-inch square pan.

Make the topping.

Measure the granulated sugar, flour, 3/4 teaspoon of the salt, and the baking powder into a bowl and whisk to combine. Drizzle the beaten egg over the dry ingredients while stirring with a fork to partially combine. The mixture will be floury and dry, with a few lumps created by adding the egg.

Prepare the peaches and assemble the cobbler.

Toss the peaches with the brown sugar, nutmeg, and the remaining 1/4 teaspoon salt. Arrange the peaches in an even layer on the bottom of the pan. Scatter the topping over the peaches as evenly as possible, given its lumpy, floury texture. Drizzle the melted butter all over, trying to get a bit into each area of the pan.

Bake.

Bake for about 50 minutes, until the topping is golden brown and the fruit is bubbling around the edges of the pan. Let the cobbler cool slightly before serving.

FRESH FRUIT, CAKE, AND CREAM

Whether the end result is a beautiful, composed dessert like a trifle, or an unassuming summer pudding, these desserts are much greater than the sum of their simple parts. Each one gets its structure from a plain cake-y item bound by juicy ripe fruit and enriched with custard or cream. The following recipes begin with soft, overripe fruit, which is nicely complemented by liqueur or a fortified wine.

A Sweet Inheritance

My name, Piper, is my mother's maiden name. For most of my life that name was the strongest connection I felt to that side of my family. My mother was born into a very eastern family who identified keenly with their geographic roots. However, as soon as my mother was married, she headed west to raise a very western family, similarly devoted to its origins. There wasn't much travel between the two coasts. As a result, I never knew my great-grandmother, Granny Piper, and have heard only a handful of stories about the "imposing Welsh woman," five feet ten inches tall, with a penchant for extravagant hats.

The last time I visited my grandmother Dorothy (Granny Piper's daughter-in-law), she'd just turned 104. We spent hours looking though her recipe box. I sat next to her as she flipped through the tidy cards, loving the sound of her nostalgic narrative. "Now this is a good one, Pipah," she'd say, with her eastern soft "r."

When we came to a card labeled "Granny Piper's Trifle," my heart beat a familial thump. I love to make trifle! My grandmother went on to explain that Granny Piper hadn't been much of a cook, but she did make a wonderful trifle.

I am pleased to know that imposing height and a name aren't the only traits I've inherited from my great-grandmother. And although I've modernized her trifle recipe with fresh fruit and a more substantial cake, I like to think Granny Piper would approve. Who knows, maybe I'll take up wearing extravagant hats!

Summer Pudding

Summer pudding is a traditional English dessert made by lining a bowl with bread, filling it with syrupy summer berries, then weighting it down and leaving it to soak overnight or for up to twenty-four hours. During the nineteenth century, it was called hydropathic pudding at health resorts, where it was served as a popular alternative to butter-rich pastries and forbidden sweets. While pastry is never forbidden in my house, I like to make this simple dessert in June and July, the height of Oregon's abundant berry season. Serve it with a dollop of lightly sweetened whipped cream (see page 137).

Summer pudding should be made in a two-quart bowl with high sides or a charlotte mold. Although most recipes call for brioche or challah, any type of rustic white bread is delicious in this recipe.

SERVES 6 TO 8

12 ounces rustic white bread

1/2 to 3/4 cup (3.5 to 5.25 ounces) granulated sugar, depending on the sweetness of the berries

3 pints (6 1/2 cups) fresh raspberries, marionberries, blueberries, or a combination

1/4 cup (2 fluid ounces) framboise or another fruity liqueur

Prepare the equipment and ingredients.

Line a 2-quart bowl or a charlotte mold with plastic wrap, leaving some overhanging on all sides. Slice the bread into about 10 slices and remove the crusts.

Sprinkle the sugar over the berries, add the framboise, and crush lightly until the berries release their juices. You'll end up with about 6 cups of syrupy fruit.

Assemble the pudding.

Press slices of bread into the mold to cover the bottom and sides completely so that none of the plastic wrap shows through. Snugly fit the pieces up against one another, filling in any holes with smaller pieces of bread. Don't worry if you need several different-size pieces; a patchwork of bread won't compromise the integrity of the whole.

Add the crushed berries with their juices, setting aside 1/2 cup juice for the top layer. Fit the remaining pieces of bread over the top, then pour the remaining berry juices over the bread and pull the extra lengths of plastic wrap up on all sides to cover and seal the top.

Weight and chill the pudding.

Place another sheet of plastic wrap over the pudding and cover it with a plate that has a slightly smaller diameter than the mold and fits just inside its rim. Put a moderately heavy object (or a couple of heavy cans) on the plate to weight the pudding down and compact it. Refrigerate the pudding overnight or for up to 24 hours.

Invert the pudding.

Wait until just before serving to invert the pudding. Fold the plastic wrap back from the bread, invert the pudding onto a plate, and remove the plastic wrap. Surprisingly, the bread and berries will have blended fully, transforming them into a true pudding. To serve, cut the pudding into wedges, like a cake.

Raspberry Port Trifle

Trifle is a dessert that begs for the cook's personal touch. Feel free to improvise, embellish, and generally take artistic license with this recipe. Use frozen or home-canned fruit in the winter months, fresh fruit and berries in the summer, or whatever you happen to have on hand. The liquor is up to you too: sherry, brandy, Marsala, bourbon, kirsch—whatever complements the fruit you're using. There's a recipe for my Granny Piper's sponge cake on page 153, but any plain cake, white or yellow, will do. Trifle made with Glazed Vanilla Bundt Cake (page 147) is out of this world. Eat half of the cake and save the rest for trifle.

I have a weakness for trifle bowls—the tall, straight sides make for perfect and visually stunning layers. If you're going to make trifles, I heartily encourage you to invest in one.

SERVES 10 TO 12 GENEROUSLY

CRÈME ANGLAISE

2 cups (16 fluid ounces) whole milk

4 egg yolks

$1/3$ cup (2.25 ounces) granulated sugar

1 teaspoon vanilla extract

$1/4$ teaspoon salt

LAYERS

2 pounds leftover plain cake

$3/4$ cup (6 fluid ounces) port

1 cup raspberry jam

2 pints (4 cups) fresh raspberries

WHIPPED CREAM

2 cups (16 fluid ounces) heavy whipping cream

2 tablespoons granulated or confectioner's sugar

1 teaspoon vanilla extract

Fresh raspberries, for garnish (optional)

Lightly toasted almonds (see page 20) or fresh fruit, for garnish (optional)

Make the crème anglaise.

Heat the milk in a heavy saucepan over medium heat until a skin begins to form on its surface, just before it comes to a simmer. Meanwhile, whisk the egg yolks with the sugar, vanilla, and salt until well blended and slightly thickened. While whisking continuously, slowly pour about 1 cup of the hot milk into the egg yolk mixture. Then, still whisking continuously, slowly pour the egg yolk mixture back into the saucepan with the remaining hot milk.

Cook the custard over medium-low heat, stirring constantly with a wooden spoon or heatproof spatula until it thickens slightly and coats the back of the spoon; this will take about 10 minutes. (If you run your finger down the spoon, the custard shouldn't run into the track.) Immediately remove the custard from the heat and pour it through a fine-mesh sieve into a 2-quart bowl. Cover with plastic wrap, placing it directly on the surface so the custard doesn't form a skin. Let the custard cool to room temperature.

Assemble the trifle.

Slice the cake into $1/2$- to $3/4$-inch-thick pieces. Arrange one-third of the slices on the bottom of the trifle bowl, pressing the cake to fill the bottom. Pour $1/4$ cup of the port evenly over the cake, then spread $1/3$ cup of the jam over the cake. Cover with a layer of raspberries, using about $1 1/3$ cups, then pour $3/4$ cup of the custard over the berries. Repeat the entire process two more times. Cover the surface of the trifle with plastic wrap and refrigerate for at least 24 hours and up to 2 days.

Make the whipped cream, garnish, and serve.

Well in advance of serving, put the whipping cream in a bowl in the refrigerator, along with a whisk. When you're ready to serve, whip the cream with the sugar and vanilla until it holds soft peaks, 5 to 7 minutes. Pile the whipped cream atop the trifle and garnish with the fresh fruit and toasted nuts.

Lost and Found

As Grand Central Bakery has grown, so has the number of individuals whose impact is key to our continued success. Laura Ohm is one of these people. Laura has a great palate, a keen intellectual interest in food, and a thing for clafouti.

Shortly after Laura and her husband, Fred, moved in together, Fred started talking about this French dessert his (French) mother made, called clafouti. Ever anxious to try new pastry, Laura had her mother-in-law, Yves, send the recipe to her. A few years ago, the original—and only—copy went missing, and Laura was sure that she'd loaned it to me. In an effort to recreate it, she tried recipes from Julia Child, M. F. K. Fisher, and others, but they failed to measure up. Finally, through painstaking trial and error, she came up with a recipe she considered to be every bit as good.

A rustic baked dessert somewhere between a custard and a soufflé, clafouti works well with different fruits and berries, though cherries and soaked prunes are traditional and, in my opinion, the yummiest. Clafouti provides a great contrast of textures, too, with a slightly chewy cake, soft baked fruit, and crunchy cracked sugar shards on top.

(P.S. I was vindicated when the original recipe turned up recently, in a dusty recipe file on Laura's bookshelf. Her new version was within 2 tablespoons of milk of her mother-in-law's original recipe!)

Clafouti

The quintessential last-minute dessert, clafouti has a dramatic, soufflé-like appearance, yet it's dead simple and truly delicious. Pop it in the oven as you sit down to dinner, and it will be ready when it's time for dessert. Make this small clafouti in an 8-inch pie pan to serve 4, or double the recipe and use a generously sized ceramic or glass pie pan to serve a crowd. Serve immediately with freshly whipped cream.

SERVES 4

$2/3$ cup (5.25 fluid ounces) whole milk

8 teaspoons plus $1/4$ cup (3 ounces) granulated sugar

2 eggs

$1\frac{1}{2}$ teaspoons vanilla extract

$1/8$ teaspoon salt

$1/3$ cup (1.75 ounces) all-purpose flour

$1\frac{1}{2}$ cups fresh pitted cherries or 1 cup halved, pitted prunes, soaked in $1/4$ cup (2 fluid ounces) brandy or Armagnac

Prepare to bake.

Preheat the oven to 400°F.

Make the batter and assemble the clafouti.

Combine the milk, the 8 teaspoons sugar, and the eggs, vanilla, salt, and flour in a blender and blend until smooth, about 30 seconds. Pour the batter into an 8-inch glass or ceramic pie pan. Add the fruit to the batter, distributing it evenly. Sprinkle the $1/4$ cup sugar over the clafouti.

Bake.

Bake until puffed and golden, 35 to 40 minutes. (Bake an additional 10 minutes for larger clafouti.) Serve immediately.

Strawberry Shortcake

While shortcake is classically associated with strawberries, these tender biscuits are a great platform for any ripe fruit in season, strawberries in May and June; marionberries, blueberries, and raspberries in July; peaches and apricots in August; and the luscious golden raspberries of late summer. For a nice touch, add a splash of liqueur to the fruit, to complement its flavor; for example, use Grand Marnier for strawberries, framboise or cassis for raspberries and blackberries, or bourbon for peaches.

Refer to the Short Dough Workshop (page 16) if this is your first attempt at biscuit making. Use different shapes of cookie cutters for a unique presentation or, for a birthday shortcake, make one big biscuit and decorate it with candles. The cream makes the dough so tender that you may want to work it a little more to keep the biscuits from falling apart.

MAKES 6 SHORTCAKES

FRUIT

2½ to 3 cups fresh strawberries

About ¼ cup (1.75 ounces) granulated sugar, depending on the sweetness of the fruit

2 tablespoons freshly squeezed lemon juice

SHORTCAKES

2 cups (10 ounces) all-purpose flour

3 tablespoons granulated sugar, plus 1 tablespoon for sprinkling (optional)

1 tablespoon baking powder

½ teaspoon salt

½ cup (4 ounces, or 1 stick) cold unsalted butter, plus 1 tablespoon for brushing (optional)

1 cup (8 fluid ounces) cold heavy whipping cream, plus 1 tablespoon for brushing (optional)

WHIPPED CREAM

1 cup (8 fluid ounces) whipping cream

2 tablespoons granulated or confectioners' sugar

1 teaspoon vanilla extract

Prepare the fruit.

Slice the strawberries or, if they're small, mash them lightly with a fork to release their juices. Sprinkle the sugar and lemon juice over the berries and let sit for at least 1 hour at room temperature or up to 6 hours in the refrigerator to draw out their juices.

Combine the dry ingredients.

Measure the flour, sugar, baking powder, and salt into a bowl with high sides or the bowl of a stand mixer and whisk to combine.

Cut in the butter.

Dice the butter into $1/2$-inch cubes. Use your hands or the paddle attachment of the stand mixer on low speed to blend the butter into the dry ingredients, mixing for 1 to 2 minutes. The mixture will resemble coarse meal with small pieces of butter sprinkled throughout.

Add the cream.

If mixing by hand, make a well in the flour mixture, pour in the cream, and mix with a fork just until the dough begins to come together in large clumps. If using a stand mixer, add the cream in one quick addition and mix only until the dry ingredients are moistened and the dough begins to come together in large clumps. This will take only a few rotations of the paddle.

Form the shortcakes.

Line a baking sheet with parchment paper. Turn the dough out onto a lightly floured surface and knead several times until it is a cohesive mass. Roll or pat the dough into a rectangle measuring about 6 by 9 inches and 1 inch thick, then cut it into six 3-inch squares using a sharp knife. Place the shortcakes on the prepared pan and refrigerate for 20 minutes. Preheat the oven to 350°F.

Bake.

Gently brush any excess flour from the shortcakes. For crisp tops, brush lightly with the cream or melted butter and sprinkle with the sugar. Bake the shortcakes for 30 to 35 minutes, rotating the pan halfway through the baking time. The shortcakes should be golden brown on top and toasty brown on the bottom. Let the shortcakes cool before splitting them.

Whip the cream.

I like to whip the cream by hand right before assembling the shortcakes; hand-whipped cream has a loose, rich texture that is more difficult to achieve using a stand mixer. Well in advance of serving dessert, put the whipping cream in a bowl in the refrigerator, along with a whisk. When you're ready for dessert, whip the cream until it holds soft peaks, 7 to 10 minutes, then whisk in the sugar and vanilla.

Assemble the shortcakes.

Use a serrated knife or a fork to split the shortcakes. Spoon about $1/4$ cup of fruit and some of the juices onto the bottom half of each shortcake. Put a nice dollop of whipped cream on the fruit, then cover with the top half of the shortcake. Spoon more fruit and whipped cream atop the shortcakes and serve right away.

6
Cake

You don't need to wait for a special occasion to bake a cake. Because Grand Central Bakery's cakes are simple and delicious, they deserve a place in the home baker's everyday repertoire.

My favorite cakes are straightforward and flavorful, made with fresh, high-quality ingredients assembled using easy, familiar techniques. Most are simply glazed, and a few are filled and frosted. Besides being fantastic for dessert, a slice of cake is lovely first thing in the morning with a cup of coffee. These cakes often taste better after sitting on the counter for a few days.

CAKE MIXING WORKSHOP.......... **144**

Cream Cheese Apple Cake 146

Glazed Vanilla Bundt Cake 147

Ganache-Glazed Chocolate
Bundt Cake 148

Polenta Pear Cake 151

Lemon Pound Cake 152

Dorothy Piper's Sunshine
Sponge Cake 153

Gingerbread................................. 154

BIRTHDAY CAKE WORKSHOP **155**

Birthday Cakes............................ **162**

Yellow Birthday Cake 162

Chocolate Birthday Cake 163

Vanilla Buttercream 164

Whipped Chocolate Ganache 164

Layer Cakes **165**

Coconut Layer Cake
with Coconut Buttercream 165

Carrot Cake 167

Old-Fashioned Spice Cake 168

CAKE MIXING WORKSHOP

Essential Equipment

You can buy all sorts of equipment for cake making, but the must-haves for the uncomplicated cake recipes in this chapter boil down to a handful of basic pieces: an electric mixer (or a really strong arm), dry and liquid measuring cups, measuring spoons, a fine-mesh sieve or sifter, a couple of small bowls, a rubber spatula or plastic bowl scraper, parchment paper, and some baking pans.

Ingredients

For consistently tasty results, always begin with the best, freshest ingredients. Choose fruit that's ripe and tasty, buy the good chocolate, and don't skimp on imitation flavorings. We use superfine sugar at the bakery, but regular granulated sugar will work just fine.

Most of the cakes we sell don't call for cake flour, which has a finer texture and lower protein content than all-purpose and bread flour. You can substitute equal amounts of cake flour for all-purpose by weight, or add an additional 2 tablespoons for every cup of cake flour used.

Technique

The cakes we sell in our cafés are all made using some variation on the same technique; we call them cream-the-butter-and-sugar cakes. The theory behind this method is that during the time it takes to cream the butter and dissolve the sugar, enough extra air is whipped into the butter to create maximum height. Then the eggs, flour, and other ingredients are added gradually and incorporated thoroughly. A beautifully mixed cake batter should be creamy and homogenous without being overworked.

Prepare the pans.

It's a bummer when a cake falls apart as you knock it out of the pan. A piece of parchment paper fitted inside the bottom of the pan ensures that the cake's bottom and sides release completely—even chocolate cakes, which are notorious for sticking. Use a light coating of butter dusted with flour on both the sides of the pan and the parchment lining on the bottom, to give the batter something to adhere to so it can rise to its full volume.

Use room temperature ingredients.

Take the eggs and butter out of the refrigerator several hours before you begin mixing a cake. All of the ingredients should be about 70°F unless the recipe specifies otherwise. Be careful not to let the butter warm up to the point that it becomes greasy.

Sift the dry ingredients.

These cake recipes call for measuring the dry ingredients first, then whisking or sifting them together. Not all cake recipes require sifting, but it helps avoid clumps in the flour and evenly distributes the salt and leavening, yielding a fine crumb.

Cream the butter and sugar.

The objective here is twofold: to dissolve the sugar into the butter for a delicate texture, and to incorporate air into the butter to create lightness. Start by beating the butter and sugar together using a stand mixer with the paddle attachment, on low speed. Gradually increase the speed to medium or medium-high, stopping once or twice during that time to scrape the bottom and sides of the bowl. Creaming should take 2 to 4 minutes, depending on the speed of the mixer and the temperature of the butter. A properly creamed butter and sugar mixture is light in color and has good loft and a fluffy texture.

Add the eggs.

Cakes of this style call for adding whole eggs to the creamed butter and sugar mixture after it's well aerated. The mixture will accept eggs gracefully if they're at room temperature and are added slowly, and the result will be a smooth, shiny batter. When cold eggs are added to creamed butter and sugar, the mixture takes on a curdled appearance.

One of the tricks I picked up at the bakery is to crack the number of eggs called for in the recipe into a liquid measuring cup or a container that makes pouring easy. This allows you to control how quickly the eggs are added and to keep little pieces of eggshell out of the batter. Everyone's made the mistake of adding eggs to creamed butter and sugar too quickly; here again, the mixture looks curdled. If this happens, increase the mixer speed and continue mixing for 1 to 2 minutes before adding the remaining eggs slowly.

Alternate additions of the dry and wet ingredients.

The final step in mixing a cake is the one that involves incorporating the remaining ingredients, wet and dry. If the additions are made all at once or too hastily, the flour can clump or the liquid can overwhelm the batter, causing the butter, sugar, and egg mixture to deflate.

The standard and most effective approach is to alternate additions by adding the dry ingredients (in 3 additions) then the wet (in 2 additions), beginning and ending with the dry ingredients. Remember, the goal is for the batter to accept these additions with ease. Add one-third of the dry ingredients to start and mix just until incorporated. Add half of the liquid ingredients and mix again before introducing another one-third of the dry ingredients and mixing until the flour is no longer visible. Add the remaining liquid ingredients, mix to incorporate, and then add the last third of the dry ingredients and mix only partially. Finish mixing by hand using a rubber spatula or plastic bowl scraper.

Any remaining ingredients, such as nuts, are usually folded in as part of this process. As you do this final mixing, scrape the bottom and sides of the bowl to recover and reintroduce any reluctant patches of butter and sugar left behind.

Bake the cake.

For filled and frosted cakes, it can be advantageous to bake the cake the day before you plan to fill and frost it. Before preheating the oven, arrange the shelves so that the cake pans can sit in or near the middle. When you put the pans in the oven, leave room for circulation between them. Rotate the pans once during baking, usually halfway through the total baking time, and begin to watch closely near the end of the baking time. Keep in mind that ovens (and thus baking times) can vary greatly from one to the next. Fortunately, a finished cake offers visible clues to its doneness: noticeable shrinking from the edges of the pan and a very slight lowering in the very middle of the cake. You can also insert a wooden skewer or cake tester into the middle of the cake like a probe. If the tester comes out clean, without any crumbs on it, the cake is done.

Knock out the cake.

Let the cake cool for about 10 to 15 minutes before removing it from the pan. Place a cardboard cake round, or the removable metal bottom from a tart pan on top of the cake and flip it upside down. If you don't feel the cake fall onto the plate, knock the pan gently on the counter once or twice to release the cake from it. If some of the cake sticks, resist the terrible temptation to scrape it off and pop it in your mouth. Instead, use a small metal spatula to carefully remove the chunk of cake from the pan and put it right back in the space it once occupied. Any visible evidence of the accident can be masked with frosting. Let your cake cool completely before proceeding to the next step.

Cream Cheese Apple Cake

Ironically, a recipe in an old Cooking Light *magazine inspired this cake. One fall we were buried in a bumper crop of the Bassetti apples that grow on our farm in Goldendale, Washington. My mother had unloaded a bunch at the bakery and I was scrambling to use the rest up when I stumbled on this recipe. I replaced the low-fat cream cheese with the real thing, used real butter instead of "lite" margarine, and threw in a few extra eggs for good measure.*

In the years since, Grand Central has baked this cake in every shape and size imaginable: as cupcakes with maple cream cheese frosting, in rounds baked in springform pans, as classic Bundt cakes, and currently in long Pullman loaf pans. At home, I like to make it in a classic 12-cup Bundt pan and sprinkle confectioners' sugar all over the top (as in this version). Because it stays moist for several days, this large cake is tailor-made for a long weekend with friends, providing dessert the first night and leftovers to nibble on for several days to come.

SERVES 14 TO 16

3 cups (15 ounces) all-purpose flour

1½ teaspoons baking powder

1 teaspoon salt

1 teaspoon ground cinnamon

1 cup (8 ounces, or 2 sticks) unsalted butter,
    at room temperature

12 ounces cream cheese, at room temperature

2½ cups (1 pound, 1.5 ounces) granulated sugar

4 eggs, at room temperature

1 teaspoon vanilla extract

1¼ pounds tart apples (3 or 4 apples), peeled
    and diced into ½-inch chunks

Confectioners' sugar, for dusting

Prepare to bake.

Preheat the oven to 350°F. Grease and lightly flour a 12-cup Bundt pan.

Combine the dry ingredients.

Sift the flour, baking powder, salt, and cinnamon into a bowl.

Cream the butter, cream cheese, and sugar.

Using a stand mixer with the paddle attachment, beat the butter, cream cheese, and granulated sugar on medium-high speed until the mixture is very light in color—almost white—and the texture is fluffy, about 8 minutes. Scrape the bottom and sides of the bowl once during the process to ensure that the butter is evenly incorporated.

Add the eggs and vanilla.

Crack the eggs into a liquid measuring cup and add the vanilla. With the mixer on low speed, slowly pour in the eggs, letting them fall in one at a time and incorporating each egg completely before adding the next. Scrape the bottom and sides of the bowl once or twice during the process.

Add the dry ingredients and apples.

With the mixer on low speed, add the dry ingredients; stop mixing as soon as the flour is incorporated. Fold the apples in by hand using a stiff spatula, then scrape the batter into the prepared pan.

Bake.

Bake for 60 to 75 minutes, rotating the pan halfway through the baking time. The cake is ready when a wooden skewer inserted in the middle comes out clean. Let the cake cool for 15 minutes before removing it from the pan. Cool completely, then cover with a thick dusting of confectioners' sugar.

Glazed Vanilla Bundt Cake

This rich white cake is glazed while it's still warm, giving it a doughnut-like appearance. It gets its volume from additional egg whites and longer whipping.

Egg whites are available in most grocery store dairy cases these days. If you choose to start with whole eggs, use the leftover egg yolks to make a simple crème anglaise (see page 137), which you can use, along with fresh berries, to dress up this cake.

SERVES 14 TO 16

CAKE

4$\frac{1}{2}$ cups (1 pound, 6.5 ounces) all-purpose flour

1 tablespoon baking powder

2 teaspoons salt

$\frac{1}{4}$ teaspoon ground nutmeg, preferably freshly grated

1$\frac{1}{2}$ cups (12 ounces, or 3 sticks) unsalted butter,
    at room temperature

2$\frac{3}{4}$ cups (1 pound, 3.25 ounces) granulated sugar

1 cup egg whites (about 7 or 8 whites),
    at room temperature

2 teaspoons vanilla extract

2 cups (16 fluid ounces) whole milk,
    at room temperature

GLAZE

$\frac{1}{2}$ cup (2 ounces) confectioners' sugar

$\frac{1}{4}$ cup (2 fluid ounces) heavy cream

$\frac{1}{4}$ teaspoon vanilla extract

Prepare to bake.

Preheat the oven to 350°F. Grease and lightly flour a 12-cup Bundt pan.

Combine the dry ingredients.

Measure the flour, baking powder, salt, and nutmeg into a bowl and sift or whisk to combine.

Cream the butter and sugar.

Using a stand mixer with the paddle attachment, beat the butter and sugar on medium-high speed until the mixture is very light in color—almost white—and the

texture is fluffy, about 7 minutes. Scrape the bottom and sides of the bowl a few times during the process.

Add the egg whites and vanilla.

Combine the egg whites and vanilla in a liquid measuring cup. With the mixer on medium speed, add the egg whites slowly (about $\frac{1}{4}$ cup at a time), completely incorporating each before adding the next. Scrape the bowl several times.

Alternate additions of the dry and wet ingredients.

Reduce the mixer speed to low. Add one-third of the dry ingredients to the mixer and incorporate on low speed, then increase the speed to medium. Add 1 cup of the milk and mix briefly to incorporate. Reduce the speed to low again, add half of the remaining dry ingredients, and mix to incorporate, then increase the speed to medium and beat for 1 minute. Repeat with the remaining 1 cup milk and the remaining dry ingredients, but stop mixing just before the flour is fully incorporated. Finish mixing by hand, using a sturdy spatula and being sure to scrape up from the bottom of the bowl.

Bake.

Pour the batter into the prepared pan. Bake for 45 minutes, then rotate the pan, lower the oven temperature to 325°F, and bake for 30 minutes more. It's ready when the sides pull away from the pan slightly and it springs back when pressed lightly in the center. The top will probably split; use a cake tester to check doneness.

Make the glaze.

Make the glaze while the cake is in the oven. Measure the confectioners' sugar, cream, and vanilla into a small bowl and whisk until smooth.

Glaze the cake.

Let the cake cool for 15 minutes before turning it out. Whisk the glaze again until completely smooth, then use it immediately. Saturate the cake completely, using a pastry brush to coat the entire surface. Apply the entire amount of glaze; it will be enough for several coats.

Ganache-Glazed Chocolate Bundt Cake

This chocolate cake is truly a marvel. Not only is it luscious and moist, it bakes up beautifully in a variety of shapes and sizes, and the batter can be frozen without affecting the cake's flavor, texture, or ability to rise. At Grand Central, we use this formula to make cupcakes, layer cakes, kugelhopfs, sheet cakes, loaves, and, my favorite, a classic 12-cup Bundt cake drizzled with chocolate ganache. I'm usually not a stickler for fancy ingredients, but this cake deserves the best chocolate you can find.

SERVES 14 TO 16

CAKE

3 ounces unsweetened chocolate, coarsely chopped
   (about ¹/₂ cup)

3 ounces semisweet chocolate, coarsely chopped
   (about ¹/₂ cup)

3 cups (15 ounces) all-purpose flour

1 cup (3 ounces) cocoa powder

1 tablespoon baking soda

¹/₂ teaspoon salt

1 cup (8 ounces, or 2 sticks) unsalted butter,
   at room temperature

2 ¹/₄ cups (1 pound) packed light brown sugar

6 eggs, at room temperature

1 tablespoon vanilla extract

1 cup (8.5 ounces) sour cream

1 cup (8 fluid ounces) lukewarm freshly brewed
   coffee (110°F to 115°F)

2 cups (12 ounces) milk chocolate chips

GANACHE

9.5 ounces semisweet chocolate, coarsely chopped
   (about 1¹/₂ cups)

³/₄ cup (6 fluid ounces) heavy cream

Prepare to bake.

Preheat the oven to 350°F. Grease and lightly flour a 12-cup Bundt pan.

Melt the chocolate.

Put the unsweetened and semisweet chocolate in a double boiler or a metal bowl suspended over a pot of barely simmering water for 5 to 7 minutes, or until the chocolate has melted and is completely smooth. Set aside to cool slightly.

Combine the dry ingredients.

Sift the flour, cocoa powder, baking soda, and salt into a bowl.

Cream the butter and sugar.

Using a stand mixer with the paddle attachment, beat the butter and sugar on medium-high speed until the mixture is very light in color—almost beige-y white—and the texture is fluffy, about 2 to 4 minutes. Scrape the bottom and sides of the bowl a few times during the process to ensure that the butter is evenly incorporated.

Add the eggs and vanilla.

Crack the eggs into a liquid measuring cup and add the vanilla. With the mixer on low speed, slowly pour in the eggs, letting them fall in one at a time and incorporating each egg completely before adding the next. Scrape the bottom and sides of the bowl once or twice during the process.

Add the chocolate.

Add the melted chocolate to the butter mixture all at once and mix on low speed until slightly combined; you don't need to fully incorporate the chocolate at this point.

(continued)

Alternate additions of the dry and wet ingredients.

Whisk the sour cream and coffee together to achieve a smooth, room temperature liquid. (Adding too much of a cold ingredient can cause the chocolate to seize.) With the mixer on low speed, add one-third of the dry ingredients until just incorporated. Add half of the sour cream mixture, mixing to combine. Repeat, using half of the remaining dry ingredients and all of the remaining wet ingredients, mixing after each addition. Add the remaining dry ingredients and stop the mixer before they're fully incorporated. Add the milk chocolate chips and finish mixing by hand, using a sturdy spatula and being sure to scrape up from the bottom of the bowl.

Happy National Bundt Cake Day!

November 15 is the day. You'll be greeted by a cheery face reminding you that this is the birthday of the Bundt cake. It is also the anniversary of the day that Grand Central Bakery introduced Bundt cakes to its lineup, fifty years after the famous cake pan was born. We celebrate with $1.00 slices of cake and the chance to enter a drawing for a 12-cup classic Bundt pan and recipes for our glazed vanilla and chocolate Bundt cakes.

Bake.

Scrape the batter into the prepared pan and bake for 60 to 75 minutes, rotating the pan halfway through the baking time. The cake is ready when it begins to pull away from the edges of the pan slightly and springs back when pressed lightly in the center. The top will probably split; use a cake tester to check doneness. Unlike with most cakes, the tester probably won't come out clean because of the melted chocolate chips. Refer to the Cake Mixing workshop on page 145 for additional doneness cues. Let the cake cool for at least 15 minutes before making the ganache.

Make the ganache.

Put the chocolate in a shallow bowl. Put the cream in a small saucepan over medium-high heat until a skin forms, then immediately pour it over the chocolate. Let the chocolate sit for a few minutes, then stir gently. The ganache should be glossy and have a smooth texture. If any chunks of chocolate remain, place the bowl over simmering water briefly and stir until melted.

Glaze the cake.

Turn the cake out and glaze it on a rack, if you have one. Place the rack on a baking sheet covered with parchment paper. Pour the ganache over the crown of the cake in one deliberate motion, distributing it as evenly as possible all the way around. Let the glaze set up for 20 minutes before transferring the cake to a plate or cake stand.

Polenta Pear Cake

This nutty cornmeal cake is made like an upside-down cake, with fresh pears baked into the batter. When it comes out of the oven, it's inverted and brushed with a sweet glaze to accent the shape and caramel-tinged edges of the pear slices on top. The cake keeps extremely well and is, in my opinion, even more delicious for breakfast than it is for dessert. I was almost tempted to include the recipe in the Breakfast and Brunch chapter. Even though we call it polenta cake, I prefer a medium grind of cornmeal.

SERVES 8

1 cup (5 ounces) all-purpose flour

1$\frac{1}{2}$ teaspoons baking powder

$\frac{1}{2}$ teaspoon salt

2 cups (10 ounces) cornmeal (medium grind)

2 firm, barely ripe pears

1 cup (8 ounces, or 2 sticks) unsalted butter,
     at room temperature

1$\frac{1}{2}$ cups (10.5 ounces) granulated sugar

6 eggs, at room temperature

1$\frac{1}{2}$ teaspoons vanilla extract

3 to 4 tablespoons apple jelly, marmalade,
     or apricot preserves

1 to 2 tablespoons water

Prepare to bake.

Preheat the oven to 350°F. Lightly grease a 10-inch round cake pan.

Combine the dry ingredients.

Measure the flour, baking powder, salt, and cornmeal into a bowl and whisk to combine.

Prepare the pears.

Use a thin paring knife to cut the pears into slices $\frac{1}{8}$ to $\frac{1}{4}$ inch thick. Fan the slices on the bottom of the prepared pan without overlapping them; there will probably be a few extra for snacking.

Cream the butter and sugar.

Using a stand mixer with the paddle attachment, beat the butter and sugar on medium-high speed until the mixture is very light in color and the texture is fluffy, about 2 to 4 minutes. Scrape the bottom and sides of the bowl a few times during the process to ensure that the butter is evenly incorporated.

Add the eggs and vanilla.

Crack the eggs into a liquid measuring cup and add the vanilla. With the mixer on low speed, gradually pour in the eggs, letting them fall in one at a time and incorporating each egg completely before adding the next. Scrape the sides of the bowl once or twice during the process.

Add the dry ingredients.

With the mixer on low speed, add the dry ingredients slowly and stop mixing just before the flour is incorporated. Finish mixing by hand, using a sturdy spatula and being sure to scrape up from the bottom of the bowl.

Bake.

Carefully pour the batter over the pears, being careful not to move them. Bake for 35 to 40 minutes, rotating the pan halfway through the baking time. The cake is ready when it pulls away from the edges of the pan slightly and springs back when pressed lightly in the center.

Cool and glaze the cake.

Immediately invert the cake onto a serving plate. Combine the jelly and 1 tablespoon of the water in a small saucepan over low heat. (Depending on whether you use jelly, marmalade, or preserves you may need to add more water to achieve the right consistency.) Cook, stirring continuously, until the mixture is a smooth and a light syrupy consistency. Brush the glaze over the pears and on the sides of the cake.

Lemon Pound Cake

I have vivid memories (circa 1974) of going to work at The Bakery with my mom. My lunch of choice in the early days was a ham and Jarlsberg cheese sandwich followed by a generous slice of this pound cake. At Grand Central we glaze it with an intensely lemony syrup, and I still like to have a slice after a ham and cheese sandwich.

SERVES 14 TO 16

CAKE

4 cups (1 pound, 4 ounces) all-purpose flour

2 teaspoons salt

1 teaspoon baking soda

1¼ cups (10 ounces, or 2½ sticks) unsalted butter, at room temperature

2½ cups (1 pound, 1.5 ounces) granulated sugar

4 eggs, at room temperature

1¼ cups (10 fluid ounces) buttermilk, at room temperature

¼ cup (2 fluid ounces) freshly squeezed lemon juice

2 tablespoons finely chopped lemon zest

GLAZE

½ cup (3.5 ounces) granulated sugar

¼ cup (2 fluid ounces) freshly squeezed lemon juice

2 tablespoons water

Prepare to bake.

Preheat the oven to 350°F. Grease and lightly flour a 10-inch tube pan.

Combine the dry ingredients.

Measure the flour, salt, and baking soda into a bowl and sift or whisk to combine.

Cream the butter and sugar.

Using a stand mixer with the paddle attachment, beat the butter and sugar on medium-high speed until the mixture is very light in color—almost white—and the texture is fluffy, about 2 to 4 minutes. Scrape the bottom and sides of the bowl a few times during the process to ensure that the butter is evenly incorporated.

Add the eggs.

Crack the eggs into a liquid measuring cup and, with the mixer on low speed, slowly pour in the eggs, letting them fall into the bowl one at a time and incorporating each egg completely before adding the next. Scrape the bottom and sides of the bowl once or twice during the process.

Alternate additions of the dry and wet ingredients.

Measure the buttermilk and lemon juice into the same liquid measuring cup used for the eggs, then stir in the lemon zest. With the mixer on low speed, add one-third of the dry ingredients, then half of the buttermilk mixture, mixing just until combined after each addition. Repeat, using half of the remaining dry ingredients and all of the remaining buttermilk. Add the remaining dry ingredients and stop the mixer before they're fully incorporated. Finish mixing by hand, using a sturdy spatula and being sure to scrape up from the bottom of the bowl.

Bake.

Scrape the batter into the prepared pan and use a spatula to smooth the top of the batter. Run a paring knife through the batter in one smooth motion 1 inch from the edge of the pan; this will help cake rise evenly. Bake for 45 minutes, then rotate the pan, turn down the oven to 325°F, and bake for 30 to 35 minutes more. The cake is ready when it pulls away from the edges of the pan slightly and it springs back when pressed lightly in the center. The top will probably split; use a cake tester to check doneness.

Make the glaze.

Make the glaze while the cake is in the oven. Put the sugar, lemon juice, and water in a small, nonreactive saucepan over medium heat. Stir and bring to a boil. Turn down the heat to low and gently simmer until the glaze thickens and becomes syrupy, about 5 minutes.

Glaze the cake.

Once the cake has cooled for 10 minutes, invert it onto a plate or the bottom of a removable metal part pan and quickly turn it back over, so that the split top is facing up. Use a skewer to poke holes all over the top and in the crack. Pour the glaze over the cake, using the entire amount. It will seem like a lot of liquid, but the warm cake will easily absorb it if you add it slowly and gradually.

Dorothy Piper's Sunshine Sponge Cake

Dorothy Piper, my maternal grandmother, was partial to sponge cake and made this one for years. She lived to be 104, and by the time she shared the recipe with me, she couldn't quite remember where she'd gotten it. I've never seen another recipe like this one. Among other things, it specifies not preheating the oven! For all its quirks and peculiarities, this recipe yields an easy, tasty sponge cake particularly well suited to trifle.

SERVES 12

10 eggs

$2/3$ cup (5.25 fluid ounces) water

$1/2$ cup (3.5 ounces) granulated sugar

1 teaspoon vanilla extract

$1^3/4$ cups plus 2 tablespoons (9.25 ounces) sifted all-purpose flour

1 teaspoon cream of tartar

$1/2$ teaspoon salt

Separate the eggs.

Separate the eggs, being careful not to let any yolk get into the whites. Set the yolks aside and put the whites in a bowl with high sides or the bowl of a stand mixer.

Make the simple syrup.

Combine the water and sugar in a small, heavy saucepan over medium-high heat and bring to a boil, stirring occasionally. Boil for about 7 minutes, or "until the mixture creates small hairs when you move it around the pan." The equivalent of Granny Piper's visual assessment is approximately 234°F, which is soft-ball stage. Turn off the heat and leave the pan on the burner.

Mix the batter.

Using a stand mixer with the whisk attachment, beat the egg whites on medium-high speed until soft peaks form. Slowly pour the hot sugar syrup into the whites and continue beating until the bowl is barely warm to the touch.

Whisk the egg yolks with the vanilla, then add to the egg white mixture. Using a sturdy spatula, fold in the flour, cream of tartar, and salt by hand.

Bake.

Pour the batter into an ungreased tube pan and put it in a cool oven. Turn the oven on at 300°F for 15 minutes, then lower the temperature to 275°F and bake for 45 minutes, until the cake is golden brown and beginning to pull away from the sides of the pan.

Gingerbread

When we were growing up, this richly spiced cake appeared at the table regularly. My mother mixed up the simple batter as she fixed dinner and threw it in the oven to bake while we ate. The aroma wafting from the kitchen was a constant reminder to save room for dessert. Serve gingerbread straight from the baking pan, topped with lightly sweetened freshly whipped cream (see page 137).

SERVES 12

3¾ cups (1 pound, 2.75 ounces) all-purpose flour

½ teaspoon salt

1 teaspoon ground cloves

1 teaspoon ground ginger

¾ teaspoon ground cinnamon

½ teaspoon finely ground black pepper

1¾ cups (12.25 ounces) granulated sugar

1½ cups (12 fluid ounces) vegetable oil or canola oil

1½ cups (1 pound, 2 ounces) molasses

3 eggs, at room temperature

1½ cups (12 fluid ounces) boiling water

2 teaspoons baking soda

3 to 4 tablespoons grated fresh ginger

Prepare to bake.

Preheat the oven to 325°F. Grease and lightly flour a 9 by 13-inch baking pan.

Combine the dry ingredients.

Measure the flour, salt, cloves, ground ginger, cinnamon, and pepper into a bowl and sift or whisk to combine.

Beat the sugar, oil, molasses, and eggs.

Using a stand mixer with the paddle attachment, beat the sugar, oil, molasses, and eggs on medium-high speed until well combined, about 2 to 4 minutes.

Finish the batter.

Add the dry ingredients all at once and mix on low speed just until they're incorporated. Pour the boiling water into a liquid measuring cup and stir in the baking soda. With the mixer on low speed, slowly add the water, being careful not to let it slosh over the sides. Add the fresh ginger and mix briefly—just one turn. Don't be alarmed by how runny the batter is.

Bake.

Pour the batter into the prepared pan and bake for 50 minutes. The cake is ready when it pulls away from the sides of the pan slightly and springs back slowly when pressed in the center.

BIRTHDAY CAKE WORKSHOP

Nothing says happy birthday like a layer cake with thickly swirled frosting and festive candles. Even nonbakers are inspired to drag out the baking books when it's time to celebrate the birthday of a loved one. These special cakes seldom appear in the Grand Central lineup, but I've definitely made my share.

In my experience, people look for cake-baking advice when they want to make a birthday cake. Over the years, I've picked up a handful of simple tricks from the many talented bakers I've worked with in our bakeries. These professional techniques will arm you with the know-how and skills to make a birthday cake that's both delectable and beautiful.

Essential Equipment

For making layer cakes, there are a few pieces of equipment that are essential:

* Two 9- or 10-inch round cake pans
* Long serrated knife
* Long metal spatula
* Cardboard rounds or the metal bottoms of tart pans

A few other pieces of equipment aren't mandatory, but they'll make the job easier, so they're nice to have:

* Offset spatula
* Rotating cake stand or lazy Susan
* Small pastry bag (at least 14 inches)
* Small piping tip for writing (#4 is a nice all-purpose size)

Most people are opinionated and traditional when it comes to choosing a birthday cake, opting for white, yellow, or chocolate cake with chocolate or vanilla frosting. This workshop includes recipes for terrific yellow and chocolate cakes (for white cake, use the Vanilla Bundt Cake batter from page 148), as well as great recipes for vanilla and chocolate frostings. It's up to you and the birthday girl or boy to choose the combination.

Because birthdays are cause for celebration and large gatherings, these birthday cakes feed a crowd. They consist of two 9- or 10-inch cakes that are split, filled, and frosted to make a spectacular four-layer cake. A cake like this can serve as many as 16, depending on everyone's appetite, enthusiasm for cake, and whether it's being served with ice cream. If this is more

(continued)

BOOST CAKE HEIGHT

GUIDE KNIFE WITH RIM OF PAN

cake than you're looking for, freeze half of the batter and make a shorter cake; it's no less festive.

If you're new to cake baking, first read the Cake Mixing Workshop (page 144), as it gives explicit details for mixing and baking a perfect cake. And before you begin the process, make room in your refrigerator or freezer to chill the layers and, eventually, the whole cake.

Level the cake.

The decision to level a cake depends upon the degree of perfection you're set on achieving. A frosted cake doesn't have to appear flawless, but you'll have better luck with the filling and frosting if it's somewhat level. A concave dip in the top of a layer can be made smooth and even with the always-pleasing solution of extra frosting, while a cake that has a lot of oven spring and emerges with a dome probably needs a trim.

The best way to level a cake top is with a serrated knife, and the easiest way to do that is by putting the cake back in the baking pan. Use the rim of the pan

A Turntable Isn't Only for Old Records

Having a rotating cake stand isn't essential, but it makes cake decorating a lot easier. There are several models available, including a standard, heavy cast-iron model used by professionals that rotates smoothly, stands about 5 inches off the counter, and is very expensive. There are also good-quality plastic versions to choose from, at about one-fifth the price. For use at home, I picked up (at a garage sale) a lazy Susan that rotates on ball bearings; these are widely available in kitchenware stores. Or use the bottom of an inverted cake pan, which is everything you need—flat, solid, and balanced— minus the rotation option.

NOTCH EDGE OF CAKE

ROTATE TO MAKE GUIDE

ROTATE AND CUT

as a guide for your knife, resting it gently on the rim while moving it across the top of the cake with a side-to-side sawing motion. If the cake sits too low in the pan, boost it up with a few cardboard rounds or a plate that fits inside the pan underneath the cake.

Split the layers.

There are several different ways to cut a cake into layers. Some of them require special equipment, but my favorite method just requires some self-assurance, a good eye, and a steady hand.

First, make a small notch in the middle of the side of the cake; when you put the layers together again, use the notches to line them up. When it's time to rebuild the cake, it's important to replace the layers in the same order and position as they were before it was split; otherwise you probably won't be able to make the layers perfectly even or level.

Hold the blade of your knife against what you estimate to be the middle of the cake. Slowly turn the cake as you allow the knife to cut a shallow groove all the way around the cake, only cutting $1/2$ to $3/4$ inch into the cake. This groove will serve as a guide for the knife as you cut all the way through the cake. Next, place one palm gently but securely on top of the cake and use the other hand to cut with a firm forward and side-to-side motion, continuing to rotate the cake and cutting in a bit further with each turn. Check occasionally to make sure that the knife is still in the groove. Separate the layers by sliding a cardboard cake round or a removable pan bottom between them.

Make the frosting.

Follow the recipe for Vanilla Buttercream (page 164) or Whipped Chocolate Ganache (page 164). The buttercream can be made ahead of time; just be sure to let it come to room temperature before whipping it for

(continued)

A DAB OF FROSTING

spreading. The whipped ganache, on the other hand, shouldn't be made until you're ready to frost the cake.

Fill the cake.

These classic birthday cakes are filled with the frosting used on the outside of the cake. The filling between the layers should be about $1/4$ inch thick.

Put the bottom cake layer on a cardboard cake round, cut side up. It's helpful to put a small dab of frosting in the center of the cake round first; this will keep the entire cake in place. Put the cake round on a rotating cake stand, lazy Susan, inverted cake pan, or even a flat plate. Begin the filling process by placing a generous dollop of frosting on the bottom layer. Using a long spatula, press firmly and use a back and forth motion to spread the frosting. Try not to lift the spatula, as it will lift the frosting with it, pulling crumbs away from the cake. When the top surface is well covered, use the spatula to evenly distribute the filling by holding it almost flat against the surface, halfway across the cake. Press lightly and rotate the cake a full circle.

Identify the notches you put in the cake before splitting it and focus on lining them up as you transfer the second layer atop the first, cut side down. Slide it onto the frosting, knowing you'll be able to move and adjust it a bit if your initial placement isn't exact. Repeat the process of filling and stacking until the cake is assembled. If the frosting is too warm, it will begin to get messy and your cake layers might slide around. If this happens, chill the cake for 5 minutes in the freezer or 15 to 20 minutes in the refrigerator after adding each layer. This ensures that the frosting sets before the next layer is placed on top.

USE NOTCHES FOR ALIGNMENT

APPLY CRUMB COAT

Crumb coat the cake.

It's discouraging to see cake crumbs showing through the finished frosting. A crumb coat ensures that the final layer goes on smooth and clean. Remove about 1 cup of frosting from the bowl to use as the crumb coasting so you won't have to worry about getting crumbs in the frosting if you double-dip your spatula. Cover the entire cake with a very thin coat of frosting to seal the crumbs to the cake.

After applying the crumb coat, put the cake on a rigid surface, like a removable pan bottom, another cardboard round, or a serving plate. Chill the entire cake in the refrigerator while you clean up the mess.

(continued)

Frost the cake.

Frosting a cake smoothly and evenly takes practice. Remember, perfect isn't the end goal—delicious is. Begin with the sides of the cake. Once the initial layer has been applied, hold the spatula parallel to the sides with the blade angled slightly outward to remove any excess frosting. Don't hesitate to start with large gobs of frosting; the excess is easily removed and will keep the crumbs from coming up. Bring the frosting up about 1/4 inch higher than the top of the cake to make a foundation for the top frosting.

Once the sides are reasonably smooth and evenly covered, place large dollops of frosting on top of the cake. Use a long spatula and a back-and-forth motion to distribute the frosting, much like the one used to fill the layers. Again, try not to lift the spatula, as this might pull away the crust. To finish the top, press the spatula firmly halfway across the cake and with the blade almost flat against it and rotate the cake stand or plate one full circle. Smooth the sides again, removing excess frosting by holding a small spatula parallel to the sides and rotating the cake once.

Write Happy Birthday.

Writing on a cake isn't something I do very often; the prospect of holding a pastry bag filled with melted chocolate over a mostly perfect cake is a frightening one. Rather than messing around making a thin icing and getting the right consistency, I prefer to use white or dark chocolate, depending on the color of the frosting.

I never write directly on the cake, because the pressure to get it right the first time makes my hand shake! Instead, I like to write on a plate, the back of a cake pan, a cookie sheet, or any other flat surface that can be covered with a piece of wax or parchment paper and fit into the refrigerator. Once you get it right and the chocolate has set up, use a small metal offset spatula to lift your chocolate message from the paper to the cake.

For printing, touch the tip to the surface. As you begin to squeeze the bag, raise the tip slightly to keep the lines even and let the chocolate fall away. Stop squeezing just before the end of the line and tug very slightly to straighten it before touching the tip back down to attach the chocolate to the surface. Release the pressure, remove the tip, and start the next line.

For script, the tip should always be touching the surface lightly. Use your whole arm, rather than just moving your hand, for smoother results.

BIRTHDAY CAKES

Yellow Birthday Cake

By now you know that I'm a zealot for a fresh egg with a bright yolk. If they're in short supply, I always save the "good" eggs for poaching and eating with toast at breakfast. But when I have a surplus, I use my best eggs for baking.

Although it seems obvious, not everyone realizes that yellow cake is different than white cake. It's especially fun to make this cake with good eggs since rich yellow yolks can't help but add up to a rich yellow cake. This cake is moist enough that it doesn't need to be brushed with syrup, and the light crumb manages to be sturdy enough for splitting and filling with your frosting of choice.

SERVES 12 GENEROUSLY

4 cups (1 pound, 4 ounces) all-purpose flour

$2^1/_4$ teaspoons salt

$^3/_4$ teaspoon baking soda

$1^1/_2$ cups (12 ounces, or 3 sticks) unsalted butter,
    at room temperature

3 cups (1 pound, 5 ounces) granulated sugar

6 eggs, at room temperature

$1^1/_2$ teaspoons vanilla extract

$1^1/_2$ cups (12 fluid ounces) buttermilk,
    at room temperature

Prepare to bake.

Preheat the oven to 350°F. Grease and lightly flour two 9- or 10-inch round cake pans or line them with parchment paper.

Combine the dry ingredients.

Measure the flour, salt, and baking soda into a bowl and sift or whisk to combine.

Cream the butter and sugar.

Using a stand mixer with the paddle attachment, beat the butter and sugar on medium-high speed until the mixture is very light in color—almost white—and the texture is fluffy, 2 to 4 minutes. Scrape the bottom and sides of the bowl a few times during the process to ensure that the butter is evenly incorporated.

Add the eggs and vanilla.

Crack the eggs into a liquid measuring cup and add the vanilla. With the mixer on low speed, slowly pour in the eggs, letting them fall in one at a time and incorporating each completely before adding the next. Scrape the bottom and sides of the bowl once or twice during the process.

Alternate additions of the dry ingredients and buttermilk.

With the mixer on low speed, add one-third of the dry ingredients, then half of the buttermilk, mixing just until combined after each addition. Repeat, using half of the remaining dry ingredients and all of the remaining buttermilk. Add the remaining dry ingredients and stop the mixer just before they're fully incorporated. Finish mixing by hand, using a sturdy spatula and being sure to scrape up from the bottom of the bowl.

Bake.

Divide the batter evenly between the prepared pans. Run a paring knife through the batter in one smooth circular motion 1 inch from the edge of the pan; this will help the cake rise evenly. Bake for 40 minutes, then rotate the pans and lower the oven temperature to 325°F. Bake for 30 to 35 minutes more. The cakes are ready when they pull away from the edges of the pans slightly and spring back when pressed lightly in the center.

Let the cakes cool for 15 minutes before turning out of the pans, then wait until they're completely cool before splitting, filling, and frosting.

Chocolate Birthday Cake

People seem to overthink chocolate cake. Most of the chocolate cakes I encounter are either too dry, or too rich, like the many flourless, molten chocolate cakes out there. This one is light and chocolaty; the high ratio of brown sugar makes it extra moist.

SERVES 12 GENEROUSLY

4 ounces unsweetened chocolate
   (2/3 cup chips or chunks)
4 ounces semisweet chocolate
   (2/3 cup chips or chunks)
2 1/2 cups (12.5 ounces) all-purpose flour
1 cup (3 ounces) unsweetened cocoa powder
1 tablespoon baking soda
1/2 teaspoon salt
1 cup (8 ounces, or 2 sticks) unsalted butter,
   at room temperature
2 1/4 cups (1 pound) packed light brown sugar
6 eggs, at room temperature
1 tablespoon vanilla extract
2 cups (16 fluid ounces) buttermilk,
   at room temperature

Prepare to bake.

Preheat the oven to 350°F. Grease and lightly flour two 9- or 10-inch round cake pans or line them with parchment paper.

Melt the chocolate.

Melt the unsweetened and semisweet chocolates together in a double boiler or a stainless steel bowl suspended over a pan with 1 inch of lightly simmering water. Set aside to cool slightly.

Combine the dry ingredients.

Sift the flour, cocoa powder, baking soda, and salt into a bowl.

Cream the butter and sugar.

Using a stand mixer with the paddle attachment, beat the butter and sugar on medium-high speed for 3 to 4 minutes, until light and very fluffy. Scrape the bottom and sides of the bowl a few times to evenly incorporate the butter.

Add the eggs, vanilla, and chocolate.

Crack the eggs into a liquid measuring cup and add the vanilla. With the mixer on low speed, slowly pour in the eggs, letting them fall in one at a time and incorporating each completely before adding the next.

Add the melted chocolate all at once and mix on low speed until slightly combined. It isn't important to fully incorporate the chocolate at this point.

Alternate additions of the dry ingredients and buttermilk.

With the mixer on low speed, add one-third of the dry ingredients, then half of the buttermilk, mixing just until combined after each addition. Repeat, using half of the remaining dry ingredients and all of the remaining buttermilk. Add the remaining dry ingredients and stop the mixer before they're fully incorporated. Finish mixing by hand, using a sturdy spatula.

Bake.

Divide the batter evenly between the prepared pans. Run a paring knife through the batter in one smooth motion 1 inch from the edge of the pan; this will help the cake rise evenly. Bake for 30 minutes, then rotate the pan and lower the oven temperature to 325°F. Bake for 30 minutes more. The cakes are ready when they pull away from the edges of the pans slightly and spring back when pressed in the center. Insert a wooden skewer into the middle of the cake to check doneness; it should come out with a few crumbs sticking to it, but no gooey batter.

Let the cakes cool for 15 minutes before turning them out of the pans, then wait until they're completely cool before splitting, filling, and frosting.

Vanilla Buttercream

Incorporating softened butter into an Italian meringue makes this buttercream smooth, airy, and easy to spread. Use it plain or as a base for any number of flavorings, including 1/2 cup of cream of coconut; 4 ounces of bittersweet chocolate, melted and cooled; 1 cup of lemon curd; or 1/2 cup of jam, preserves, or lightly sweetened fruit puree.

MAKES 4 1/2 TO 5 CUPS (MORE THAN ENOUGH TO FILL AND FROST ONE 9- OR 10-INCH LAYER CAKE)

1 cup plus 1 additional egg white (about 9 whites),
    at room temperature
2 cups (14 ounces) granulated sugar
1/2 teaspoon salt
3 cups (1 1/2 pounds, or 6 sticks) unsalted butter,
    at warm room temperature (about 70°F)
1 1/2 teaspoons vanilla extract

Heat the egg whites, sugar, and salt.

Combine the egg whites, sugar, and salt in a bowl that fits snugly over a saucepan with about 1 1/2 inches of simmering water; the bowl shouldn't be resting on or touching the water. Use a heatproof rubber spatula to stir the mixture gently until it becomes opaque, with lots of little bubbles. This should take about 8 to 10 minutes; the temperature will be approximately 160°F. It will smell slightly of cooked eggs.

Beat and cool the egg white mixture.

Remove the bowl from the heat and, using a stand mixer with the paddle attachment, beat on high speed for about 7 minutes, until the bowl is no longer hot to the touch and the mixture is glossy, white, and holds medium-firm peaks.

Finish the frosting.

Add the softened butter, 1 tablespoon at a time, mixing briefly between additions. When the butter is incorporated, add the vanilla and any additional flavor-

ings you'd like. If the frosting does not look creamy, keep mixing it. The buttercream will eventually come together.

Whipped Chocolate Ganache

Classic ganache is made with equal parts heavy cream and chocolate, which is slightly too stiff a consistency for making a fluffy whipped version that spreads nicely on a cake. The small amount of additional cream in this recipe makes it more spreadable than a typical ganache. Besides the extra cream, the only difference between this ganache and the one poured over the Ganache-Glazed Chocolate Bundt Cake (page 148) is that this one manages to be rich and airy at the same time because is beaten. This is a quick and easy solution for frosting a cake when you don't have time to make a buttercream frosting.

MAKES 4 1/2 CUPS (ENOUGH TO FILL AND FROST ONE 9-INCH LAYER CAKE)

1 pound (2 2/3 cups) coarsely chopped
    bittersweet chocolate
2 1/4 cups (18 fluid ounces) heavy cream
1/2 teaspoon vanilla extract

Make the ganache.

Put the chocolate in a shallow bowl. Bring the cream to a boil, then immediately pour it over the chocolate. Let the chocolate sit for a few minutes, then stir gently. The ganache should be glossy and have a smooth texture. If any chunks of chocolate remain, place the bowl over simmering water briefly and stir until melted.

Whip the ganache.

Using a stand mixer with the whisk attachment, whip the ganache on medium-high speed until thickened, with a spreadable consistency, between 7 and 12 minutes. Use the ganache right away.

LAYER CAKES

When I have a little extra time or have been charged with providing dessert for a special occasion, I make one of these classic American layer cakes. Each has a specified filing and frosting, but all three can be assembled as outlined in the Birthday Cake Workshop on page 155.

Coconut Layer Cake with Coconut Buttercream

This tender yellow cake is packed with coconut, split and layered with pastry cream, and frosted with a cream of coconut–spiked buttercream. Delicious at any time of year, it's an Easter tradition at the bakery and in my family. It involves a few more steps than the simple cakes, but it's worth the extra effort. Follow the assembly instructions in the Birthday Cake Workshop, substituting the pastry cream for buttercream between layers.

Since I usually bake it for an Easter dinner crowd, this recipe makes a large cake. Cut it in half (or freeze half of the batter for another time) and use a single tall-sided 8-inch cake pan for a smaller cake.

SERVES 16

CAKE

1 cup (3 ounces) unsweetened coconut flakes

4 cups (1 pound, 4 ounces) all-purpose flour

2 teaspoons baking powder

2 teaspoons salt

2 cups (1 pound, or 4 sticks) unsalted butter, at room temperature

2 cups (14 ounces) granulated sugar

6 eggs, at room temperature

2 teaspoons vanilla extract

2 cups (16 fluid ounces) whole milk, at room temperature

2 cups (6 ounces) sweetened flake coconut

2 cups (8 ounces) unsweetened macaroon-cut coconut

PASTRY CREAM

1¼ cups (10 fluid ounces) half-and-half

½ cup (3.5 ounces) granulated sugar

3 egg yolks

2 tablespoons cornstarch

2 teaspoons vanilla extract

COCONUT BUTTERCREAM

½ cup egg whites (about 4 egg whites), at room temperature

1 cup (7 ounces) granulated sugar

¼ teaspoon salt

1½ cups (12 ounces, or 3 sticks) unsalted butter, at warm room temperature (about 70°F)

½ cup (4 fluid ounces) cream of coconut

1 teaspoon vanilla extract

Prepare to bake.

Preheat the oven to 350°F. Grease and lightly flour two 9- or 10-inch round cake pans and line the bottom of each with a parchment circle. (Use one of the cake pans to trace and cut two parchment paper circles.)

Toast the unsweetened coconut flakes.

Line a sheet pan with parchment paper, then spread the unsweetened coconut flakes on it in an even layer. Toast until the coconut has a nutty aroma and some of the edges are dark, about 15 minutes.

Combine the dry ingredients.

Measure the flour, baking powder, and salt into a bowl and sift or whisk to combine.

(continued)

Cream the butter and sugar.

Using a stand mixer with the paddle attachment, beat the butter and sugar on medium-high speed until the mixture is very light in color—nearly white—and fluffy, about 2 to 4 minutes. Scrape the bottom and sides of the bowl to evenly incorporate the butter.

Add the eggs and vanilla.

Crack the eggs into a liquid measuring cup and add the vanilla. With the mixer on low speed, slowly pour in the eggs, letting them fall in one at a time and incorporating each completely before adding the next. Scrape the bottom and sides of the bowl once or twice.

Alternate additions of the dry and wet ingredients.

Measure the milk into the same liquid measuring cup used for the eggs and vanilla. With the mixer on low speed, add one-third of the dry ingredients, then half of the milk, mixing just until combined after each addition. Repeat, using half of the remaining dry ingredients and all of the remaining milk. Add the remaining dry ingredients and stop mixing when incorporated.

Finish the batter.

Fold in the sweetened flake and macaroon-cut coconuts by hand, using a sturdy spatula and taking care to mix only minimally.

Bake.

Divide the batter between the prepared pans. Bake for about 40 minutes. The cakes are ready when the edges pull away from the pans and a wooden skewer inserted in the center comes out clean. Let the cakes cool for 10 minutes before inverting onto cardboard cake circles or the bottoms of tart pans.

Make the custard for the pastry cream.

In a heavy, nonreactive saucepan over medium-high heat, bring the half-and-half to a simmer. Whisk the sugar, yolks, and cornstarch together in a bowl, then gradually add the hot half-and-half, a few ounces at a time. Pour the mixture back into the saucepan.

Finish the pastry cream and chill.

Cook the mixture over medium heat, stirring constantly, until it comes to a simmer and begins to thicken, about 5 minutes. When it is ready, the pastry cream will coat the back of a wooden spoon. Pour into a clean bowl, then stir in the vanilla. Cover with plastic wrap, placing it directly on the surface so the pastry cream doesn't form a skin. Chill for 4 hours.

Heat the egg whites, sugar, and salt for the buttercream.

Combine the egg whites, sugar, and salt in a bowl that fits snugly over a saucepan with about $1^1/_2$ inches of simmering water; the bowl shouldn't be resting on or touching the water. Whisk the mixture until it begins to thicken and becomes opaque, with lots of little bubbles. This should take 5 to 7 minutes; the temperature will be approximately 160°F.

Beat and cool the egg white mixture.

Remove the bowl from the heat and, using a stand mixer with the paddle attachment, beat on high speed for about 7 minutes, until the bowl is no longer hot to the touch and the mixture is glossy, white, and holds medium-size peaks.

Finish the frosting.

Add the softened butter, 1 tablespoon at a time, mixing briefly between additions. When the butter is incorporated, add the cream of coconut and vanilla. If the frosting does not look creamy, keep mixing it. The buttercream will eventually come together.

Fill and frost the cake.

Split the cakes and divide the frosting between the layers and top. (See the Birthday Cake Workshop, page 155, for instructions.)

Carrot Cake

Our version of perennially popular carrot cake is chock-full of ingredients and finished with tangy cream cheese frosting. I like to bake it in the middle of winter, when my enthusiasm for apples and pears is waning and the next seasonal fruits are still in the distant future.

A 6-inch round cake pan is somewhat unusual, and you may not have one in your collection—yet. Consider adding one; it makes a terrific small layer cake. Layer cakes are always more fun, and this size is just right for 6 to 8 people. Double this recipe for a full-size cake with fewer layers.

SERVES 6 TO 8

CAKE

1¹⁄₂ cups (7.5 ounces) all-purpose flour

¹⁄₂ cup (2.5 ounces) whole wheat flour

³⁄₄ teaspoon baking soda

¹⁄₂ teaspoon salt

1¹⁄₂ teaspoons ground cinnamon

¹⁄₂ teaspoon ground nutmeg

1¹⁄₂ cups (10.5 ounces) granulated sugar

³⁄₄ cup (6 fluid ounces) vegetable oil or canola oil

2 eggs, at room temperature

³⁄₄ teaspoon vanilla extract

2¹⁄₄ cups grated carrots (about 4 carrots)

¹⁄₂ cup (1.5 ounces) sweetened flake coconut

¹⁄₂ cup (2 ounces) macaroon-cut coconut

6 ounces fresh or canned pineapple, drained and coarsely chopped

³⁄₄ cup (3 ounces) walnuts, lightly toasted and coarsely chopped (see page 20)

FROSTING

5 ounces cream cheese, at room temperature

3 tablespoons unsalted butter, at room temperature

1¹⁄₂ cups (6 ounces) confectioners' sugar

Prepare to bake.

Preheat the oven to 350°F. Grease and lightly flour two 6-inch round cake pans and line them with rounds of parchment paper.

Combine the dry ingredients.

Measure the all-purpose flour, whole wheat flour, baking soda, salt, cinnamon, and nutmeg into a bowl and whisk to combine.

Mix the sugar and oil.

Using a stand mixer with the paddle attachment, combine the sugar and oil on medium speed until well blended and slightly lighter in color, about 4 minutes. The mixture will have a sandy texture and won't appear particularly smooth.

Add the eggs and vanilla.

Crack the eggs into a liquid measuring cup and add the vanilla. With the mixer on low speed, slowly pour in the eggs, letting them fall in one at a time and incorporating each egg completely before adding the next. Scrape the bottom and sides of the bowl once or twice during the process.

Finish the batter.

With the mixer on low speed, add the dry ingredients slowly and mix just until incorporated. Fold in the carrots, both kinds of coconut, and the pineapple and walnuts by hand using a sturdy spatula.

Bake.

Divide the batter between the pans. Bake for about 45 minutes, rotating the pans halfway through the baking time. The cakes are ready when they pull away from the edges of the pans slightly and spring back when pressed lightly in the center. Let the cakes cool for 10 to 15 minutes before removing them from the pans, then wait until they're completely cool before splitting the layers, filling, and frosting.

(continued)

Make the frosting.

Using a stand mixer with the paddle attachment, beat the cream cheese and butter on medium speed until smooth and well combined, with no visible lumps, about 3 to 5 minutes. Add the confectioners' sugar and mix on low speed until well incorporated, smooth, and spreadable, about 2 minutes.

Fill and frost the cake.

Split the cakes and divide the frosting between the layers and top. (See the Birthday Cake Workshop, page 155, for instructions.)

Old-Fashioned Spice Cake

The funny truth about me and spice cake is that I used to think it came from a box. It was one of only a few mixes in my mother's larder. This recipe for a homemade version duplicates the familiar spice mixture and is enhanced by a sweet apple compote and a rich cream cheese frosting. This recipe makes a 6 inch by 4-inch layer cake, but if you don't have 6-inch pans, put the batter in a 10 inch pan and make a slightly shorter cake. You can still split and fill it, or just frost the top and sides.

SERVES 6 TO 8

CAKE

1$\frac{1}{2}$ cups (7.5 ounces) all-purpose flour

$\frac{3}{4}$ teaspoon baking powder

$\frac{3}{8}$ teaspoon baking soda

$\frac{1}{4}$ teaspoon salt

1$\frac{1}{2}$ teaspoons ground cinnamon

1 teaspoon ground cardamom

$\frac{1}{4}$ teaspoon ground ginger

9 tablespoons (4.5 ounces, or 1$\frac{1}{8}$ sticks) unsalted butter, at room temperature

1$\frac{1}{4}$ cups (8.75 ounces) packed light brown sugar

2 eggs, at room temperature

$\frac{3}{4}$ teaspoon vanilla extract

1 cup (8.5 ounces) sour cream, at room temperature

COMPOTE

1$\frac{1}{2}$ pounds apples (about 3 large apples)

2 tablespoons freshly squeezed lemon juice

$\frac{1}{4}$ cup (2 ounces, or $\frac{1}{2}$ stick) unsalted butter

$\frac{1}{4}$ cup (1.75 ounces) granulated sugar

$\frac{1}{4}$ cup (2 fluid ounces) Calvados or apple cider

FROSTING

5 ounces cream cheese, at room temperature

3 tablespoons unsalted butter, at room temperature

1$\frac{1}{2}$ cups (6 ounces) confectioners' sugar

2 tablespoons maple syrup

Prepare to bake.

Preheat the oven to 350°F. Grease and lightly flour two 6-inch round cake pans and line them with rounds of parchment paper.

Combine the dry ingredients.

Measure the flour, baking powder, baking soda, salt, cinnamon, cardamom, and ginger into a bowl and whisk to combine.

Cream the butter and sugar.

Using a stand mixer with the paddle attachment, beat the butter and sugar on medium-high speed until well combined, about 4 minutes. The butter won't lighten in color or texture significantly, and the appearance will be sandy due to the high ratio of sugar to butter. Scrape the bottom and sides of the bowl a few times during the process to ensure that the butter is evenly incorporated.

Add the eggs and vanilla.

Crack the eggs into a liquid measuring cup and add the vanilla. With the mixer on low speed, slowly pour in the eggs, letting them fall in one at a time and incorporating each egg completely before adding the next. Scrape the bottom and sides of the bowl once or twice during the process.

Alternate additions of the dry ingredients and the sour cream.

With the mixer on low speed, add one-third of the dry ingredients, then half of the sour cream, mixing just until combined after each addition. Repeat with half of the remaining dry ingredients and all of the remaining sour cream. Add the remaining dry ingredients and stop the mixer just before the flour is fully incorporated. Finish mixing by hand using a sturdy spatula and being sure to scrape up from the bottom of the bowl.

Bake.

Divide the batter between the prepared pans. Run a paring knife through the batter once in a single, smooth motion 1 inch from the edge of the pan; this helps the cake rise evenly. Bake for about 40 minutes, rotating the pans halfway through the baking time. The cakes are ready when they pull away from the edges of the pans slightly and spring back when pressed in the center. Let the cakes cool for 15 to 20 minutes before turning out of the pans, then wait until they're completely cool before splitting the layers, filling, and frosting.

Make the compote.

Peel, core, and halve the apples, then slice them about $1/4$ inch thick and toss the slices with the lemon juice. Melt the butter in a large, heavy sauté pan or skillet over medium-high heat until bubbly, then add the apples and sauté, tossing occasionally, until tender, for 5 to 8 minutes. Sprinkle with the sugar and stir gently with a wooden spoon. Lower the heat to medium and continue cooking, stirring occasionally, until the butter and sugar have reduced to a thick syrup. The apples should be transparent and completely caramelized yet firm to the touch. Remove from the heat and add the Calvados. Return to the heat and cook for 3 to 5 minutes to let the alcohol burn off (or let the cider reduce if using cider). The syrup should be thick and substantially reduced. Let the compote cool before filling the cake.

Make the frosting.

Using a stand mixer with the paddle attachment, beat the cream cheese and butter on medium speed until smooth and well combined, without any visible lumps, 3 to 5 minutes. Add the confectioners' sugar and mix on low speed until well incorporated, about 2 minutes. With the mixer on low speed, add the maple syrup and mix just until smooth and spreadable.

Fill and frost the cake.

Split the cakes and divide the frosting between the layers and top. (See the Birthday Cake Workshop, page 155, for instructions.)

7

Time for Pie

Anyone who has tried knows that baking a pie is certainly not "as easy as pie." However, with professional guidance and a bit of practice, anyone can master this hallmark of an accomplished home baker. This chapter includes holiday classics like pumpkin pie and pecan pie, as well as thorough and encouraging instructions for how to make pies from fresh fruits in season.

If you're new to pie baking, go straight to the Flaky Pastry Workshop (page 174) for detailed information about how to make a delicate, flaky, all-butter crust for your pie. Or, if you're just a little nervous about the process, read the tips on rolling, filling, and forming a pie (page 175). The recipes in this chapter each yield one 9- or 10-inch pie. I find heavy enameled and Pyrex pie pans oddly appealing; I must have four or five and am tempted to buy another when I see one at a garage sale. But they don't make the best pie crust. Use the cheaper lightweight variety for the flakiest crust; it allows the heat to transfer quickly. If you have a metal pie pan, I recommend using that rather than Pyrex. (The metal transfers heat more quickly than glass, creating a crisp, delicate crust.)

FLAKY PASTRY WORKSHOP 172

All-Butter Flaky Pie Dough 173

Rough Puff Pastry 176

Double-Crust Pies 182

Rhubarb Pie 183

Strawberry Rhubarb Pie 183

Marionberry Pie 184

Blueberry Pie 184

Raspberry Pie 185

Gooseberry Pie 185

Peach Pie 186

Apple Pie 186

Cherry Pie................................... 187

Single-Crust Pies 188

Fresh Strawberry Pie 188

Lemon Meringue Pie 189

Holiday Pies 190

Apple Brandy Mince Pie 191

Pumpkin Pie 192

Bourbon Pecan Pie 192

Tarte Tatin 194

FLAKY PASTRY WORKSHOP

Pie dough and puff pastry are two frequently used building blocks in a baker's repertoire. Although I use them in different applications, they share a certain number of characteristics, the first of which is the same good ingredients. The differences between the two are more a matter of the proportions of ingredients and the techniques used.

Ingredients

The ingredients for flaky pastry doughs are simple and straightforward: flour, sugar, salt, butter, water, and lemon juice. But because there are so few, it's important to choose and prepare them carefully.

FLOUR

The main difference between the various all-purpose flours you find in the grocery store is the amount of gluten each contains. Gluten is the protein that creates strength and chewiness in baked goods. Normally those adjectives are reserved to describe bread, so it's logical that bread flour has the highest percentage of gluten, while cake and pastry flour have the lowest percentage.

I know great bakers who insist on making pie dough with pastry flour. Since the technique used to make pie dough removes any possibility of developing gluten, I don't find it necessary to use low-gluten flour. For simplicity's sake, I recommend unbleached all-purpose flour for making pie dough at home.

Unbleached all-purpose flour is also my favorite for making puff pastry. It has more gluten-forming proteins than bleached flour or cake flour, enabling it to provide extra support for the fragile layers of butter and dough. Although gluten plays an important role in making good puff pastry, stay away from high-protein flour formulated specifically for bread; it will make your pastry tough.

SUGAR

Sugar, even in small amounts, gives pastry a barely recognizable hint of sweetness and the ability to caramelize, turning it a tempting shade of golden brown.

SALT

Salt is critical for flavor in any recipe. Without it, your pastry will be bland. If you use salted butter, use only half the amount of salt called for in the recipe.

BUTTER (SHORTENING)

The definition of shortening describes the all-important role fat plays in pie crust, puff pastry, and short doughs: minimizing the development of gluten strands (shortening them, in essence) when moisture is added to flour. Pie dough requires shortening, and for me, butter is the only choice. It imparts the best flavor and gives pastry a superior mouthfeel.

Butter is the most important ingredient in puff pastry; it plays an essential role in both the flavor and the texture of the finished product. I use European-style butters (Plugrá, Challenge, and Straus Family Creamery are a few that are available nationally) because they're enriched by a culture much like cheese, giving them a more dynamic flavor. Their high butterfat ratio and lower moisture content make European-style butters pliable and easy to handle, good qualities for success in making puff pastry.

Although I highly recommend using unsalted European-style butter, I have made perfectly delicious puff pastry from salted table butter when that's what was in the refrigerator.

WATER

Water provides hydration and keeps the dough together. Start with ice water, and keep it cold. It isn't necessary to used bottled or filtered water unless the mineral content of your tap water is particularly high.

LEMON JUICE

Lemon juice serves two purposes: It keeps the dough from oxidizing and turning a dull color, and it relaxes the gluten strands, which prevents the dough from becoming tough or elastic, allowing you to roll it without the dough bouncing back.

(continued)

All-Butter Flaky Pie Dough

I grew up in a household where pie dough was made with half butter, half margarine. My mother believed that including some vegetable shortening was the ticket to a flaky crust. As her daughter, I readily adopted and held that belief until I met Julie Richardson.

Julie runs a wonderful Portland bakery called Baker and Spice and is one of a handful of incredibly accomplished bakers with whom I've had the good fortune to work. When she moved to Portland in the early days of Grand Central, Julie and I worked together at the bakery, in production. During that time, she schooled me in the merits of all-butter pie dough, and since then I've never looked back. Use

this technique and I think you'll agree: the flavor, texture, and mouthfeel of a crust made with butter as the only shortening is unparalleled.

The following instructions might appear exhausting; don't worry, they're merely exhaustive. A practiced pie baker working quickly and decisively can make tender pie dough in minutes. After you've made a few batches of dough, the principles at work will become evident and you'll feel comfortable and confident taking shortcuts. If you're learning to make dough, follow the step-by-step instructions and allow time to chill your dough at every appropriate point. The more you make pastry dough, the better you'll get.

YIELD	One 10- to 12-ounce disk	Two 10- to 12-ounce disks	Three 10- to 12-ounce disks	Four 10- to 12-ounce disks
ALL-PURPOSE FLOUR	1$^1/_4$ cups (6.25 ounces)	2 $^1/_2$ cups (12.5 ounces)	3$^3/_4$ cups (1 pound, 2.75 ounces)	5 cups (1 pound, 9 ounces)
GRANULATED SUGAR	1 tablespoon	2 tablespoons	3 tablespoons	4 tablespoons
SALT	1 teaspoon	2 teaspoons	1 tablespoon	1 tablespoon plus 1 teaspoon
BUTTER	$^1/_2$ cup (4 ounces, or 1 stick)	1 cup (8 ounces, or 2 sticks)	1$^1/_2$ cups (12 ounces, or 3 sticks)	2 cups (1 pound, or 4 sticks)
WATER	3 tablespoons	$^1/_3$ cup (2.75 fluid ounces)	$^1/_2$ cup (4 fluid ounces)	$^2/_3$ cup (5.25 fluid ounces)
LEMON JUICE	1$^1/_2$ teaspoons	1 tablespoon	1 $^1/_2$ tablespoons	2 tablespoons

Technique

A perfect crust is tender and flaky, yet sturdy enough to be rolled and shaped into a pie. Think of the butter and flour as building blocks for flakiness. It probably isn't the best metaphor for pastry, but I like to visualize concrete and aggregate. Flour and water are the cement, and the butter pebbles are the aggregate. You're trying to create dough in which the hydrated flour and the butter exist together in the same mass without being homogenized.

The most important tip for success when making pie dough is to keep the ingredients cold. Make a little bit of room in your refrigerator or freezer before you get started. Warm, greasy butter is the enemy of tender crust; if it melts into the flour, you'll get a tough, crispy crust that's more like a cracker. The ingredients should be cold during every state of mixing. If you're a novice, chill everything to begin with, and don't hesitate to put your dough in the refrigerator at any point if it begins to warm up.

Prepare the ingredients.

Measure the flour, sugar, and salt into a bowl and refrigerate for at least 2 hours or up to overnight.

Dice the cold butter into $1/2$-inch cubes and toss them with the flour. Fill a drinking glass with ice and cold water. Put the lemon juice into a liquid measuring cup, then add the specified amount of cold water to the lemon juice right before pouring it into the pie dough. Be careful not to add any of the ice.

Cut in the butter.

Pie dough can be mixed by hand or with a stand mixer. I prefer to use my hands if I'm making a small quantity; it's just as fast and there's less cleanup. When I'm making several pies or a big batch of dough for my freezer, I pull out my KitchenAid.

By hand: When mixing pie dough by hand, you must move quickly so that the heat from your hands doesn't warm up the butter. Use your fingertips, and thumbs to rub the butter together with the chilled dry ingredients. Press the cubes of butter into flat chips with each movement. The butter should be cold enough that you're coating the butter pieces with the flour. Stop mixing when the texture of the flour changes from silky to mealy.

With a stand mixer: Use a stand mixer with the paddle attachment on the lowest speed to cut the butter into the flour. After 1 to 2 minutes, the silky texture of the flour will become mealy. Chunks and chips of flattened butter ranging from the size of lentils to the size of lima beans will remain. If the mixture doesn't feel cool to the touch, chill it before proceeding.

Hydrate the dough.

As with using butter that's too warm, adding too much water will result in overworked, tough dough; a small amount of water is all that's necessary to encourage the dough to come together. Because flour and butter both contain varying degrees of moisture, the amount of water it takes to bring pie dough together also varies. I recommend holding back about one-fourth of the total amount of the cold water mixed with lemon juice to use at the very end of mixing if needed.

By hand: Use a fork to make a well in the flour mixture. Drizzle in three-fourths of the cold water mixed with lemon juice while gradually pulling the dry ingredients into the middle with the fork and mixing gently. Check the hydration of the dough by gathering a small fistful; if it holds together, it's ready. If it's dry or crumbly, mix a little longer before adding more water, 1 tablespoon at a time, aiming for dry patches.

With a stand mixer: With the mixer running at the lowest speed, drizzle in three-fourths of the cold water mixed with lemon juice. Check the hydration of the dough by gathering a small fistful; if it holds together, it's ready. If it's dry or crumbly, mix a little bit longer (2 or 3 rotations) before adding more water, 1 tablespoon at a time, aiming for the dry patches.

Form the disks.

When the dough has the proper amount of water, it will come together with minimal effort and no deliberate packing. Form the dough into 10- to 12-ounce disks, gathering and pressing with the palms of your hands and keeping in mind that you're building horizontal layers for flakiness. My favorite way to do this is on a piece of plastic. Then I use the wrap to pull the dough in tight and contain any dry, floury patches, which will hydrate further by continuing to absorb the liquid as the dough rests in the refrigerator.

Chill the dough.

It's important to wrap the dough tightly and chill it at this point, before attempting to roll it out. Time in the refrigerator ensures that the butter doesn't warm up and also allows the dough to relax. Beginners should let the dough chill for at least 1 to 2 hours, or it can sit in the refrigerator for several days before you use it. More experienced pie bakers will know when to hurry things along. Always return the dough to the refrigerator to rest and chill if you're having trouble rolling it.

Roll out the dough.

In order to make a pie, you'll need to take a disk of dough and transform it into a flat circular sheet. It sounds simple enough, but rolling dough is a skill that takes time to develop; mastery and perfection only come with practice. Each time you roll dough, it gets easier. Work quickly and deliberately, so that the dough doesn't have time to soften. If it becomes too soft or sticky, or if you find yourself getting frustrated and needing a break, slip the dough onto a baking sheet, cover it, and refrigerate or freeze it until firm.

When rolling pie dough, begin by lightly flouring a smooth, solid work surface. Roll directly on your countertop or, if it's tiled or has an irregular surface like slate, use a large wooden cutting board or a slab of marble or smooth stone.

Unwrap the chilled dough and, with the rolling pin in the middle of the disk, press down and out using firm, steady pressure as you begin to roll. Give the disk a quarter turn and roll out again, always starting from the middle. Turn the dough frequently, adding a light dusting of flour to the surface or to the rolling pin if the dough begins to stick. Continue rotating and rolling, adding flour as necessary, until the diameter is at least 1 inch greater than the top of the pie pan you're planning to line with it. The dough should be about $1/8$ inch thick.

Form the pie.

After rolling the bottom crust, fold it in half to transfer it to the pie pan. Place the fold in the center of the pan and, without stretching the dough, pull the top layer of dough across to cover the other side of the pan. Ease it in, pressing gently against the sides and into the edges. Fill the shell and refrigerate. Repeat the roll-out for the top crust.

(continued)

Rough Puff Pastry

Having a stash of puff pastry in my freezer makes me feel secure. This miraculous marriage of butter and flour is the key to a quick, flaky tarte Tatin, a batch of berry turnovers, or the perfect chicken potpie crust, no matter how limited my time may be.

Some of the cooks I respect most tell me that ready-made puff pastry is one ingredient they will buy. They scoff at the notion that puff pastry can be *made easily in a home kitchen. The solution is rough puff pastry, which refers to a technique for making lovely puff pastry without the time, special equipment, or precision required for classic puff pastry. The simple formula and straightforward technique in this workshop are proof that making puff pastry at home doesn't have to be complicated or time-consuming.*

YIELD	About 1 pound	About 2 pounds	About 3 pounds
ALL-PURPOSE FLOUR	1 1/2 cups (7.5 ounces)	3 cups (15 ounces)	4 1/2 cups (1 pound, 6.5 ounces)
GRANULATED SUGAR	1 tablespoon	2 tablespoons	3 tablespoons
SALT	1 teaspoon	2 teaspoons	1 tablespoon
BUTTER	3/4 cup (6 ounces, or 1 1/2 sticks)	1 1/2 cups (12 ounces, or 3 sticks)	2 1/4 cups (1 pound, 2 ounces, or 4 1/2 sticks)
WATER	1/2 cup (4 fluid ounces)	3/4 cup (6 fluid ounces)	1 cup (8 fluid ounces)
LEMON JUICE	1 1/2 teaspoons	1 tablespoon	1 1/2 tablespoons

Technique

Puff pastry owes its dramatic appearance and flaky texture to lamination. For a better understanding of the process, it's helpful to compare the structure of laminated dough to a cross section of plywood: Microscopic layers of dough and butter are stacked up repeatedly, one on the other, without mingling. As the dough bakes, the butter releases steam, which is trapped by the layers of dough, causing the pastry to puff. In the case of rough puff, this structure is achieved by cutting large chunks of butter into the dry ingredients, where they are distributed randomly, and then folding the dough repeatedly.

Prepare the ingredients.

Measure the flour, sugar, and salt into the bowl you'll use for mixing and refrigerate for at least 2 hours or up to overnight.

Cut the butter into 1-inch chunks. Fill a drinking glass with ice and cold water. Put the lemon juice into a liquid measuring cup, then add the specified amount of cold water to the lemon juice right before pouring it into the pie dough. Be careful not to add any of the ice.

Cut in the butter.

Perfectly mixed rough puff pastry dough is, by nature, a bit of a mess. There will be irregular chunks of butter and floury dry patches no matter which method you choose. Don't lose faith; the end result is always stunning.

Rough puff dough can be mixed by hand or with a stand mixer. I prefer to use my hands if I'm making a small quantity; it's just as fast and there's less cleanup. When I want to stock up, I pull out my KitchenAid to mix a large batch.

By hand: Working quickly, use your fingertips and thumbs to rub the butter pieces with the chilled dry ingredients. Stop mixing when the texture of the flour begins to change from silky to mealy. There should still be chunks of flattened butter ranging from the size of a nickel to the size of a quarter.

With a stand mixer: Using a stand mixer with the paddle attachment on medium-low speed, add the butter all at once and mix for 1 minute. The texture of the flour will go from silky to shaggy, and the dough will still contain some larger chunks of butter. You're likely to find unincorporated flour at the bottom of the bowl and dry patches throughout.

Hydrate the dough.

As with using butter that's too warm, adding too much water will result in overworked, tough dough; a small amount of water is all that's necessary to encourage the dough to come together. Because flour and butter both contain varying degrees of moisture, the amount of water it takes to bring rough puff pastry dough together also varies. I recommend holding back about one-fourth of the total amount of the cold water mixed with lemon juice to use at the very end of mixing if needed.

By hand: Use a fork to make a well in the flour mixture. Drizzle in three-fourths of the ice water and lemon juice while gradually pulling the dry ingredients into the middle with a fork and mixing gently. Check the hydration of the dough by gathering a small fistful; if it holds together, it's ready. If it's dry or crumbly, mix a little longer before adding more water, 1 tablespoon at a time, testing the dough after each addition by pinching it.

With a stand mixer: With the mixer running at the lowest speed, drizzle in three-fourths of the cold water mixed with lemon juice. Check the hydration of the dough by gathering a small fistful; if it holds together, it's ready. If it's dry or crumbly, mix a little longer (2 or 3 rotations) before adding more water, 1 tablespoon at a time, testing the dough after each addition by pinching it.

(continued)

Form and chill the dough.

Bringing the dough together into a rough but cohesive mass is the first step in developing the horizontal structure of puff pastry.

Pull out a length of plastic wrap, leaving it attached to the roll. Begin building layers by loosely arranging handfuls of dough on top of one another. Use the heel of your hand or a bench knife to pat and guide the dough into the center of the piece of plastic wrap. Gradually form the dough into a 1-inch-thick rectangle using the heel of your hand. (Poking and prodding the dough with your fingers or a utensil interrupts the development of the layers.) The thickness of the rectangle is what matters here, not its dimensions.

When you have a rough rectangle of dough, fold the bottom flap of the plastic wrap up around it, then fold the two sides into the center, tugging firmly on the ends and pulling to coax the dough to hold its shape. Tear the plastic wrap and wrap it tightly around the dough, using the heel of your hand to lightly pack the dough as you do so. Chill for at least 2 hours.

Add the folds.

The microscopic layers of butter and dough in puff pastry are created by rolling the rectangle of dough and folding it like a letter, also known as giving it turns. The effects of this process are twofold: It builds additional layers by stacking the flattened dough back onto itself, and it develops the gluten, which creates

elasticity in the dough. The resulting miniature gluten bubbles trap the steam from the melting butter. The frequency of bubbles determines the height and flakiness of puff pastry.

To begin the process, lightly flour a work surface. Arrange the rectangle so that the short ends are at the top and bottom of the work surface. Roll the dough out to three times its original length; it will be about $1/4$ inch thick. Always roll the pastry into a square or rectangular shape, and roll in only one direction. The dough may be difficult to work with or fall apart as you make the first fold. Use a dough scraper and your hands to redistribute the dough, pat the pieces together, and keep the rectangle true. Take the bottom edge of the dough and fold it two-thirds of the way up the rectangle. Bring the top edge down to meet the new bottom edge, like a business letter. Wrap or cover the dough and refrigerate it for 20 minutes after the first turn.

or shape it, and stack it with pieces of parchment paper between the layers. Save the scraps, fitting them together, stacking, and rolling out again to achieve a 1-inch thickness. (Wrap or cover this pieced-together dough and allow it to rest in the refrigerator for 20 minutes before rolling it out.)

Alternatively, you can roll the whole sheet out, cover it with parchment, roll it up, and freeze it, dividing large batches into two or more pieces.

Puff pastry can be frozen for up to a year in a freezer that stays close to 0°F. Double wrap the dough in plastic or store it in a resealable bag. Once it's defrosted, the dough shouldn't sit in the refrigerator for more than 2 days, or its ability to puff will be slightly diminished. Put it back in the freezer as soon as possible if you can't use it. The dough can be refrozen twice after its initial freezing.

(continued)

Take the dough out of the refrigerator and arrange it so that the seam is on the right, and the short ends are at the top and bottom. Repeat the process of rolling, folding, and refrigerating two more times for a total of three folding processes. As you further develop the gluten in the dough, it will want to shrink or spring back when it's rolled. It is crucial to let the dough rest after each fold. If it becomes elastic or difficult to roll out in the middle of a fold, let it relax in the refrigerator for 15 minutes.

Feel free to interrupt the process of adding folds at any point, as long as you pick up where you left off within the next 24 hours or so. If you wait longer, the dough may begin to oxidize slightly. The flavor shouldn't be affected if it's well wrapped.

Finishing and storing the dough.

After it has all of its folds, roll the dough out to the desired finished thickness on parchment paper. Cut

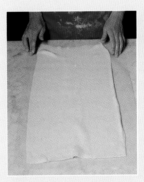 

Freezing an Unbaked Pie

We sell over one thousand pies the day before Thanksgiving alone. Customers often ask, "Did you make all of those today?" The answer is yes, and no. All one thousand-plus pies were baked that day, but they were assembled and frozen whole at some point in the preceding weeks. This is a great trick to use at home, too.

With a frozen pie, the crust starts to bake before the fruit begins to defrost, and the pie takes longer to bake, which means the bottom crust browns nicely and gets crispy. When you have a bit of extra time, or when you're already planning to make a pie anyway, gather enough ingredients to make a second one. If you don't have a spare pie pan to leave in the freezer, line one with foil or plastic wrap. Assemble the pie as usual and freeze it. When it's fully frozen, lift the pie from the pan, wrap it so it's airtight, and put it back in the freezer. When you're ready for a fresh pie, unwrap it, put it back in the pan in which it was formed, and pop the pie in the oven; you don't even have to defrost it.

Weaving a Lattice Crust

No pie is prettier than one topped with a classic open lattice crust. Roll the dough for a lattice crust into more of an oval shape, at least 10 by 12 inches, then cut it into 8 to 12 (depending on how fine a weave you want) even strips, $3/4$ to 1 inch wide. Arrange half of the strips evenly over the filling. Gently fold back every other strip slightly past the center and lay another strip on top of the pie, perpendicular to the first set of strips. Unfold the strips, returning them to their original position so that they lie flat on top of the perpendicular strip. Working in the same direction, fold back the strips that weren't folded back the first time, lay a second perpendicular strip on top, then return them to their original position. Repeat the process in this manner on the other side of the pie, remembering to alternate the strips that are folded back so that they weave in and out. Trim away any uneven ends and crimp the edges.

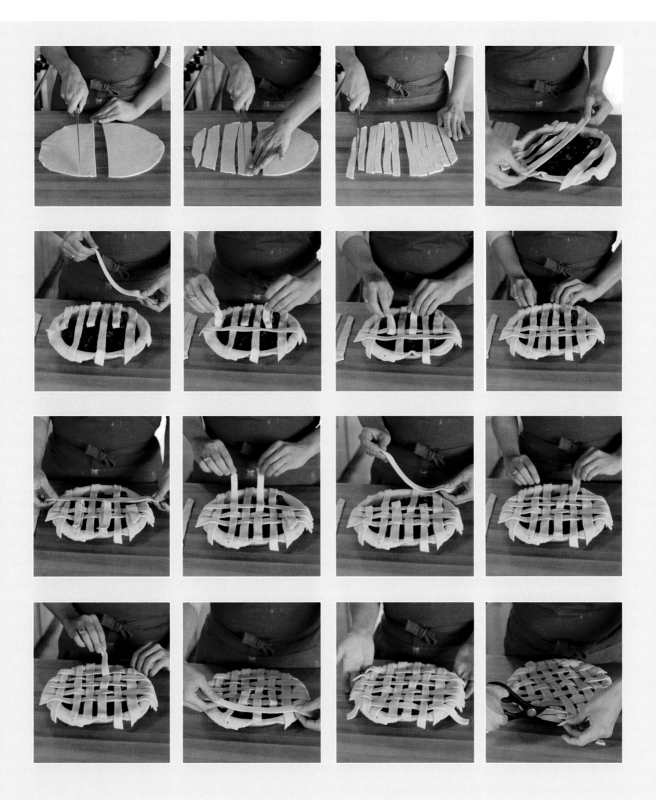

DOUBLE-CRUST PIES

I love old-fashioned double-crust pies, and they're one of my favorite things to bake. I make pies throughout the year with whatever fruit is in season, but I'm never ashamed to fill a pie with frozen berries or good canned cherries when nice local produce isn't available. The process for putting a fruit pie together is more or less the same for all types of fruit, but the amounts of sugar, thickener, and additional flavorings vary from one fruit to the next. I've included simple recipes for my favorite fruit pies, but don't let my preferences limit your creativity. Also, I prefer a less sweet pie, but if you've got tart fruit or you like your pie on the sweet side, add a bit more sugar. Taste your filling as you go, and you'll know exactly how much sugar the fruit needs. Use these recipes as formulas to guide you, don't view them as set in stone. Let whatever fruit is beautiful and fresh at the market inspire you.

Making a Double-Crust Pie

Roll out and refrigerate the bottom crust while you roll out the top crust; the diameter should be about $1/2$ inch greater than the top of the pie pan.

Remove the bottom crust from the refrigerator and add the filling. If the top crust isn't sticky, slip your hands under it, palms down, and lift it onto the top of the pie, centering it as you lower it. Trim the edges, if necessary, to match up with the bottom crust, or about $1/2$ inch past the edge of the pan. Tuck the overhang of the top crust under the bottom crust and press down around the edges to seal it. Crimp or flute the border using your fingers or a fork, then use a paring knife to cut about 5 steam vents into the top crust, to allow the pressure created by the bubbling filling underneath to be released. This will prevent the pie from bursting open and spilling filling.

If you have the time, it can be advantageous to chill a formed pie for up to 1 hour. However, I don't recommend leaving it longer, as the filling may begin to soak into the dough, preventing it from crisping and browning in the oven.

Rhubarb Pie

The British call rhubarb "pie plant," which is fitting, as pie is the most popular way to prepare this vegetable. And no wonder—it makes a perfect, tangy, bright pie.

SERVES 6 TO 8

2 disks All-Butter Flaky Pie Dough (page 173)
1½ pounds rhubarb stalks
1½ cups (10.5 ounces) granulated sugar
3 tablespoons all-purpose flour
1 teaspoon vanilla extract
Pinch of salt

Prepare to bake.
Preheat the oven to 375°F.

Prepare the filling.
Cut the rhubarb crosswise into ³⁄₄-inch pieces; you should have about 6 cups total. Add the sugar, flour, vanilla, and salt and toss to combine.

Form and bake the pie.
Roll out the dough according to the directions on page 175. Pour the filling into the bottom crust and top with a lattice or solid crust. Crimp or flute the edges, and if using a solid top crust, cut a few steam vents.

Bake for 30 minutes, then rotate the pan and lower the oven temperature to 350°F. Bake for 30 minutes more, until the crust is a rich golden brown and the filling is bubbling.

Strawberry Rhubarb Pie

In Oregon, rhubarb is the first produce that arrives in early spring for making pies, followed shortly thereafter by wonderful strawberries. Hood, Shuksan, Totem, and the many everbearing varieties are some of our favorites at the bakery. The timing is a happy coincidence since, when the two are combined, they make a fabulous pie.

SERVES 6 TO 8

2 disks All-Butter Flaky Pie Dough (page 175)
1 pound rhubarb stalks
1 pint (2 cups) fresh strawberries
1 cup (7 ounces) granulated sugar
2 tablespoons cornstarch
1 tablespoon freshly squeezed lemon juice

Prepare to bake.
Preheat the oven to 375°F.

Prepare the filling.
Cut the rhubarb crosswise into 1-inch pieces; you should have 3 to 4 cups total. Hull the strawberries and slice them in half if they're large. Combine the rhubarb, strawberries, and sugar and toss gently until evenly mixed. Combine the cornstarch and lemon juice and stir to make a slurry, then add it to the fruit and stir gently.

Form and bake the pie.
Roll out the dough according to the directions on page 175. Pour the filling into the bottom crust and top with a lattice or solid crust. Crimp or flute the edges, and if using a solid top crust, cut a few steam vents.

Bake for 30 minutes, then rotate the pan and lower the oven temperature to 350°F. Bake for 30 minutes more, until the crust is a rich golden brown and the filling is bubbling.

Marionberry Pie

Because marionberries freeze especially well, we use frozen Willamette Valley marionberries to make this pie at the bakery during the winter. It's absolutely delicious and a welcome slice of summer during the rainy season. Substitute any variety of blackberries if you can't find marionberries.

SERVES 6 TO 8

2 disks All-Butter Flaky Pie Dough (page 173)
2 pints (4 cups) marionberries
1/2 cup (3.5 ounces) granulated sugar
2 tablespoons cornstarch
1 tablespoon freshly squeezed lemon juice

Prepare to bake.

Preheat the oven to 375°F.

Prepare the filling.

Gently toss the marionberries with the sugar. Combine the cornstarch and lemon juice and stir to make a slurry, then add it to the berries and stir gently.

Form and bake the pie.

Roll out the dough according to the directions on page 175. Pour the filling into the bottom crust and top with a lattice crust.

Bake for 30 minutes, then rotate the pan and lower the oven temperature to 350°F. Bake for 30 minutes more, until the crust is a rich golden brown and the filling is bubbling.

Blueberry Pie

The amount of sugar you need will vary according to whether you're at the beginning, middle, or end of the blueberry season. Lemon zest brightens up this sweet summery pie wherever you are in the berry season.

SERVES 6 TO 8

2 disks All-Butter Flaky Pie Dough (page 173)
2 pints (4 cups) fresh blueberries
1/2 to 3/4 cup (3.5 to 5.25 ounces) granulated sugar
2 tablespoons finely chopped lemon zest
2 tablespoons cornstarch
1 tablespoon freshly squeezed lemon juice

Prepare to bake.

Preheat the oven to 375°F.

Prepare the filling.

Toss the berries with the sugar and lemon zest. Combine the cornstarch and lemon juice and stir to make a slurry, then add it to the berries and stir gently.

Form and bake the pie.

Roll out the dough according to the directions on page 175. Pour the filling into the bottom crust and top with a solid crust. Crimp or flute the edges and cut a few steam vents.

Bake for 30 minutes, then rotate the pan and lower the oven temperature to 350°F. Bake for 30 minutes more, until the crust is a rich golden brown and the filling is bubbling.

Raspberry Pie

I have a weakness for raspberry pie and love the way a hint of vanilla complements the fragrant flavor of fresh berries. If the berries are ripe and particularly sweet, begin by adding just a small amount of sugar, and only add more as needed.

SERVES 6 TO 8

2 disks All-Butter Flaky Pie Dough (page 173)
2 pints (4 cups) fresh raspberries
1/2 to 3/4 cup (3.5 to 5.25 ounces) granulated sugar
2 tablespoons cornstarch
2 tablespoons water
1 teaspoon vanilla extract

Prepare to bake.

Preheat the oven to 375°F.

Prepare the filling.

Gently toss the raspberries with the sugar. Combine the cornstarch, water, and vanilla and stir to make a slurry, then add it to the raspberries and stir gently.

Form and bake the pie.

Roll out the dough according to the directions on page 175. Pour the filling into the bottom crust and top with a lattice crust.

Bake for 30 minutes, then rotate the pan and lower the oven temperature to 350°F. Bake for 30 minutes more, until the crust is a rich golden brown and the filling is bubbling.

Gooseberry Pie

Gooseberries have nasty thorns and are uncommonly sour. They might even be considered hostile . . . until they're baked into a pie. These days it's easy to find gooseberries at the farmers' market, so save yourself the trouble (and pain) of picking them from the bush. Gooseberry pie requires a heavy hand with the sugar, but the end result is undeniably one of the great treats of summer. Start with less sugar than the recipe calls for and add more to taste; the final amount will depend on the sweetness of the gooseberries.

SERVES 6 TO 8

2 disks All-Butter Flaky Pie Dough (page 173)
2 pints (4 cups) fresh gooseberries
1 to 1 1/2 cups (7 to 10.5 ounces) granulated sugar
1/4 cup (1.25 ounces) all-purpose flour

Prepare to bake.

Preheat the oven to 400°F.

Prepare the filling.

Toss the gooseberries with the sugar and flour.

Form and bake the pie.

Roll out the dough according to the directions on page 175. Pour the filling into the bottom crust and top with a solid crust. Crimp or flute the edges and cut a few steam vents.

Bake for 30 minutes, then rotate the pan and lower the oven temperature to 375°F. Bake for 30 minutes more, until the crust is a rich golden brown and the filling is bubbling.

Peach Pie

When I was growing up, the skin on the peaches we ate was covered with thick fuzz, and my mother insisted on scalding and skinning them before baking them into a pie. Today's peaches are virtually fuzz free and can be sliced up skin and all, which makes for an easier and much prettier pie. If you can find a freestone variety like Red Haven or Elberta, the job will be even simpler.

SERVES 6 TO 8

2 disks All-Butter Flaky Pie Dough (page 173)

2 pounds peaches (about 5 large peaches)

1/2 cup (3.5 ounces) granulated sugar

1/4 cup (1.75 ounces) packed light brown sugar

2 tablespoons cornstarch

1 teaspoon vanilla extract

Prepare to bake.

Preheat the oven to 375°F.

Prepare the filling.

Slice the peaches 1/2 inch thick; you should have about 4 to 5 cups. Gently toss with the sugars and let stand for about 10 minutes, until the peaches begin to release their juices. Use a few tablespoons of the juice to make a slurry with the cornstarch and vanilla, then add it to the peaches and stir gently.

Form and bake the pie.

Roll out the dough according to the directions on page 175. Pour the filling into the bottom crust, pressing down gently to fill any spaces without fruit. Cover with a solid crust, crimp or flute the edges, and cut a few steam vents.

Bake for 30 minutes, then rotate the pan and lower the oven temperature to 350°F. Bake for 30 minutes more, until the crust is a rich golden brown and the filling is bubbling.

Apple Pie

We use an assortment of apples in our pies. In my opinion, the best apple pies are made with fruit that's tart, sweet, and firm. As they come into season, we feature the best, freshest varieties with those qualities. Gravensteins and Transparents come first, Pink Ladies are last, and in between there are innumerable delicious versions. I tend to like apples with a predominantly tart flavor, including Granny Smith and Honeycrisp.

SERVES 6 TO 8

2 disks All-Butter Flaky Pie Dough (page 173)

2 pounds firm, tart apples (about 4 to 5 large apples)

3/4 cup (5.25 ounces) granulated sugar

1/2 cup (3.5 ounces) packed light brown sugar

1 teaspoon ground cinnamon

1 tablespoon freshly squeezed lemon juice

Prepare to bake.

Preheat the oven to 375°F.

Prepare the filling.

Peel and core the apples and slice them 1/4 to 1/2 inch thick; you should have about 8 cups. Toss the apples with the sugars, cinnamon, and lemon juice, then set aside for an hour or so, until they begin to release some of their juices. This helps prevent the apple slices from shrinking in the oven as they lose their juices, which creates large gaps between the crust and the fruit.

Form and bake the pie.

Roll out the dough according to the directions on page 175. Pour the filling into the bottom crust and shake carefully so the apples settle into the pan, then cover with a solid crust. Crimp or flute the edges, and cut a few steam vents.

Bake for 30 minutes, then rotate the pan and lower the oven temperature to 350°F. Bake for 30 minutes more, until the crust is a golden brown and the filling is bubbling.

Cherry Pie

We bake cherry pie in the middle of the winter at Grand Central. I know, it's not cherry season in February, but cherries are one of a few items on which we've chosen to "compromise." They freeze well, and we buy them pitted, because it's just not good business to pay a trained baker to pit cherries. Besides, I find them to be the perfect antidote to that gray space between November and March, when there's nothing coming into season anytime soon and apples and pears have lost their appeal.

Since pitting cherries is a ridiculously messy, tedious task I wouldn't wish on my worst enemy, I used canned or frozen sour cherries in my pies at home. Then Ellen taught me a clever way to pit cherries using a paper clip and a wine cork (see the sidebar). I guess I'm willing to admit that a pie made from fresh sour cherries is worth the stained fingers and some extra work.

SERVES 6 TO 8

2 disks All-Butter Flaky Pie Dough (page 173)

4 cups pitted sour cherries, fresh, frozen, or canned (with juice)

3/4 cup (5.25 ounces) granulated sugar

1 teaspoon almond extract

1 tablespoon freshly squeezed lemon juice

3 tablespoons instant tapioca or cornstarch

1/4 teaspoon salt

Prepare the filling.

Toss the cherries with the sugar, then stir in the almond extract and lemon juice. Allow the mixture to macerate for at least 10 minutes, or up to 3 hours. Add the tapioca and salt once the cherries have released some of their juices. If you're using canned cherries, measure out 1/2 cup of the cherry juice and discard the rest. Stir the tapioca and salt into the reserved cherry juice until dissolved, then stir it into the cherries.

Form and bake the pie.

Roll out the dough according to the directions on page 175. Pour the filling into the bottom crust and top with a lattice crust.

Bake for 30 minutes, then rotate the pan and lower the oven temperature to 350°F. Bake for 30 minutes more, until the crust is a rich golden brown and the filling is bubbling.

Pitting Cherries

Open a large paperclip so that it makes a skinny S. Bend it back and forth in the middle until it breaks into two long open loop shapes. Push the smaller of the loops into one end of a cork until it protrudes about 1/2 inch. Using the cork for leverage, plunge the paperclip loop into the stem end of the cherry, hook the pit, and ease it out. This method has the distinct advantage of puncturing the cherry on only one side.

SINGLE-CRUST PIES

Any single crust pie is improved by blind baking the crust; it insures that the buttery flavor comes through and the crust remains crisp. Like many steps in pie baking, blind baking can be done well ahead of time. A baked crust will be just fine if it sits out for up to two days. If it's going to be longer until you bake your final pie, store the crust in the freezer wrapped tightly with plastic wrap.

Fresh Strawberry Pie

This recipe comes from Joan Ohm, mother of Laura Ohm, Grand Central Bakery's pastry commissary and kitchen manager. When Laura was growing up, during the first or second week of summer vacation her mom would get her out of bed "way too early." They would go to the U-pick strawberry fields, where Laura would, predictably, eat more than she picked. Luckily for Laura, her industrious and efficient mother would get them out of the fields and headed home with a few flats of berries in no time. This is the pie Joan always made when they got home and I know it's the recipe that comes to Laura's mind when she glimpses the first strawberries of the season.

SERVES 8

1 All-Butter Flaky Pie Dough shell (page 173),
   blind baked (see sidebar at right)
3 pints (6 to 7 cups) fresh strawberries, hulled
1 cup (7 ounces) granulated sugar
3 tablespoons cornstarch
1 tablespoon freshly squeezed lemon juice
Lightly sweetened whipped cream (see page 137),
   for serving

Prepare the filling.

Combine 3 cups of the strawberries with the sugar and cornstarch in a saucepan over medium-low heat and cook, stirring constantly, until the sugar dissolves and the mixture comes to a simmer. Turn down the heat to low and mash the berries with the back of a large spoon as they continue to simmer for about 3 minutes, until the mixture is thick and glossy.

Fill the pie.

Arrange the remaining strawberries decoratively in the pie crust. Pour the filling over the berries and let the pie sit for about 30 minutes, until the filling sets up. Serve with the sweetened whipped cream alongside.

Blind Baking a Crust

Prebaking, or blind baking, usually involves pricking the shell all over with a fork to prevent it from rising and blistering, then lining it with a piece of foil or parchment paper and filling it with dried beans, rice, or metal or ceramic pie weights. The weights and liner are removed several minutes before the baking time is over to allow the crust to become pale golden brown and slightly dry.

To blind bake a pie crust, preheat the oven to 375°F, then roll out the pie dough and fit it into the baking pan (see page 175). Use a fork to prick the bottom of the crust, then crimp the edges of the crust and chill it for 30 minutes. Cover the chilled crust with a piece of parchment paper or foil, then fill the pan with 2 to 3 cups of dried beans. Lower the oven temperature to 350°F and bake the crust for 25 minutes. Remove the crust from the oven, carefully lift out the parchment paper and beans, and return the crust to the oven for 5 minutes.

Lemon Meringue Pie

My sister, Megan, is the lemon meringue pie aficionado of the family. She developed a soft spot for the classic tart custard and sweet meringue combination when she was nine years old and spent the summer with our grandmother in Sudbury, Massachusetts, where Dorothy Piper was known for her mean lemon meringue pie.

When she thinks of lemon meringue pie, Megan still pictures that firm, bright, meringue-topped yellow triangle from our Betty Crocker cookbook. Having made countless pies of her own, however, she traded that recipe in long ago. This one has a delicate filling, which makes for a slightly loose pie. If there's a lonely disk of pie dough kicking around in your freezer, this is a great single-crust recipe.

SERVES 8

1 All-Butter Flaky Pie Dough shell (page 173),
    blind baked (see sidebar, opposite)

FILLING

5 egg yolks

1 cup (7 ounces) granulated sugar

3 tablespoons cornstarch

1/2 teaspoon salt

1/2 cup (4 fluid ounces) water

1/2 cup (4 fluid ounces) whole milk

3/4 cup (6 fluid ounces) freshly squeezed lemon juice

2 tablespoons (1 ounce, or 1/4 stick) unsalted butter

3 tablespoons finely chopped lemon zest

MERINGUE

5 egg whites

3/4 cup (5.25 ounces) granulated sugar

1/2 teaspoon cream of tartar

1/8 teaspoon salt

Make the filling.

Whisk the egg yolks, sugar, cornstarch, and salt together in a bowl. Heat the water and milk in a heavy, nonreactive saucepan over medium heat, and once the liquid is hot but not boiling, temper the egg mixture by adding the hot liquids to it very slowly while whisking continuously.

Pour the mixture back into the saucepan, add the lemon juice, then turn down the heat to low and stir continuously using a heatproof spatula to scrape across the bottom and get into the edges and corners of the pan. Bring the mixture just to a lazy boil and simmer for 1 full minute, then immediately strain through a fine-mesh sieve into a clean bowl. Fold in the butter and lemon zest. Let the custard cool until no longer hot to the touch, then pour the warm filling into the prebaked pie crust and let the pie cool for at least 1 hour before finishing. (If the meringue is piled on the filling before it is cool, it will weep.)

Make the meringue.

Preheat the oven to 325°F.

Put the egg whites in a clean, dry bowl. I like to use a stand mixer with the whisk attachment, but a strong arm and a proper whisk can do the job too. Add the sugar, cream of tartar, and salt and whip until the sugar is completely dissolved and the whites hold soft peaks. Spoon the meringue over the lemon filling in generous dollops.

Bake.

The only purpose of putting this pie in the oven is to caramelize and set the meringue topping; 20 to 25 minutes at 325°F should do the trick. Pull the pie from the oven when the meringue has a rich golden color and doesn't jiggle. Let the pie sit for several hours before serving.

HOLIDAY PIES

Grand Central Bakery sells more pies between Thanksgiving and Christmas than we do the rest of the year combined. When it comes to the holidays, we're traditionalists and stick to familiar renditions of favorites like pecan and pumpkin. I've included a third recipe too, for a pie that suffers from a bad reputation: mincemeat. It is a paragon of winter flavors and aromas and is never missing from our family's holiday table.

Apple Brandy Mince Pie

My family has always enjoyed this modern adaptation of mincemeat, which contains no meat and no suet. Perhaps this variation, with its festive mixture of apples, dried fruit, and nuts lightly spiced and gently doused with spirits, deserves a PR campaign to overcome the resistance of skeptics. I can't imagine the holidays without it. The filling can be made in the fall, when the apples arrive, and canned for use later in the season.

SERVES 8

2 disks All-Butter Flaky Pie Dough (page 173)

3 tablespoons unsalted butter

1 pound apples (about 2 large apples), peeled, cored, and diced into 1/2-inch cubes

3/4 cup (4 ounces) currants

3/4 cup (4 ounces) golden raisins

1/2 cup (2 ounces) walnuts, lightly toasted and coarsely chopped (see page 20)

1/4 cup (1.75 ounces) packed light brown sugar

1/4 cup (2 fluid ounces) brandy

1/2 cup (4 fluid ounces) apple cider

2 tablespoons molasses

1 tablespoon freshly squeezed lemon juice

1 teaspoon finely chopped lemon zest

1 teaspoon pumpkin pie spice (see page 33)

1/8 teaspoon salt

Make the filling.

Melt the butter in a large, heavy saucepan over medium heat. Add the remaining ingredients, stirring well to combine and evenly distribute the liquids and spices. Bring the mixture to a boil, then turn down the heat to low, cover, and simmer until the apples are soft, about 20 minutes. Let the mixture cool before pureeing half of it in a food processor or blender. Add the pureed portion back to the chunky mixture and chill completely before filling the pie.

Form and bake the pie.

Preheat the oven to 375°F.

Roll out the dough according to the directions on page 175. Pour in the filling and top with a lattice crust.

Bake for 30 minutes, then rotate the pan and lower the oven temperature to 350°F. Bake for 30 minutes more, until the crust is a rich golden brown and the filling is bubbling.

Pumpkin Pie

This recipe makes a very traditional pumpkin pie. It calls for canned pumpkin, which is a dependable, quality product. But if you're up for it, substitute 2 cups of roasted, pureed fresh pumpkin or squash.

SERVES 8

1 All-Butter Flaky Pie Dough shell (page 173),
    blind baked (see page 188)
1 15-ounce can pumpkin puree, or 2 cups roasted,
    pureed fresh pumpkin
1½ cups (12 fluid ounces) half-and-half
2 eggs
½ cup (3.5 ounces) granulated sugar
¼ cup (1.75 ounces) packed light brown sugar
1 teaspoon ground ginger
1 teaspoon ground cinnamon
¼ teaspoon ground cloves
Pinch of salt

Prepare to bake.

Preheat the oven to 325°F.

Make the filling.

Combine the pumpkin, half-and-half, eggs, granulated sugar, brown sugar, ginger, cinnamon, cloves, and salt in a large bowl and whisk until the mixture is homogenous, creamy, and smooth.

Fill and bake the pie.

Pour the filling into the pie crust. Bake for 30 minutes, then rotate the pan and lower the oven temperature to 300°F. Bake for 30 minutes more, until the filling is set and the top of the pie is just beginning to caramelize.

Bourbon Pecan Pie

We feature this popular pie from Thanksgiving through Christmas. Toast the pecans before adding them to the filling to bring out their flavor.

SERVES 8

1 All-Butter Flaky Pie Dough shell (page 173),
    blind baked (see page 188)
1 cup (11.5 ounces) light corn syrup
¾ cup (5.25 ounces) packed light brown sugar
2 tablespoons unsalted butter
¼ cup (2 fluid ounces) bourbon
1 teaspoon vanilla extract
3 eggs, at room temperature
1½ cups (5.25 ounces) pecan halves, lightly toasted
    (see page 20)

Prepare to bake.

Preheat the oven to 325°F.

Prepare the filling.

Put the corn syrup and brown sugar in a heavy saucepan over medium heat and cook, stirring occasionally, until the sugar dissolves. Remove from the heat and add the butter, bourbon, and vanilla. Let the mixture cool, then add the eggs and whisk until smooth.

Fill and bake the pie.

Arrange the pecan halves on the bottom of the crust, then carefully pour the filling over them. Bake for 45 minutes, until the filling is set, rotating the pan halfway through the baking time.

My First Tarte Tatin

I discovered the ease and elegance of tarte Tatin one weekend in Goldendale, at our family farm east of the Cascades in Washington State. We have an apple orchard there with fifty unique trees that produce big, bumpy Bassetti apples. The mother of these apples came from a tree that grew south of Seattle in the 1930s, outside the childhood home of my mother's husband, Fred. The tree was there when the Bassetti family moved in and, as far as anybody knew, it had always been there, producing large, tasty, misshapen apples.

It was never identified officially, but apple experts said the tree was probably a cousin of the king. We call its offspring Bassetties. While very delicious, Bassetties are irregular in size, and the trees are inconsistent in their level of productivity. Some years we're overwhelmed; others, we hold tight to the few boxes the orchard produces. When we have a good year, my family gathers at the farm for a weekend of cider pressing.

The year I made my first tarte Tatin was a good year. Boxes of apples were stacked all over the kitchen and garage. I love a traditional double-crust apple pie as much as the next person, but we had already eaten one that weekend and I wanted to try something different. I don't remember who mentioned tarte Tatin, but it sounded like a great idea, so I went straight to my mother's cookbook collection, in search of a recipe.

I remember feeling discouraged immediately. The recipe began with detailed directions for caramelizing the sugar and cooking the apples in the pan at a temperature described only as "just right." It went on and on like this for two full pages. It seemed overly fussy, and I wasn't sure I'd be able to pull it off.

Always looking for a shortcut, I thought about the delicious caramel that develops in the bottom of a pan of cinnamon rolls, the happy result of combining brown and white sugar in equal parts. I decided to go for it and skipped the first two steps. Instead, I melted butter with equal parts of brown and white sugar, then I arranged my apples on top, packing them closely, and covered them with a disk of Rough Puff Pastry. Since I was using a generous amount of pastry and lumpy Bassetties, I baked my tart for well over the prescribed hour, nervously awaiting the outcome.

When it was finally ready, I pulled my tarte Tatin from the oven and let it sit for a few minutes before flipping it out onto a large plate. The results were stunning! (Though I did burn myself with molten caramel.) The apples kept their shape wonderfully and were richly colored with the caramel. And they were so tender that a fork cut through them effortlessly. Because I had baked the pastry on top rather than underneath the fruit, it puffed beyond my dreams and was unbelievably delicate and flaky. But the best part was discovering the places where I had tucked the pastry down around the apples, causing the caramel to bubble up and bake into the crust. I've made many a tarte Tatin since, and I'm always pleased with the results. And I still serve myself the piece with the most caramel on the crust.

Tarte Tatin

This French upside-down pie has become my signature dessert. I try to time the rest of the meal so that I can put the tart in the oven as we sit down to dinner. Few desserts are as dramatic or delicious as a tarte Tatin served hot from the oven with freshly whipped cream.

Classic tarte Tatin is made with apples, but I've also had great success using everything from apricots to pineapple. Baking the fruit in caramel with a crust on top brings out the very best in any firm, slightly tart fruit.

I'm often asked what kind of apple makes the best tarte Tatin, to which I always answer, "The one with the best flavor and texture at the time." In the late summer and beginning of fall, this might mean an early variety like Gravenstein. Later in the season, there are oodles of good choices. I'm partial to Cameo, Honeycrisp, and, during the winter months, Pink Lady apples.

SERVES 8 TO 10

1 pound Rough Puff Pastry (page 176)

2 tablespoons unsalted butter

½ cup (3.5 ounces) granulated sugar

½ cup (3.75 ounces) packed light brown sugar

½ teaspoon ground cinnamon

½ teaspoon vanilla extract

2 to 3 pounds tart, firm apples (4 to 6 large apples)

Lightly sweetened whipped cream (see page 137)
    or vanilla ice cream, for serving

Prepare to bake.

Preheat the oven to 375°F.

Prepare the caramel.

Melt the butter in a 10-inch cast-iron or enameled skillet over medium heat. (I use a Le Creuset enameled brazier, also called a wide French oven.) Add the granulated sugar and brown sugar and stir. When the sugars begin to melt and bubble together, remove the pan from the heat and add the cinnamon and vanilla. Don't worry if the caramel begins to separate; it will come back together in the oven.

Prepare the apples.

Set one apple aside. Peel and halve the remaining apples or, if they're unusually large, quarter them. Place the apples in the caramel, rounded side down, packing them as tightly as possible and filling in any gaping holes with apple chunks. Peel and thinly slice the remaining apple, then shingle the slices to create a single layer covering the larger apple pieces underneath.

Roll out the pastry.

On a lightly floured surface, roll out the pastry to a thickness of ⅛ inch. Cut a circle from the dough that measures 12 to 13 inches in diameter and place it over the apples, tucking the edges down inside the pan. If you don't plan to bake the tart immediately, refrigerate it.

Bake.

Bake the tart for 20 minutes, then lower the oven temperature to 350°F and bake for 30 to 40 minutes more, until the crust is a deep, rich brown.

Let the tart cool for about 5 minutes, but don't wait much longer than 10 minutes to turn it out, or the caramel will set up and harden, causing everything but the crust to stick stubbornly to the pan. To turn out the tart, use a round platter somewhat larger than the pan. Place it on top of the pan and, in one swift, deliberate movement, invert the tart so that the crust is sitting on the platter and the beautifully caramelized apples are on top. Be extremely careful as you attempt this maneuver; sugar burn is the worst kind. Serve with a dollop of lightly sweetened whipped cream or a small scoop of vanilla ice cream.

Index

A

All-Butter Flaky Pie Dough, 173–75
Almonds
    Almond Anise Biscotti, 62–63
    Fresh Berry Crumble, 131
    Megan's Apricot Almond
        Granola, 51
    Pink Almond Macaroons, 87
    Seasonal Rustic Fruit Tarts, 122–25
    toasting, 20
    Vanilla Almond Cookies, 66
Anne's Bran Muffins, 28
Apples
    Anne's Bran Muffins, 28
    Apple Brandy Mince Pie, 191
    Apple Crisp, 130
    Apple Pie, 186
    Cream Cheese Apple Cake, 146
    Old-Fashioned Spice Cake, 168–69
    Seasonal Rustic Fruit Tarts, 122–25
    Tarte Tatin, 193–94
Apricots
    chopping dried, 20
    Megan's Apricot Almond
        Granola, 51
    Seasonal Rustic Fruit Tarts, 122–25
Artichokes
    Seasonal Strata, 101
Artisan Pizza, 111–12
Asparagus
    Seasonal Rustic Savory Tarts,
        103, 105
    Seasonal Strata, 101

B

Bacon
    Seasonal Rustic Savory Tarts,
        103, 105
The Bakery Cinnamon Rolls, 42–45
Baking pans, 9
Baking powder, 6
Baking sheets, 9, 11
Baking soda, 6
Banana Nut Bread, 32
Beef
    Steak and Onion Hand Pie
        Filling, 108
Belgian Waffles (Gaufres
    Bruxelloises), 47
Bell peppers
    Seasonal Strata, 101
Bench knives, 11
Ben's Pan Pizza, 113
Berries. *See also individual berries*
    buying, 7
    freezing, 7
    Fresh Berry Crumble, 131
    Seasonal Rustic Fruit Tarts, 122–25
    Sour Cream Coffee Cake, 30
    Summer Pudding, 135
Biscotti, Almond Anise, 62–63
Biscuit cutters, 24
Biscuits, Buttermilk, 96
Black Cherry and Raspberry Kuchen,
    48–50
Blind baking, 188

Blueberries
    Blueberry Muffins, 27
    Blueberry Pie, 184
    Summer Pudding, 135
Bourbon Pecan Pie, 192
Bowl scrapers, 11
Bran
    Anne's Bran Muffins, 28
    Megan's Apricot Almond
        Granola, 51
Bread
    Banana Nut Bread, 32
    Bread Pudding Muffins, 29
    Buttermilk Biscuits, 96
    Clover Rolls, 95
    Cornbread, 97
    Cranberry Orange Pecan Bread, 34
    freezing quick, 9
    Irish Soda Bread, 25
    Pumpkin Bread, 33
    Rosemary Bread Pudding, 100
    Seasonal Strata, 101
    South of the Border Cornbread, 97
    Summer Pudding, 135
Breakfast Crepes à la Ben, 37
Butter
    brown, 125
    creaming sugar and, 55, 144
    freezing, 7
    types of, 6, 172
Buttercream. *See* Frostings and icings
Buttermilk Biscuits, 96

C

Cakes
  birthday, 155–63
  Black Cherry and Raspberry Kuchen, 48–50
  Carrot Cake, 167–68
  Chocolate Birthday Cake, 163
  Coconut Layer Cake with Coconut Buttercream, 165–66
  Cream Cheese Apple Cake, 146
  Dorothy Piper's Sunshine Sponge Cake, 153
  freezing batter for, 8
  Ganache-Glazed Chocolate Bundt Cake, 148–50
  Gingerbread, 154
  Glazed Vanilla Bundt Cake, 147
  layer, 165–69
  Lemon Pound Cake, 152–53
  making, 144–45
  Old-Fashioned Spice Cake, 168–69
  Polenta Pear Cake, 151
  Raspberry Port Trifle, 135
  Sour Cream Coffee Cake, 30
  Yellow Birthday Cake, 162
Cake stands, rotating, 156
Carrots
  Anne's Bran Muffins, 28
  Carrot Cake, 167–68
  Chicken Potpie, 115–16
  Root Vegetable and Mushroom Potpie, 117
  Salmon and Leek Potpie, 116–17
Cheese. See also Cream cheese
  Classic Leek and Cheese Quiche, 105
  Corn Pudding, 98
  Seasonal Rustic Savory Tarts, 103, 105
  Seasonal Strata, 101
  South of the Border Cornbread, 97
Cherries
  Black Cherry and Raspberry Kuchen, 48–50
  Cherry Pie, 187
  Clafouti, 138
  pitting, 187
Chicken Potpie, 115–16

Chiles
  Seasonal Rustic Savory Tarts, 103, 105
  South of the Border Cornbread, 97
  Spicy Potato Hand Pie Filling, 108
Chocolate
  Chocolate Birthday Cake, 163
  Chocolate Mint Sandwich Cookies, 83
  Cocoa Nib Cookies, 69
  Ganache-Glazed Chocolate Bundt Cake, 148–50
  Hazelnut Macaroons, 88–89
  Oatmeal Chocolate Chip Cookies, 56
  Triple-Chocolate Cookies, 61
  Whipped Chocolate Ganache, 164
Cinnamon Rolls, The Bakery, 42–45
Clafouti, 138
Classic Buttery Shortbread, 78
Classic Leek and Cheese Quiche, 105
Clover Rolls, 95
Cobbler, Peach, 133
Cocoa Nib Cookies, 69
Coconut
  Carrot Cake, 167–68
  Coconut Layer Cake with Coconut Buttercream, 165–66
  Coconut Macaroons, 89
Coffee Cake, Sour Cream, 30
Cookies
  Almond Anise Biscotti, 62–63
  Chocolate Mint Sandwich Cookies, 83
  Classic Buttery Shortbread, 78
  Cocoa Nib Cookies, 69
  Coconut Macaroons, 89
  decorating, 76–80
  Favorite Lemon Bars, 91
  freezing baked, 9
  freezing dough for, 8, 55
  Ginger Molasses Cookies, 60
  Ginger Oat Cookies, 67
  Graham Cracker Sandwich Cookies, 84
  Hazelnut Macaroons, 88–89
  Hazelnut Poppy Seed Cookies, 73
  Lacy Oatmeal Cookies, 90

  Lemon Cream Sandwich Cookies, 85
  macaroons, 86–89
  making, 55
  Oatmeal Chocolate Chip Cookies, 56
  Oatmeal Raisin Cookies, 59
  Orange Nutmeg Cookies, 70
  Peanut Butter Cookies, 58
  Peanut Butter Sandwich Cookies, 82
  Pistachio Cranberry Cookies, 72
  Salty Peanut Cookies, 74
  sandwich, 81–85
  Sesame Cookies, 75
  shortbread, 64–80
  Triple-Chocolate Cookies, 61
  Vanilla Almond Cookies, 66
Corn
  Seasonal Rustic Savory Tarts, 103, 105
  South of the Border Cornbread, 97
Cornmeal
  Cornbread, 97
  Corn Pudding, 99
  Polenta Pear Cake, 151
  South of the Border Cornbread, 97
Cranberries
  Cranberry Orange Pecan Bread, 34
  Pistachio Cranberry Cookies, 72
  Seasonal Rustic Fruit Tarts, 122–25
Cream cheese
  Carrot Cake, 167–68
  Cream Cheese Apple Cake, 146
  Lemon Cream Sandwich Cookies, 85
  Old-Fashioned Spice Cake, 168–69
Crème Anglaise, 135
Crepes
  Breakfast Crepes à la Ben, 37
  making, 36
Crisps
  Apple Crisp, 130
  Rhubarb Crisp, 132
Crumble, Fresh Berry, 131
Currants
  Apple Brandy Mince Pie, 191
  The Bakery Cinnamon Rolls, 42–45
  Irish Soda Bread, 25

D

Dorothy Piper's Sunshine Sponge
Cake, 153
Dutch Babies, 39

E

Eggplant
Seasonal Strata, 101
Eggs
buying, 6
Egg Wash, 20
freezing leftover yolks and
whites, 7
Equipment, 9, 11–13

F

Favorite Lemon Bars, 91
Figs
chopping, 20
Seasonal Rustic Fruit Tarts, 122–25
Flavorings, 5
Flaxseeds
Megan's Apricot Almond
Granola, 51
Flour
measuring, 5
types of, 4–5, 172
Food processors, 12
Freezers
items for, 7–9
types of, 11
Fresh Berry Crumble, 131
Fresh Huckleberry Tart, 121
Fresh Strawberry Pie, 188
Frostings and icings
Coconut Buttercream, 165–66
Royal Icing, 78
Vanilla Buttercream, 164
Whipped Chocolate Ganache, 164
Fruit. *See also individual fruits*
dried, 20
Grand Central Bakery Scones, 21
Seasonal Rustic Fruit Tarts, 122–25
Sour Cream Coffee Cake, 30

G

Ganache, Whipped Chocolate, 164
Ganache-Glazed Chocolate Bundt
Cake, 148–50

Gaufres Bruxelloises (Belgian
Waffles), 47
Ginger
Gingerbread, 154
Ginger Molasses Cookies, 60
Ginger Oat Cookies, 67
Glazed Vanilla Bundt Cake, 147
Gooseberry Pie, 185
Graham Cracker Sandwich
Cookies, 84
Grand Central Bakery Jammers,
22–24
Grand Central Bakery Scones, 21
Granola, Megan's Apricot Almond, 51
Greens
Seasonal Rustic Savory Tarts,
103, 105
Seasonal Strata, 101

H

Hand pies
freezing, 9
Savory Hand Pies, 106–7
Spicy Potato Hand Pie Filling, 108
Steak and Onion Hand Pie
Filling, 108
Hazelnuts
Hazelnut Macaroons, 88–89
Hazelnut Poppy Seed Cookies, 73
toasting and skinning, 89
Huckleberry Tart, Fresh, 121

I, J

Icings. *See* Frostings and icings
Irish Soda Bread, 25
Jammers, Grand Central Bakery,
22–24

K

Knives, 12
Kuchen, Black Cherry and Raspberry,
48–50

L

Lacy Oatmeal Cookies, 90
Leeks
Classic Leek and Cheese
Quiche, 105

Root Vegetable and Mushroom
Potpie, 117
Salmon and Leek Potpie, 116–17
Seasonal Rustic Savory Tarts,
103, 105
Seasonal Strata, 101
Lemons
Favorite Lemon Bars, 91
Lemon Cream Sandwich
Cookies, 85
Lemon Crumble Tart, 126–28
Lemon Curd, 126, 128
Lemon Meringue Pie, 189
Lemon Pound Cake, 152–53

M

Macaroons
Coconut Macaroons, 89
Hazelnut Macaroons, 88–89
Pink Almond Macaroons, 87
Marionberries, 131
Marionberry Pie, 184
Summer Pudding, 135
Measuring
cups and spoons, 12
scoop and sweep technique, 5
by weight, 11–12
Megan's Apricot Almond Granola, 51
Microplane graters, 12
Mince Pie, Apple Brandy, 191
Mixers, 11
Mixing bowls, 11
Muffins
Anne's Bran Muffins, 28
Blueberry Muffins, 27
Mushrooms
Chicken Potpie, 115–16
Root Vegetable and Mushroom
Potpie, 117
Seasonal Rustic Savory Tarts,
103, 105
Seasonal Strata, 101

N

Nectarines
Seasonal Rustic Fruit Tarts, 122–25
Nuts. *See also individual nuts*
chopping, 20
freezing, 7

Grand Central Bakery Scones, 21
grinding into meal, 88
toasting, 20

O

Oats
    Apple Crisp, 130
    Fresh Berry Crumble, 131
    Ginger Oat Cookies, 67
    Lacy Oatmeal Cookies, 90
    Megan's Apricot Almond
        Granola, 51
    Oatmeal Chocolate Chip
        Cookies, 56
    Oatmeal Raisin Cookies, 59
    Rhubarb Crisp, 132
    Sour Cream Coffee Cake, 30
Old-Fashioned Spice Cake, 168–69
Oranges
    Cranberry Orange Pecan Bread, 34
    Orange Nutmeg Cookies, 70
Ovens, 12–13

P

Pan liners, 12
Parchment paper, 13
Parsnips
    Root Vegetable and Mushroom
        Potpie, 117
Pastry bags, 80
Pastry brushes, 13
Pastry Cream, 165–66
Peaches
    freezing, 7
    Peach Cobbler, 133
    Peach Pie, 186
    Seasonal Rustic Fruit Tarts, 122–25
Peanuts and peanut butter
    Peanut Butter Cookies, 58
    Peanut Butter Sandwich
        Cookies, 82
    Salty Peanut Cookies, 74
Pears
    Polenta Pear Cake, 151
    Seasonal Rustic Fruit Tarts, 122–25
Peas
    Spicy Potato Hand Pie Filling, 108
Pecans
    Bourbon Pecan Pie, 192

Cranberry Orange Pecan Bread, 34
Pecan Sticky Buns, 46
Seasonal Rustic Fruit Tarts, 122–25
toasting, 20
Pie dough
    All-Butter Flaky Pie Dough, 173–75
    freezing, 8
    ingredients for, 172–73
Pies
    Apple Brandy Mince Pie, 191
    Apple Pie, 186
    blind baking crusts for, 188
    Blueberry Pie, 184
    Bourbon Pecan Pie, 192
    Cherry Pie, 187
    double-crust, 182–87
    freezing, 9, 180–81
    Fresh Strawberry Pie, 188
    Gooseberry Pie, 185
    Lemon Meringue Pie, 189
    Marionberry Pie, 184
    pans for, 170
    Peach Pie, 186
    Pumpkin Pie, 192
    Raspberry Pie, 185
    Rhubarb Pie, 183
    single-crust, 188–89
    Strawberry Rhubarb Pie, 183
    weaving lattice crust for, 180–81
Pineapple
    Carrot Cake, 167–68
Pink Almond Macaroons, 87
Pistachio Cranberry Cookies, 72
Pizzas
    Artisan Pizza, 111–12
    baking, 111
    Ben's Pan Pizza, 113
    toppings for, 112
Plums
    Seasonal Rustic Fruit Tarts, 122–25
Polenta Pear Cake, 151
Popovers, 38
Poppy Seed Cookies, Hazelnut, 73
Potatoes
    Seasonal Rustic Savory Tarts,
        103, 105
    Spicy Potato Hand Pie Filling, 108
Potpies
    Chicken Potpie, 115–16

crust for, 114
pans for, 117
Root Vegetable and Mushroom
    Potpie, 117
Salmon and Leek Potpie, 116–17
Pound Cake, Lemon, 152–53
Prunes
    chopping, 20
    Clafouti, 138
Puddings
    Bread Pudding Muffins, 29
    Corn Pudding, 99
    Rosemary Bread Pudding, 100
    Summer Pudding, 135
Puff pastry
    Chicken Potpie, 115–16
    freezing, 8
    Root Vegetable and Mushroom
        Potpie, 117
    Rough Puff Pastry, 176–79
    Salmon and Leek Potpie, 116–17
    Savory Hand Pies, 106–7
    Tarte Tatin, 193–94
Pumpkin
    Pumpkin Bread, 33
    Pumpkin Pie, 192
    Pumpkin Pie Spice, 33

Q, R

Quiche, Classic Leek and Cheese, 105
Raisins
    Anne's Bran Muffins, 28
    Apple Brandy Mince Pie, 191
    Oatmeal Raisin Cookies, 59
Raspberries
    Black Cherry and Raspberry
        Kuchen, 48–50
    Pink Almond Macaroons, 87
    Raspberry Crumble Tart, 128
    Raspberry Pie, 185
    Raspberry Port Trifle, 135
    Summer Pudding, 135
Rhubarb
    freezing, 7
    Rhubarb Crisp, 132
    Rhubarb Pie, 183
    Seasonal Rustic Fruit Tarts, 122–25
    Strawberry Rhubarb Pie, 183
Rolling pins, 13

Rolls
The Bakery Cinnamon Rolls, 42–45
Clover Rolls, 95
Root Vegetable and Mushroom
Potpie, 117
Rosemary Bread Pudding, 100
Rough Puff Pastry, 176–79
Royal Icing, 78

S
Salmon and Leek Potpie, 116–17
Salt, 5
Salty Peanut Cookies, 74
Savory Hand Pies, 106–7
Scales, 11
Scones, Grand Central Bakery, 21
Seasonal Rustic Fruit Tarts, 122–25
Seasonal Rustic Savory Tarts, 103, 105
Seasonal Strata, 101
Sesame Cookies, 75
Shortcakes, Strawberry, 140–41
Short dough
chilling, 18
equipment for, 16
freezing, 18
ingredients for, 16
overworked, 18
technique for, 16–19
Sieves, 11
Skewers, bamboo, 11
Sour Cream Coffee Cake, 30
South of the Border Cornbread, 97
Spatulas, 13
Spices, 5
Spicy Potato Hand Pie Filling, 108

Squash
Seasonal Rustic Savory Tarts,
103, 105
Seasonal Strata, 101
Steak and Onion Hand Pie
Filling, 108
Sticky Buns, Pecan, 46
Strata, Seasonal, 101
Strawberries
Fresh Strawberry Pie, 188
Gaufres Bruxelloises (Belgian
Waffles), 47
Seasonal Rustic Fruit Tarts, 122–25
Strawberry Rhubarb Pie, 183
Strawberry Shortcake, 140–41
Sugar
creaming butter and, 55, 144
types of, 5
Summer Pudding, 135
Sunflower seeds
Megan's Apricot Almond
Granola, 51
Sunshine Sponge Cake, Dorothy
Piper's, 153

T
Tarts
freezing, 9
Fresh Huckleberry Tart, 121
Lemon Crumble Tart, 126–28
Raspberry Crumble Tart, 128
Seasonal Rustic Fruit Tarts, 122–25
Seasonal Rustic Savory Tarts,
103, 105
Tarte Tatin, 193–94
Tomatoes
Seasonal Strata, 101
Trifle, Raspberry Port, 135
Triple-Chocolate Cookies, 61

V
Vanilla
extract, 6
Glazed Vanilla Bundt Cake, 147
Vanilla Almond Cookies, 66
Vanilla Buttercream, 164
Vegetables. See also individual
vegetables
Seasonal Rustic Savory Tarts,
103, 105
Seasonal Strata, 101

W
Waffles, Belgian (Gaufres
Bruxelloises), 47
Walnuts
Apple Brandy Mince Pie, 191
Banana Nut Bread, 32
Carrot Cake, 167–68
Seasonal Rustic Fruit Tarts, 122–25
toasting, 20
Whipped Chocolate Ganache, 164
Whipped Cream, 135, 140–41
Whisks, 13

Y
Yeast, 5, 41
Yellow Birthday Cake, 162

Z
Zesters, 12
Zucchini
Seasonal Rustic Savory Tarts,
103, 105
Seasonal Strata, 101